CSS FOR
WEB DESIGNERS ONLY

Donna L. Baker

WILEY

John Wiley & Sons, Inc.

CSS For Web Designers Only

Published by
Wiley Publishing, Inc.
111 River Street
Hoboken, NJ 07030
www.wiley.com

Copyright © 2006 by Wiley Publishing, Inc., Indianapolis, Indiana

Published simultaneously in Canada

Library of Congress Control Number: 2006923796

ISBN-13: 978-0-471-78867-6

ISBN-10: 0-471-78867-8

Manufactured in the United States of America

10 9 8 7 6 5 4 3 2 1

1K/SR/QW/QW/IN

about the author

Donna L. Baker is a seasoned author and graphic designer. She designed her first Web site in 1991, and has been actively developing her skill and expertise ever since. She has taught college-level courses and corporate training sessions on all aspects of Web design for several years.

Donna has authored many books on Web design and graphic design software, including numerous Wiley titles. Examples of her work are available from her Web site at www.donnabaker.ca as well as numerous online sources such as CreativePro.com and Adobe.com.

She lives with her family on the south shore of Lake Winnipeg, North America's "inland sea."

credits

Acquisitions Editor
Michael Roney

Project Editor
Sarah Hellert

Technical Editor
Yolanda Burrell

Copy Editor
Scott Tullis

Editorial Manager
Robyn Siesky

Business Manager
Amy Knies

Vice President & Executive Group Publisher
Richard Swadley

Vice President & Publisher
Barry Pruett

Project Coordinator
Jennifer Theriot

Graphics and Production Specialists
Jennifer Click
Lynsey Osborn
Melanee Prendergast
Brent Savage
Amanda Spagnuolo

Cover Design
Mike Trent

Proofreading
Leeann Harney

Indexing
Lynnzee Elze

For my pal "R"

preface

"CSS For Web Designers Only" sums up this book succinctly. Its about CSS, its focus is Web design- ers, and I have tried to write and address the material to meet the needs of this group of designers.

It's an interesting approach to writing a book. Although an author always has a defined target group to which the book is addressed, in this case I have the pleasure of writing it more personally.

My perspective is to write as though I were talking to a colleague, rather than setting forth instructions and processes. For that reason, you see phrases like "I prefer to do this," and "In my opinion, *xx* is the way to go," and so on.

I have focused the content to meet the overall goal of looking at the subject from the perspective of a practicing Web designer, and considered several common questions as guides to developing the content. What do I want to know? What do I need to know? Why should I care? And a big one: How can I do it faster/better/more efficiently?

The book is presented in several functional areas, and covers CSS issues ranging from choosing and developing a column layout to designing a Web page for television screens.

I don't think you can design a style sheet in isolation from the page's code, and for that reason there are some references to XHTML for specific topics like definition lists and DOCTYPE. The focus isn't on JavaScript or other programming languages, although there are a few scripts in the book.

You see a few structures throughout the book, designed to offer information in specific ways, including code samples and descriptions, notes, tips, and Question and Answer sections.

CODE SAMPLES

In addition to the numerous CSS examples, I have also included XHTML examples as reference when necessary.

My personal preference for writing a style uses a specific layout that separates the styles from one another, shows me the style name separately, and also shows me the punctuation clearly — techniques I developed over years of troubleshooting angst. Here's an example of how I would write a style for my own work:

```
blockquote {
    background-image:url(bar_bkgd.jpg);
    background-repeat:repeat-x;
    background-position: bottom;
}
```

Notice the name of the style and opening bracket are on their own line, each property is indented and on its own line, and the closing bracket again has its own line.

CODE DESCRIPTIONS

In many cases, code descriptions are contained within the lines of the text, and you can see them in a different typeface.

Where there are several lines, the code is laid out in its own style on the page; if the code example is quite lengthy, it is defined as a List for the chapter.

GLOSSARY

The glossary in this book isn't an encyclopedia. Instead, I designed it as a mini-reference, rather than using a standard glossary and then pages and pages of appendices listing selectors, properties, and values.

My glossary is based on an assumption that you don't need me to define `background-color` as a unique glossary entry, but that it would be nice to have a collection of properties that you can refer to when designing your styles.

What you will find in the glossary are shortcut properties that describe the syntax and possible content for the shortcut, a single listing for many or all of the separate properties, and separate listings for properties that have some sort of unusual feature or syntax requirement.

For example, there are four background entries:

> background properties, which describes the different types of properties you can apply to a background

> background, which describes the shortcut attribute and how to write it

> `background-position`, which describes how to define a location on the page, and is a separate entry because of its complexity

> `background-repeat`, another background property that has a separate entry, again because of its complexity

NOTES AND TIPS

What's a book without notes and tips? A novel I suppose.

I have used two types of notes. Notes are bits of ancillary information that applies to the content of the page, but isn't a specific activity or function.

Tips are called "Pro Tips" and are one of my favorite elements of the book. There are a squillion ways to make work simpler, easier, less convoluted, and more fun. You pick up tips from your colleagues and other resources all the time — and this book is one of those resources.

Q & A

Each chapter ends with a Question and Answer section. First I ask me a question, and then I give me an answer. Hmm.

The questions and answers are associated with the content in the chapter, but are not necessarily part of the stream of information. You can think of the Q & A as a huge Pro Tip.

In some cases, there might be a question about a workaround for a particular browser that is too extensive to add to the body, but important enough to include in the book.

In other cases, the section includes answers to questions that might arise when you are working with a particular style or property.

Here's a question from Chapter 8 for example: "I want to use links within table cells, but they don't seem to be displaying the `a:hover` pseudo-class appearance, although the styles work perfectly with other links. Is there anything I can do to make the links behave correctly?"

The answer to the question describes why the problem occurs and a solution. So what is the solution? You'll have to turn to Chapter 8.

acknowledgments

I want to thank my family: my daughter Erin for her unique perspective on the world; her pal and Auntie Bev, who has done so much for us; and my Deena for hanging out online on a daily basis. Special thanks to my extraordinary husband Terry, who maintained his sense of humor through the writing of this book as well as building a new house.

This book was made special by contributions from a stellar cast of Web aficionados. My thanks to Faruk Ateş, Denyer, Chris Ware, and my dear friend Margaret Werdermann.

Kudos to the good folks at Wiley. I want to thank Mike Roney for signing the book and keeping me on track. Thanks to Scott Tullis for making the words make sense, and Yolanda Burrell for making the content make sense. Really special thanks to Sarah Hellert, the project editor. It has been a pleasure, and anyone who can manage a constant stream of "Today's question is . . ." e-mails is A-OK in my book." "My book," get it?

Thank you to my buddies Abby and Daisy. And finally, as always, thanks to Tom Waits for playing the tunes in my life.

contents at a glance

contents

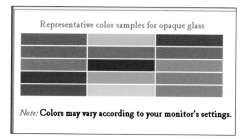

Representative color samples for opaque glass

Note: **Colors may vary according to your monitor's settings.**

chapter **2 Font and Letter Styling** **25**

A newly completed piece in Smalti glass, tile on fiberglass mesh, 23 x 18 inches.

"The glass is cool, with an almost buttery texture, and markedly different coloring on each side..."

chapter **3 Designing Stylish Text** **43**

chapter **4 Images with Style, and Styles with Images . . . 63**

Although this youngster has a good stance and
uneven coloring on her face makes her unsuita

Part II Layouts and Positioning   79

chapter **5 Positioning Content Using CSS** **81**

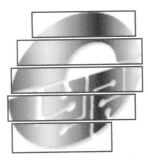

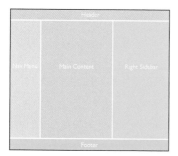

Part III Structured Page Elements   121

chapter 7 Making a List, and Checking It Twice 123

Here are some garnish ideas:

- chopped dates, raisins, or other dried fruit
- shredded coconut
- granola
- chopped nuts
- sesame seeds
- sunflower seeds

chapter **8 Table Tune-Ups** **139**

GDD can be used to:

Assess the suitability of a region for production of a crop

Estimate the growth-stages of crops or life stages of insects

Help estimate the yields of cereals and canola

Estimate the heat stress on crops such as canola

Predict maturity and cutting dates of forage crops

Estimate the protein content of cereals and the oil content of ca

chapter **9 Building Interesting Forms** **153**

chapter **10 Designing Text and Visual Hyperlinks** **167**

Part IV Workflows   193

chapter **11 Testing Pages and Dealing with Browsers** . . . **195**

chapter **12** **Designing Style Sheets for Print and Other Media** **215**

appendix **A About the Contributors** **235**

appendix **B CSS Properties and Values** **243**

Pro Glossary **259**

PAGE CONTENT

Chapter 1

MAKING CSS WORK FOR YOU

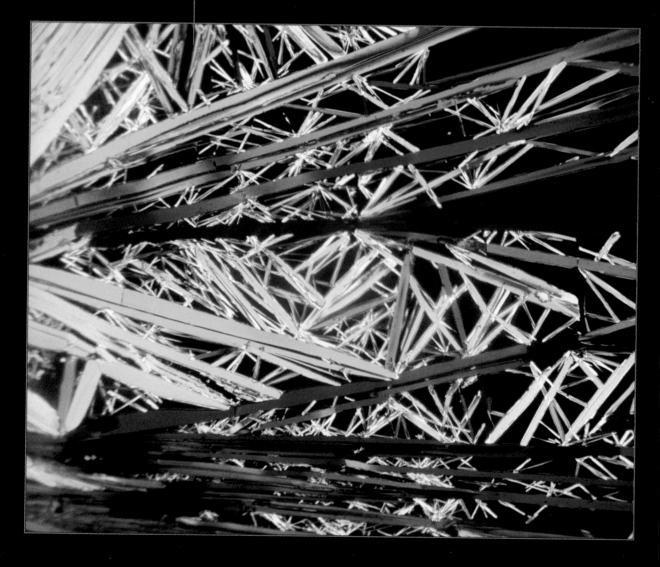

Cascading Style Sheets (CSS) is an open and freely available standard developed to separate presentation and content on a Web site. The standard is developed and published by the World Wide Web Consortium (W3C), a group made up of organizations, industries, manufacturers, and others involved in the development of the Internet.

CSS came on the scene in 1996 with the release of CSS Level 1. CSS Level 2 was released in 1998 and builds on CSS Level 1, supporting more styles and expanding to include different types of media output. CSS 3 is currently in development, and is destined for release in a number of modules addressing different categories of styles, such as selectors, color, or print.

The point of separating presentation and content is that updating and changing the appearance needs to be done only once to a style sheet, and the changes are automatically passed to the browser when the page is displayed. If you can remember the "old days" of Web page building before the time of CSS, you'll appreciate how valuable it is to have a centralized function to update the styles used on a page. Read how guest contributor Margaret Werdermann used a consistent method for producing customized style sheets for her clients.

CSS is paired with the XHTML standard. XHTML reformulates HTML with XML syntax and without any presentation attributes. CSS is supported to different degrees by different browsers, and different browser versions.

DESCRIBING WEB PAGE CONTENT

When you write CSS styles you use numerous properties for defining the placement of content on the page. CSS uses the *box model* as the basis for describing everything displayed on a Web page.

You don't have to understand the intricacies of the box model to write CSS, but appreciating how it works will improve your ability to predict how a style looks, and save you tweaking and adjusting time.

NOTE

For full details on the box model, check out the World Wide Web Consortium's CSS2 or CSS3 specifications. Both of these documents make terrific bedtime reading.

There is always one box on a page; each element added to the page adds another box. As you can see in figure 1-1 where I have drawn an overlay of the boxes used in this simple Web page, boxes can be nested within other boxes within other boxes . . . .

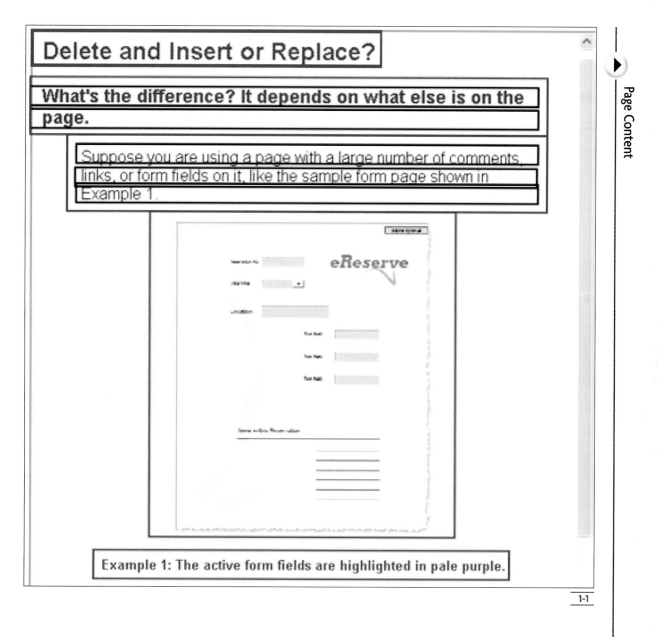

Delete and Insert or Replace?

What's the difference? It depends on what else is on the page.

Suppose you are using a page with a large number of comments, links, or form fields on it, like the sample form page shown in Example 1.

eReserve

Example 1: The active form fields are highlighted in pale purple.

1-1

IDENTIFYING THE BOX COMPONENTS

Each box has a content area holding text, images, or other material. The content optionally has padding, border, and margin areas that you specify by assigning style properties.

The characteristics of a box are shown in figure 1-2, and include:

> **Margins.** A margin is the outermost element of a box.

> **Borders.** The border is inside and adjacent to the margin.

> **Padding.** Padding is the space inside the border and surrounding the content.

Margins | Borders | Padding | Padding background | Content background | Contents

1-2

Width composed of left and right values and content

Height composed of top and bottom values and content

1-3

> **Padding background.** The color or image assigned to the padding space.

> **Content background.** The color or image assigned to the background surrounding the content.

> **Content.** The actual content viewed on the Web page is the innermost element in a box.

DEFINING THE BOX'S SIZE

Planning layouts means you have to know what makes up the overall height and width of a box. In figure 1-3, you can see that:

> The overall width of the box is made up of the left margin, left border, left padding, content width, right padding, right border, and right margin.

> The overall height of the box is the sum of the top margin, top border, top padding, content height, bottom padding, bottom border, and bottom margin.

Box Model Issues

The current CSS standards identify the `width` and `height` properties of a box as the content area of the box only. The total box width is made up of the content area, as well as padding, borders, and margins. Unless the `width` property is specified, the total box width is the same as the `content area` of the surrounding container element.

Unfortunately, all CSS-enabled versions of Internet Explorer before IE6 function under a different box model where the padding and borders are included as part of a width or height total. Only if the elements don't use borders or padding do the two models jive.

Page layout problems and the headaches accompanying them arise when a box uses an assigned `width` and either (or both)

`borders` or `padding` is defined. The standard box model causes the overall box width to increase, and in the IE model the `content area` is decreased by the same amount.

For example:

```
{width:400px; padding:20px;
border:5px;}
```

If you look at this object in a standards-compliant browser, the box from border edge to border edge is 450px, the sum of 400 + (20*2) + (5*2).

In older versions of IE, all the values are combined within the width value for a total of 400px, and the actual width of the content area shrinks to 350px, the remainder of 400px – (20*2 + 5*2).

LOCATING CSS INFORMATION

Style Sheets are templates, very similar to templates in desktop publishing applications that contain rules defined for page elements, or *selectors*.

PLACING CODE INLINE

Using a style inline is comparable to how HTML was written in the past, where presentation details were included along with the page's content in the body of the page.

The style is written as an attribute for the tag. For example, if I want to use a `<p>` style in a page, like the brown text shown in figure 1-4, the tag is written as:

```
<p style= "font-family: 'Gill Sans
Extra Bold', 'Arial Black',
sans-serif; color:#663300;"> What's
the difference? It depends on what
else is on the page. </p>
```

On the upside, inline CSS lets you:

> Add style information quickly to a specific tag. If the paragraph scripted above were the only instance of content that used that particular `color` and `font-family` properties, then it's easy to add it to the `<p>` tag.

> Decrease clutter in your site's code. A style applied to only one element isn't included in other style listings, which makes organizing and locating your other styles simpler.

On the downside:

> Using inline CSS is a real pain to maintain because you have to scan a page's code for the style's information.

> Often you work with multiple paragraphs on the page that use the same style. Using inline CSS means repeating the style information for each paragraph, as shown in figure 1-5, which hardly contributes to streamlined code.

Delete and Insert or Replace?

What's the difference? It depends on what else is on the page.

Suppose you are using a page with a large number of comments, links, or form fields on it, like the sample form page shown in Example 1.

1-4

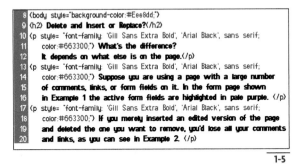

1-5

> You can't reuse common elements. For example, if you have a heading that uses the same color and font family as a type of paragraph, you have to define that heading separately, rather than naming a single style and applying it to different elements.

PRO TIP

In general, I find inline CSS difficult to maintain and hard to troubleshoot, but it does have its place. I have used an inline tag when I am creating a "one-off" page where the content is specific to the page as opposed to a site, and where the style is specific to a single instance of a tag.

EMBEDDING THE STYLES

Rather than adding styles to each individual element on a page, you can include them as a `style` element within the page's `<head>` tags.

The `<p>` example described in the previous section can be moved to a page's `<head>` section, as shown in figure 1-6.

On the upside:

> Embedding the styles on a page is the best way to ensure your styles' information is always included with your page's code, like the example shown in figure 1-6.

> Including the styles in a single block is simple to maintain and troubleshoot on a page-by-page basis.

```
3  <head>
4  <title>Tips for Managing PDF Pages</title>
5  <meta http-equiv="Content-Type" content="text/html; charset=iso-8859-1" />
6  <style type="text/css">
7  .intro {
8      font-family: "Gill Sans Extra Bold", "Arial Black", sans-serif;
9      color: #663300;
10 }
11 </style>
12 </head>
```

1-6

On the downside:

> Styles can't be shared across pages on a site, meaning you have to copy and paste the code from one page to another.

> When styles need updating, you have to update the code on each page containing a copy of the styles.

PRO TIP

Hide the styles from non-CSS browsers by commenting out the `<style>` tag on the HTML page.

LINKING TO AN EXTERNAL FILE

Rather than including any of the style information in the page, write a style sheet as a separate file, linked to your Web pages by tags included in the `<head>` tag.

A style sheet is linked to a Web page using this code:

```
<link href="name_of_stylesheet.css"
rel="stylesheet" type="text/css" />
```

The link requires three attributes including:

1. `type`. The `type` attribute defines the `MIME_type` of the target URL. In the case of an attached style sheet, the type is `text/css`; other types can include `text/javascript` or `image/jpg`.

2. `rel`. The `rel` attribute defines the relationship between the current document and the targeted document, such as a style sheet.

3. `href`. The `href` attribute uses the URL of the CSS file as its value.

On the upside:

> Maintaining all the styles in a single file is a convenient way to keep track of a page or site's presentation.

> Incorporating your styles in a single file shows you what you have named different styles, preventing duplication in naming and possible errors.

> Collecting all the styles in a single file lets you see the relationships among the styles, making it simpler for you to identify and take advantage of the existing styles. For example, figure 1-7 shows the same page as that displayed in figure 1-4. In the external style sheet, the brown text is defined as a style, which is then applied to the main heading on the page. The caption under the image, which uses the default `<h5>` tag, also has the style applied.

Delete and Insert or Replace?

What's the difference? It depends on what else is on the page.

Suppose you are using a page with a large number of comments, links, or form fields on it, like the sample form page shown in Example 1.

Example I: The active form fields are highlighted in pale purple.

NOTE

For interest and a more cohesive page I also assigned a style to the default `<blockquote>` tag to add padding and a border at the left and bottom edges of the block.

On the downside:

> A style sheet must be accessible by the pages to which it is linked. If a viewer takes a page offline for example, they won't have the linked styles — so much for your carefully crafted page presentation.

> Having all the styles for a site in a single file can be difficult to organize logically.

> Collecting all of a site's styles in a single file can make it difficult to pinpoint a style you want to modify.

APPLYING AN IMPORTED STYLE SHEET

You can import as many style sheets files as you want and override imported styles using embedded styles, but I don't recommend it except in an environment using a structured style sheet scheme.

When you are trying to find the source of an error and have to pass through numerous hierarchical layers, you'll see why. It is probably well worth the time it takes to rebuild the sheet for the page or site.

You can add more than one style sheet to a Web page by linking a style sheet using an *at-rule*. The rule begins with the @ symbol (hence the name) followed by an alphanumeric keyword, which can also include dashes or underlines.

If you want to add an additional style sheet to an existing one, write:

```
@import url(extrastyles.css);
```

Instead of using a linked style sheet on a Web page, use the at-rule. On your Web page, the ⟨style⟩ tag is written similar to:

```
<style type="text/css">
@import url(extrastyles.css);
</style>
```

NOTE

At-rules have other uses as well, such as defining media — for example, @print for a printer. Other forms include @font-face to define and embed an external font and @page to apply styles to printed pages.

MAINTAINING PAGE STYLES OFFLINE

You can use both linked and embedded styles in a page. You may want to provide both options in cases where a file is viewed offline, such as a lesson or tutorial article.

To include an embedded style sheet within the Web page that lists the basic elements of the page design, follow these steps:

1. Attach and test the page using your site's style sheet.

2. Embed a subset of the styles using a ⟨style⟩ element within the ⟨head⟩ tag.

3. Delete or comment the code that defines the style sheet. In the example shown in figure 1-8, the code is hidden with comments.

```
3  <head>
4  <title>Tips for Managing PDF Pages</title>
5  <meta http-equiv="Content-Type" content="text/html; charset=iso-8859-1" />
6  <!-- <link href="ch01.css" rel="stylesheet" type="text/css" /> -->
7  <style type="text/css">
8  .intro {
9      font-family: "Gill Sans Extra Bold", "Arial Black", sans-serif;
10     color: #663300;
11 }
12 </style>
```

1-8

4. Test the page to make sure the applicable styles are embedded.

5. Reinsert the code defining the style sheet, or remove the comments.

Writing CSS Syntax

CSS syntax, as anyone reading this book already knows, is made up of a selector, a property, and a value, and is expressed as:

```
selector {property: value}
```

The *selector* is usually the HTML element or tag you are defining, the *property* is the attribute you are modifying, and the *value* is the description you are applying to the defined property. Together the selector and the property/value are known as a *ruleset*.

Keep yourself straight! Naming styles functionally is usually easier to understand than naming them according to appearance. Naming a style `schedulebottomrow` is simpler to figure out than `doublelinedarkblue`, especially if your site's color scheme is dark blue and you use several table and form structures.

NOTE

Don't start a class or ID name with a number because Mozilla/Firefox browsers won't recognize the style.

Styling Elements

Instances of the same element, such as `<h4>` tags, can be assigned a unique style. In this case, use the name of the element as the name of the style on the style sheet.

For example, my style for the `<h3>` tag shown on the Web page in figure 1-9 uses a different font-variant and color than the other heading styles, and is written as:

```
h3 {
color:#996633;
font-variant: small-caps;
}
```

Timesaving Tips

- If the file is in a program that offers a PDF the PDFMaker with its current settings.

- If the file is in a program without a PDFMa opens the program and prints the file usir Converter.

- Unless you have content placed on the sy option From Clipboard Image is grayed c

- When converted, the file is named accorc name but isn't yet saved in its PDF forma

Generating PDF Files

In Acrobat 7 you can generate PDF files from wit the Create PDF task button to access several or

1-9

Writing and Using Multiple Styles for an Element

More than one style can be associated with an element. For example, in figure 1-10 you can see two paragraph styles, one introducing the Samples section of the page, and the other describing the first sample. On the style sheet associated with the page the styles for the paragraphs are named `p.basic` and `p.glossaryrow`.

Using the element followed by a period and the style name identifies the style as specific to the tag.

Applying a Rule to Specific Instances

To zero in on page content and apply styles with razor-like precision, take a look at *contextual* selectors. A contextual selector is a string of individual selectors that produces a search pattern.

Samples

Here are sample SWF movies from the book. If you can't see the sample movies, and are using Internet Explorer, check your security settings in the Tools > Internet Options > Security settings dialog box:

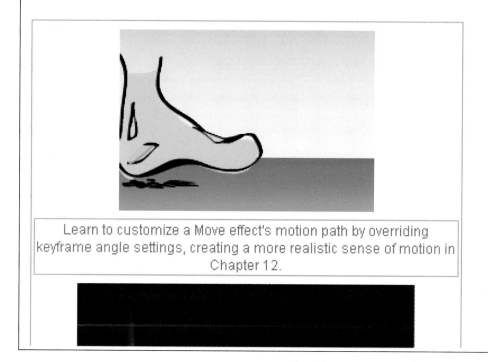

Learn to customize a Move effect's motion path by overriding keyframe angle settings, creating a more realistic sense of motion in Chapter 12.

1-10

Only the last element in the pattern is modified, and only when it meets the listed criteria. You are free to define contextual selectors in a number of ways. The price of this freedom is that contextual selectors can be difficult to write and apply, and errors that occur can be very hard to locate.

Here are two variations on the contextual selector theme. The appearances on a Web page are shown in figure 1-11.

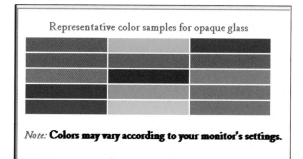

Representative color samples for opaque glass

Note: **Colors may vary according to your monitor's settings.**

1-11

The first example is written as:

```
div table caption {color:#006699}
```

The element `<caption>` is shown on the page as a medium blue, and styles the table's caption at the top of the page. However, the style only applies in the context of the element `<table>` which occurs in the context of the element `<div>`.

Specify two or more contextual situations separated by commas, written as:

```
div table caption, h4 em
    {color:#006699}
```

The element `<caption>` is shown in medium blue, and the element `<em>` is also medium blue when it occurs in the context of `<h4>`. The line below the table uses the `<h4>` style; the `<em>` tag applies only to the word "Note"; the rest of the heading uses the page's basic style.

WRITING ID SELECTORS

With the `id` selector you can define the same style for different HTML elements using a single rule.

For example, a rule can be applied as an `id` attribute to any element that I choose, such as the figure caption, part of the numbered list, and the horizontal rule shown in figure 1-12.

The style shown in the figure is written as:

```
#accent {
color: #3399CC;
background-color: #E9E9E9;
}
```

Before using an `id` selector, determine whether you want it to apply to one element or use it more generally. Either write a generic attribute that is applied like the example, or specify the elements to which it can apply. For example, the selector `p#accent` can be applied only to `<p>` tags having the rule `id="accent"`.

NOTE

In addition to regular classes and elements, you can also work with and write styles for pseudo-classes and pseudo-elements. Read about pseudo-classes in Chapter 10, and pseudo-elements in Chapter 2.

Figure 1-1. Choose an option from the task button's menu.

Click the Create PDF task button to display the menu and follow these steps:

1. **Click the first option, From File, to display the Open dialog box.**
2. **Locate the file you want to convert to PDF.**
3. Click Open. You'll see a progress bar window as Acrobat executes a macro that opens the file in the native program and converts it to a PDF.
4. The converted file opens in Acrobat. Choose File > Save to save the file as a PDF.

1-12

Making CSS Work for You

CLAIMING AN INHERITANCE

Web pages are structured hierarchically. The `<html>` element is the top of the heap, also known as the *ancestor*. The rest of the page descends from this top-level element.

Like any family, child elements can inherit properties from their parents. In the case of a Web page, the inherited properties result in the default style for the element. For example, a `<table>` element's style is inherited by `<tr>` and `<td>` tags.

If you don't want inherited properties to be assumed by a child element, specify a style for the child element. In the example shown in figure 1-13, alternate `<tr>` tags use unique styles.

To capitalize on inheritance, you can use a *parent-child* selector to apply properties in defined parent-child relationships. Write the selector by listing two or more selectors separated by a tilde (~).

An example is shown in figure 1-14. In the sample page, the `<em>` element is used within both a `<p>` and an `<h2>` tag.

The style is written as:

```
body ~h2 ~em {font-family:Arial,
   Helvetica, sans-serif;}
```

As a result, only the element within the `<h2>` tag is styled.

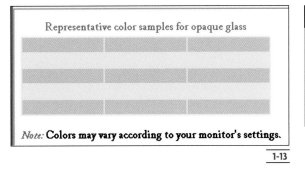

Representative color samples for opaque glass

Note: **Colors may vary according to your monitor's settings.**

1-13

PRO TIP

A property may be assigned an `inherit` value, which means that it uses the same value as that displayed by its parent.

You can use the `inherit` value for properties that aren't normally inherited, such as backgrounds.

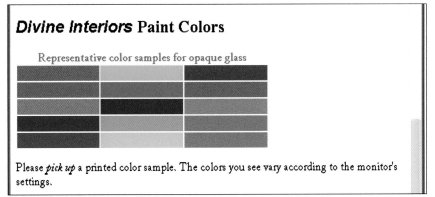

Divine Interiors Paint Colors

Representative color samples for opaque glass

Please *pick up* a printed color sample. The colors you see vary according to the monitor's settings.

1-14

CASCADING STYLES

You may have experience using CSS and building Web pages without understanding how the cascade rules are applied.

The CSS cascade is a sorting system made up of rules that organize declarations so there are no conflicts in presentation. When several rules apply, the one with the greatest importance, or *weight*, takes precedence, allowing the browser to solve conflicting rules and display the content correctly.

Style sheets come from three sources, including:

> The author writing the style sheet, who defines the styles either in the document or linked from an external file.

> Users, who can specify style information as well, such as applying a contrasting color scheme-based style sheet.

> User agents, such as Web browsers, who apply a default style sheet before any other style sheets.

WEIGHT ASSIGNMENTS

Each *style rule,* or property and value combination, you assign to a style is assigned a weight. More than

one rule can apply to the same style and are applied in order of weight.

SORTING STRATEGIES

Aside from sorting styles by origin, there are other types of sorts upon which the final displayed style is based. In ascending order, the other types of sorting include:

> **Specified selector.** A selector such as `img.left` overrides a general selector such as `img`.

> **Specified order.** If two rules have the same origin, weight, and specificity, the latter specified rule is used.

> **Defined importance.** Declarations with increased weight take precedence over declarations with normal weight.

REDEFINING IMPORTANCE

By default, rules in an author's style sheet override those in a user's style sheet. As listed previously, an `!important` declaration is more important than a normal declaration, and can be used by both author and user style sheets.

The ability to control appearance is extremely useful when designing for those viewers with special visual requirements, such as using high-contrast colors schemes or very large font sizes.

For example, the Web page shown in figure 1-15 shows the application of my styles to the numbered list.

If you look at the same page in figure 1-16, you see the text is much larger and black, resulting from a user's style defining the size and color as `!important`.

Figure 1-1. Choose an option from the task button's menu.

Click the Create PDF task button to display the menu and follow these steps:

1. Click the first option, From File, to display the Open dialog box.
2. Locate the file you want to convert to PDF.
3. Click Open. You'll see a progress bar window as Acrobat executes a macro that opens the file in the native program and converts it to a PDF.
4. The converted file opens in Acrobat. Choose File > Save to save the file as a PDF.

`1-15`

PRO TIP

If you declare a shorthand property as `!important` you declare all its component properties as `!important` as well.

Figure 1-1. Choose an option from the task button's menu.

Click the Create PDF task button and follow these steps:

1. Click the first option, From Fil dialog box.
2. Locate the file you want to co
3. Click Open. You'll see a prog Acrobat executes a macro tha native program and converts
4. The converted file opens in A Save to save the file as a PDF

`1-16`

BUILDING A BUSINESS SUITE OF STYLES

*D*esigning styles for your own site is a problem, but how about designing suites of different types of online education materials for numerous clients? Education consultant and training developer Margaret Werdermann has developed a plan that works for her business.

For my business, I have one basic style sheet that I build on and customize for each project. I use this same sheet, not to make all my sites look the same — in fact, the sites I create are always very different from each other — but, instead, as a mental checklist.

In the design phase of a project, I'll go through the basic style sheet, discussing each style and the attributes I commonly set for it. I ask myself, "What do I want to do with this style to make it work best for this design and layout?"

This method was really born of necessity. It took only a couple of projects "reinventing the wheel" to realize that starting from scratch with a blank style sheet might sound terribly creative; but, in fact, it's just a colossal waste of time. Now, I start with my basic "menu" of styles, each given its own "flavor" for a particular project. Then, because every project ends up having some unique twist, I add to that project's basic sheet. Some of the additions are only really relevant to that project, and they just stay on that sheet. Others, I can see a use for future projects, and they get added to the master style sheet to be used again.

So now I bet you're thinking, "If one master style sheet is a good idea, wouldn't it be a good idea to just prefabricate, say, half a dozen different style sheets and let your customers choose from them?" I mean, it would probably be a lot easier to say, "Choose A, B, or C" than to go through the work of customizing the basic style sheet for each project individually, right? Well, that's true, and I know there are places out there that do exactly that; but I never have and never will.

My customers expect customized sites that express the personalities of their organizations. I feel I owe it to them to get to know them well and make sure their sites work perfectly with their content and appeal to their individual target audiences. You can't do that with a cookie-cutter design.

SORTING ELEMENTS

It can be confusing to keep track of what you are working with sometimes, particularly if you are using multiple style sources, like an inline style and an external style sheet.

To keep track, remember the order of priority:

1. An inline style attribute overrides all other styles.

2. A `style` element embedded in a page overrides linked and imported sheets.

3. The `link` element attached as an external style overrides imported styles.

4. The `@import` statement has lowest priority. Imported style sheets cascade with each other in the order in which they are imported.

FIGURING OUT PROPERTY VALUES

Contrary to the title, this isn't a discussion on real estate! A Web browser is more complex software than it may appear at first glance.

To display what you see on a Web page, a browser follows these steps:

1. The document is parsed and a document tree is constructed.

2. The value for each property is calculated.

3. The value is assigned to every property applicable in the target media type.

All properties on a style sheet have a default *initial* value assigned to the root element of the document tree. Common examples are the link colors, underline decoration, and the appearance of headings, shown in the example in figure 1-17.

Delete and Insert or Replace?

What's the difference? It depends on what else is on the page.

Keep fields intact by **replacing pages.** View more examples.

1-17

The displayed value for a property results from a calculation that may include up to four steps depending on the circumstances of the style sheets in use. The calculations are based on these values, listed in order:

1

Making CSS Work for You

Using Attribute Selectors

Attribute selectors are more specific than general selectors and may be useful in situations using multiple style sheets, like the sets of style sheets written for sites that include a storefront, technical information, and other presentation requirements.

The selector can be defined in varying degrees of specificity as:

> An attribute assigned to an element. A style is applied only if both the element and attribute are present. For example, p[title] would apply the style only to a <p> tag that also used the title attribute.

> The attribute and value. A style is applied only if the element uses a specific class. For example, p[class=intro] would assign the style only to those <p> tags that also use the intro class attribute.

> The attribute and value parts. A style is applied only if the attribute value is an exact match of the specified value. For example, the style named p[class="marcom phase2 intro"] assigns the style only to those paragraphs using the specific named class containing the words "marcom phase2 intro". Writing the style name as p[class~="phase2"] applies the style to those paragraphs using the "marcom phase2 intro" class as well as others using the "phase2" term as part of the class name.

---

1. The *specified* value the CSS specification defines is assigned by a browser based on this order:

   a. If the cascade results in a value, use the value.

   b. If the property is inherited and isn't part of the document tree, use the computed value of the property's parent element.

   c. If neither case is true, use the property's initial value.

2. The *computed* value is determined by inheritance. For example, em lengths are computed to pixel or absolute lengths; URI locations are made absolute.

3. The *used* value results from converting to an absolute value. If you are writing a style that uses percentage values for a table width, like the table examples in figure 1-18, the width of the table depends on the width of the browser window. Regardless of the browser window's size, the table is displayed at 50 percent of its width.

4. The *actual* value displays the property using local settings. Ordinarily, the used value is the same as the actual value. If you are using a black-and-white monitor, for example, regardless of the color settings specified in the style sheet, you'll see only shades of gray.

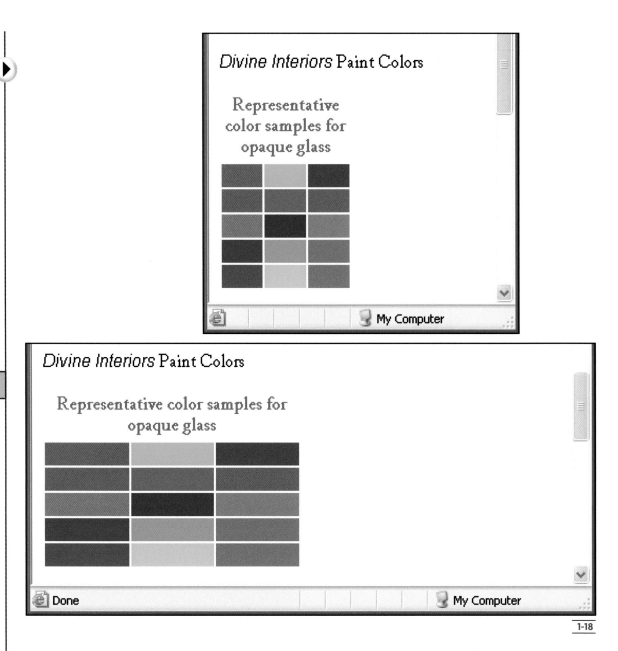

Divine Interiors Paint Colors

Representative color samples for opaque glass

1-18

TAKING CONTROL OF YOUR STYLE SHEET

Writing styles and using the principles of CSS is both fascinating and complex. There are a few methods you can use to make your style sheet as clear and usable as possible.

Although there isn't one best way to proceed, after writing a batch of styles for a new project, I evaluate my style sheet using these steps as a basic checklist:

1. Combine rulesets to omit directions or locations such as "top," "bottom," or "left." If I have written styles in "longhand" for an element, such as a `<blockquote>`, I combine the rulesets to condense the style.

2. Group selectors where styles are repeated. If I realize that `<h2>` and `<h4>` use the same properties and values, I group their styles.

3. Write shorthand properties to simplify the style sheet. Once a style is written and I have seen all the elements both in writing and applied to the page, I usually replace the long style with a shorthand version.

4. Add comments. Lots of comments. I add comments as reminders for myself, such as why I am using one method rather than another, or as headings if I am sorting the styles according to their use in the site.

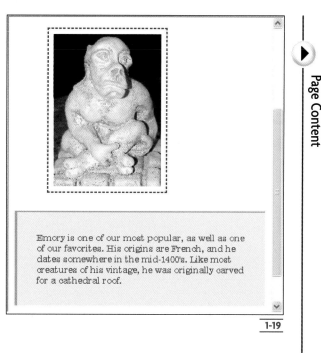

1-19

COMBINING RULESETS

The CSS box model lets you specify elements on different sides, such as the left or top, right or bottom.

Here's an example. Figure 1-19 shows a paragraph that uses padding and borders. The style `p.callout` is written as:

```
p.callout {
color:#993333;
background-color:#E6E6CC;
padding-top: 30px;
padding-right: 30px;
padding-bottom: 30px;
padding-left: 30px;
border-top: 2px;
border-right: 0px;
border-bottom: 0px;
border-left:4px;
border-color: #CC9933;
border-style: solid;
}
```

When rulesets are applied uniformly to all margins, for example, I prefer to condense the length of the style by omitting the location in the property. Condensing the style `p.callout` shortens it to:

```
p.callout {
color:#993333;
background-color:#E6E6CC;
padding: 30px;
border-left:4px;
border-top: 2px;
border-bottom: 0px;
border-right: 0px;
border-color: #CC9933;
border-style: solid;
}
```

GROUPING SELECTORS

Grouping selectors is an easy way to keep track of similar types of styles such as headings, and saves time spent repeating the styles' rules and troubleshooting.

There are three categories of groups. Check to see if you are using the grouping methods as often as you could:

1. An element, such as a margin or border, can be condensed into a single line by removing the side designation in the property's name, such as "left" or "right" in the property and specifying the dimensions for each side of the object in this order: top, right, bottom, left. For example, the `p.callout` style listed earlier can be condensed further by combining the border widths separated by spaces, written as:

```
p.callout {
color:#993333;
background-color:#E6E6CC;
padding: 30px;
border: 2px 0px 0px 4px;
border-color: #CC9933;
border-style: solid;
}
```

2. A number of selectors that share a style, such as headings, are separated by commas. For example, if you want all the headings in a page to use the same text color, write:

```
h1, h2, h3, h4, h5, h6 {
  color: #0066CC
}
```

3. The most common way to group selectors is to write two or more declarations attached to the same style separated by a semicolon. For example, to define font characteristics for a paragraph, write:

```
p {
  font-family: Verdana, Arial, san
  serif;
  font-weight: bold;
  color: #999999;
}
```

WRITING SHORTHAND PROPERTIES

Once you get into the swing of writing CSS, as in many other things in life, you start to look for ways to streamline your work.

Fortunately, you can specify styles using shorthand properties that decrease the length of your style sheet and save keystrokes and bandwidth. The requirement is that the properties apply to the same style.

Figure 1-20 shows a heading with the following style applied:

```
h1 {
  font-family:"BrushScript
  BT","Times New Roman", serif;
  font-size: 36px;
  font-weight: bolder;
  color:#990000;
}
```

Replicas are available in a wide range of colors and finishes. Choose a rough stone finish, like the one shown in the picture, for the most authentic reproduction.

Emory's Family Tree

Emory is one of our most popular, as well as one of our favorites. His origins are French, and he dates somewhere

1-20

The shorthand version of the style separates the values by spaces. It is condensed into a single `font` property written as:

```
h1 {
    font:"BrushScript BT","Times New
     Roman",serif
    bolder 36px #330066;
}
```

COMMENTING ON STYLE SHEETS

You may not realize how important comments are until you are faced with revising work you haven't dealt with in recent memory. It's even worse if you are starting from someone else's work.

Insert comments anywhere in a style sheet by enclosing the code or notes you want to hide using /* COMMENT */ on the style sheet. A comment can be added anywhere you can insert white space. In fact, the comments themselves are treated as white space with one exception: You can't nest a comment within another comment.

If you aren't sure how or when to use comments, imagine you are printing a page of data that has no headings, no references, and no instructions. Any or all of these situations may be perfect places to use comments.

Is there a specific order that's best to use for writing a style? Does it matter? When?

For the most part, writing a style is a matter of convenience, habit, and workflow. If it works for you, that's the best method. A browser reads a style in order — the last command or line read is considered the newest.

There are a couple of examples of situations where the order is critical. The most common example is using pseudo-element styles for `<a>` states. The order must list the `a:link` and `a:visited` states first, then the `a:hover` state, and finally the `a:active` state. Explore more in Chapter 10.

Devising workarounds for some browser inconsistencies also requires ordering style properties in a specific way.

What takes precedence — HTML attributes or CSS properties?

CSS properties take precedence over HTML attributes. If both properties and attributes are specified, the HTML attributes are used in browsers without CSS support, but have no effect in CSS-enabled browsers.

How can the box model display issue described in this chapter be resolved?

Several fixes have been developed for preventing the IE box model resizing issue described in this chapter in the sidebar "Box Model Issues." One method produces a workaround based on two `width` properties that must be written in order. The first is a `width` read by all browsers; all those except IE 5x will display the `width` property's value.

```
box {
width:400px;
padding:20px;
border:5px;
width/**/:/**/ 350px;
}
```

By placing empty comment tags (`/**/`) before the colon, IE5.0 ignores the command. Likewise, by placing these empty comment tags after the colon, IE5.5 will ignore the command. By using these two rules in conjunction with each other, the command is hidden from IE5.x.syntax.

Chapter 2

FONT AND LETTER STYLING

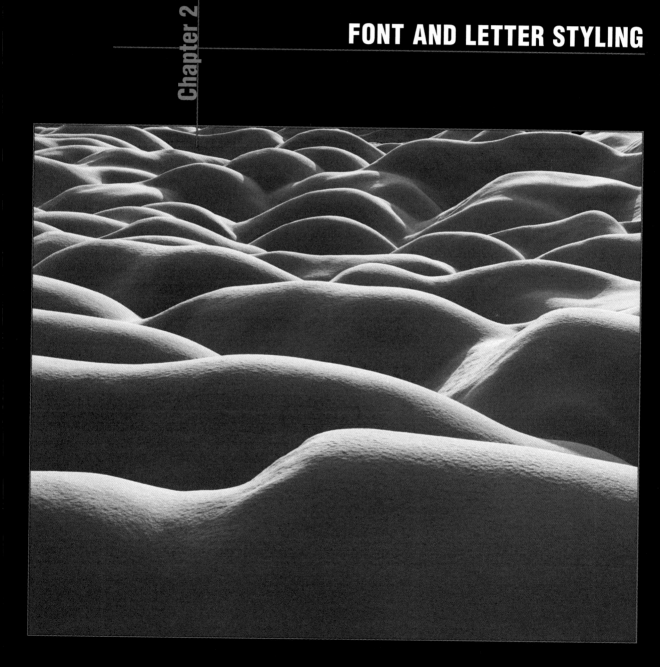

Some Web sites need as much careful attention to the text and its appearance as to its content, while content may be king on other sites. At the other extreme, where text is used graphically, the words become the most important feature of the page.

For most Web sites, the goal is to design font and text options that enhance the message of the site, while not distracting from the content. For example, a block of text using an italic font looks different enough from the rest of the content to draw attention to it, which is the point of using the italics. On the other hand, if the entire page uses italic text, the importance of the text disappears, and the page is more difficult to read.

Along with the appearance of the letters themselves, the colors, weight, spacing, and other characteristics of the text on the page contribute to guiding the reader through your site.

Font properties are inherited. As described in Chapter 1, inheritance means any CSS property that isn't specified for an element uses a property assigned a value for a parent element.

CHARACTERIZING FONTS

In CSS terms, *fonts* are not the same as *text*. Fonts and text are much the same as characters and paragraphs: font properties refer to the letters in the words themselves, while text styles refer to collections of letters.

Fonts are styled using the properties listed in Table 2-1. Keep in mind that not all viewers are using browsers capable of interpreting CSS at all, and at this point in time, very few support CSS3. The table includes properties introduced in CSS1 as well as additional properties introduced in CSS2.

Table 2-1: CSS Font Properties

Font Properties Introduced in CSS1

Property	Description
font-family	A list of font or generic names arranged in order of priority as values for the property.
font-style	Defines the vertical angle of the font.
font-variant	Specifies how the text content is capped.
font-weight	Defines the weight of the font by description or a numerical value.
font-size	The size of the font defined using one of several types of measurement, such as pixels or points.

Font Properties Introduced in CSS2

Property	Description
font-stretch	Defines the spacing between letters horizontally in a line of text; the property applies to both expanding and condensing the text.
font-size adjust	The value defines the aspect ratio of the font, or the ratio between the height of the lowercase letter *x* and the height of the font-size. The aspect ratio is important when using fonts at a small size.

Coming to a Browser Near You

CSS3 contains new font properties, including the `font-effect` property that allows styling with common word processing effects, such as embossing or engraving.

A number of font properties pertain to the amount of emphasis placed on character, including `font-emphasize`, `font-emphasize-position`, and `font-emphasize-style`. These properties are used with East Asian documents to apply accents to the characters, specify whether the accent precedes or follows the characters, and identify a string of text. I don't work with East Asian documents, but I understand how valuable proper character emphasis is to prevent misinterpretation of text meaning.

The `font-smooth` property specifies whether fonts are anti-aliased when displayed. The options include using always or never as well as defining a font size as a threshold for smoothing the characters. I am looking forward to finally having font smoothing available, which I am sure is the case for any of us involved in graphic design who are accustomed to working with programs that produce smooth font displays.

The `font-size` property has existed since CSS1; in CSS3 a coordinating property named `font-size-adjust` is defined. For designers working with small-sized fonts, it's a valuable way to control a font's aspect ratio — you can have the best of both worlds. You can use a small font and font family according to the page's design, and yet adjust the aspect ratio to read the characters clearly in a browser window.

The values may be written as:

> A size, such as small or xx-large
> A relative size, such as larger or smaller
> A length such as a number of points or pixels
> A percentage based on the font size of the parent element such as 50% or 130%

CSS3 also allows `none` as a value for font properties.

PRO TIP

Content on a page may contain characters from more than one font, such as alphanumeric characters and mathematical symbols. Your browser will look for characters in the first font listed in the property, then the second, and so on, until the character is found and displayed.

DEFINING A FONT FAMILY

Usually the first font or text decision to make is the font family you plan to use for the site. A *font family* is the CSS property defining a font by name.

Follow these steps to define a font family and write its style:

1. Decide on the fonts you want to use. The syntax for a font family is written as:

```
{
font-family: "font choice a", "font
 choice b", generic font-family;
}
```

The `font-family` rule is interpreted by a Web browser in order of the values listed, like the Garamond font shown in figure 2-1. The style for the block of text next to the thumbnail image is written as:

```
{
font-family: Garamond, "Times New
  Roman", Times, serif;
}
```

2-1

2. Ensure a browser can read the listed font names properly. Enclose the proper name of a font in quotation marks for clear identification if the name contains white space. In the example shown in figure 2-1, Times New Roman is the only named font that contains more than one word and needs quotation marks.

When a browser interprets the page, it correlates the names on the list with fonts installed on the viewer's system, displaying the first font available.

3. Specify the generic font you want to include in the font set. Minimally, every computer is going to have a generic serif font, which is used to display the content on the page, as in the example shown in figure 2-2.

2-2

DISPLAYING GENERIC FONTS

The generic serif font, although heavier and not quite the same visually as the first choice Garamond, is definitely superior to showing the text in a generic monospace font, like the example shown in figure 2-3.

2-3

You aren't limited in the number of fonts you can name as values, aside from practicality. It isn't likely that the average viewer will notice an appreciable difference between Gill Sans and Arial font, both of which are shown in figure 2-4. Not only will the average reader not notice much difference, writing long strings of font names is time-consuming, and certainly doesn't contribute to streamlined code in any way.

In ordinary circumstances where I want the look of a named font, the style property lists the named font; one or even two similar fonts that may be available to the user if they don't have my named font; and then the generic font as a set of three values.

On the other hand, if you are designing to a corporate template, you usually have to define the template's fonts first and then follow up with generics.

Because every computer will minimally display a generic serif, sans-serif, and monospaced font, include one of the options in your font-family declaration as the last value in the string.

2-4

NOTE

Writing a font-family style is often a judgment call. How important is the font? In the example written in the previous section, the style includes two alternate fonts if the viewer doesn't have Garamond.

Notice that the alternate fonts are Times New Roman and Times, much the same in appearance but named differently. Listing both means the viewer's browser will display either of the Times fonts available.

USING OTHER GENERIC FONTS

In addition to the generic serif, sans-serif, and monospaced font types, there are two more font types that you may see or use in a Web page's styles.

Standards-compliance requires that a generic font be listed at the end of the `font-family` value's string. That's fine as part of a string, but there's no way to predict the text appearance if you write only the generic font as the value. Unlike serif or sans-serif, which use a single, easily identifiable appearance, the Fantasy and Cursive generic font types aren't standardized.

The two types include:

> **Fantasy.** A fantasy font is a highly stylized decorative font, and isn't going to give you predictable results because there isn't a default font appearance. The browser has to read the value and then decide which of the system's fonts should be displayed to fulfill the `fantasy` value in the style.

> **Cursive.** A cursive font is a font that looks like handwriting or printing. Because there are hundreds of fonts defined in the cursive category, assigning the value to the font by name in your style is going to be more successful than writing a generic style.

Examples of both default Fantasy and Cursive fonts are shown in three browser windows in figure 2-5. The upper pair is the Internet Explorer 6 interpretation of the styles; the central pair is how Firefox 1.5 displays the styles; and the lower pair is the result of Netscape Navigator 7 reading the styles.

This is an example of using fantasy as the font-family value.

This is an example of using cursive as the font-family value.

This is an example of using fantasy as the font-family value.

This is an example of using cursive as the font-family value.

This is an example of using fantasy as the font-family value.

This is an example of using cursive as the font-family value.

2-5

PRO TIP

Suppose you want to display a cursive font, and list Bradley Hand and Brush Script as your first and second choice values. You need a generic font as the last in the string of values.

Sometimes I use the generic cursive as the generic in the string. If the text appearance isn't critical, but perhaps the layout spacing is important, choosing either a serif or sans-serif generic lets you understand how most viewers will see the page display; the same sort of control isn't possible using the cursive generic.

DESIGNING A FONT SET

"Less is more." Like most things in good design, look for colors, fonts, and graphic details that are cohesive and contribute to the page's message.

Follow these steps to design your font set:

1. Decide on the color scheme. Use color for interest and emphasis, but limit the number of colors on a page. A small number of coordinated colors is attractive, while a large assortment of colors is distracting and takes away focus from the content. In the example shown in figure 2-6, brown is used for the main heading as well as the menu items at the lower left; the text in the blockquote and the body of the page is black.

2. Similarly, limit the number of fonts on a page. Use bold or italic text for emphasis or particular purposes, such as the introductory blockquote shown in figure 2-6.

3. Choose fonts that are easy to read on-screen. The example in figure 2-6 uses Papyrus font for the heading and blockquote text. It is an artistic font, yet easy to read.

4. Choose fonts that match the type of site or its content. The top line of text in figure 2-7 uses the Millennium font, better suited to less artistic subject matter — this font would look good on a science fiction Web site. The central line of text uses a font named Whatevur, and its informal, irreverent, and blocky appearance could make it a good choice for a teen opinion blog or forums. The bottom line of text uses the AirCut font. Although this font is suitably artistic for the subject matter of the page, it's difficult to read on-screen because the letters are quite thin.

Cherub Series, January 2005

Page Content

I have completed several photographic studies in recent years. The cherub group, including four images, is from January 2005.

Shot from north side, 10 am　　　Shot from south side, 10 am

6 Jan
2006

Next

Home

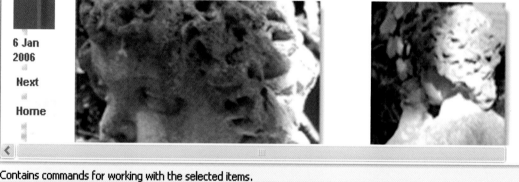

Contains commands for working with the selected items.

2-6

CHERUB SERIES, JANUARY 2005

Cherub Series, January 2005

Cherub Series, January 2005

2-7

STYLING FONT WEIGHTS AND APPEARANCES

Customize the font display using one or more common font properties, listed in Table 2-1. A simple way to create a suite of headings and link appearances for a site is using a combination of font properties applied to the same font.

SPECIFYING A FONT STYLE

The `font-style` property defines the slant of the characters displayed in your Web browser. The default `normal` style is upright, sometimes called "roman." Unless a different style is specified, all text is shown in normal style.

The other font styles are variations on a positive slant: `oblique` style slants the text several degrees in a positive direction; `italic` style slants it further in a positive direction.

The differences between `oblique` and `italic` are slight to none. Some browsers don't recognize `oblique` at all, and automatically insert `italic` text. In figure 2-8, for example, the quote looks the same whether the style specifies `oblique` or `italic` font style.

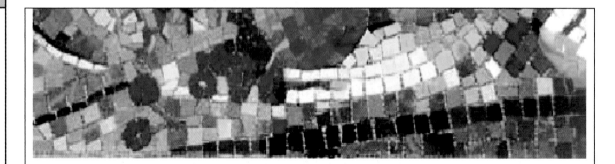

A newly completed piece in Smalti glass, tile on fiberglass mesh, 23 x 18 inches.

"The glass is cool, with an almost buttery texture, and markedly different coloring on each side..."

2-8

USING FONT VARIANTS

There are only two variations on the font variants theme. Text is either shown as normal, using upper- and lowercase letters depending on how the content is typed; or small-caps, where all lowercase letters are converted to uppercase letters having a smaller font size than the original uppercase letters.

Using a small-cap variation looks good when applied to <h2> level heading styles, and also for link styles. This book shows an example of using small caps for a second-level heading.

DEFINING A FONT WEIGHT

Fonts can display weights, or different stroke widths. A font at its default weight technically uses the font-weight: normal property and value.

Font weight is defined either as a comparison or as a value. As a comparison, you can write font-weight: bold for heavier text than the default, and font-weight: bolder for even heavier text. Use font-weight: lighter for a slimmer version of the default text, like the upper title shown in the example in figure 2-9. For comparison, the lower sample of the title shows the original style's weight, which I found too heavy for the page.

In the example, the modified <h1> style is about the same size as the <h2> style would appear on the page, but I always adjust the default headings. I don't use the <h2> style instead of a modified <h1> level style, nor do I usually create classes for headings rather than modifying the default appearance of the heading.

Be inspired ~

Be inspired ~

Finishing a piece is inspiring at any time. When you have an opportunity to work with the perfect mosaic material, it's even more special.

2-9

If you plan to modify the default headings, which I recommend for simplicity whenever possible, the goal is to maintain the relationship among the headings' appearances. Alternatively, you can define a font-weight value in increments from 100 to 900 inclusive. The increments don't have a unit of measurement, such as pixels or inches. A value of 100 is the thinnest, 400 is equivalent to a normal weight, and 700 is equivalent to bold weight.

PRO TIP

A properly structured page starts with a first-level heading followed by a hierarchy of headings decreasing in prominence.

The better the page's structure, the easier it is to use by screen readers and other assistive devices.

DEFINING FONT SIZES

Probably the most common properties applied in font styles pertain to font sizes, described in your styles as a *length*. Length can be either horizontal or vertical, and *relative* or *absolute*. Relative units specify a value according to another value; absolute lengths provide a value based on a specific unit of measure.

A length value is formatted as +1.3em and is composed of:

> The sign character with (+) as the default. Since a positive number is implied you don't have to include the symbol; for a negative value you need to preface the number with a (-) symbol.

> The number for the length's value, which can include decimal values.

> An identifier for the unit of measure used, such as px or em. If the length is 0, the identifier is optional.

PRO TIP

It is legal to use negative length values but I don't recommend it. Negative values unnecessarily complicate your styles, and browsers may be unable to display your intended style correctly.

USING RELATIVE LENGTH VALUES

Relative length units specify a value for one element relative to another element's property. Defining relative lengths is the way to go when a page is both displayed on-screen and printed because relative units scale more accurately than absolute units.

The types of relative units to choose from include:

> Units of measure, such as pixels and em units.

> Percentages, either greater than or less than 100 percent.

> Keywords that change the size of a font based on a comparison, such as larger or smaller.

Sizing using relative values

I generally use relative size values to allow viewers' browsers to resize the content as necessary. Control over display sizes lets my viewers accommodate poor eyesight or lighting conditions, or different qualities of monitor displays.

The three units of measure that define lengths in relation to other units include:

> **em.** The em unit is the same as the value of the font-size property of an element. If your style's parent element uses a 12pt (point) font as the default, for example, then 1em = 12pt height, as you can see in figure 2-10. Use em units for both vertical and horizontal measurement.

> **ex.** The ex unit is based on the height of a font's lowercase *x*, defined as the font's *x-height*. In figure 2-10, the lowercase *x* shows a height of 9pt, meaning that 1ex = 9pt height.

> **px.** Pixels are the native unit of measurement for a monitor; the visual size of a pixel is relative to the viewing device or monitor. Pixels are terrific for defining on-screen sizes, but steer clear of pixels as a unit of measurement for content destined for printing. Using pixels can result in printing problems, sometimes showing a single dot for a character.

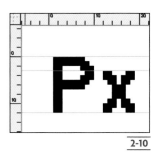

2-10

Sizing using percentage values

It doesn't really matter what font or range of sizes are used for text and headings on a page, as you can see in figure 2-11. Instead, it's the relationship among the elements that is important.

We customarily define the relative importance of content we read based on text size. That is, seeing a very large heading means you are at the start of a section, chapter, or unit; progressively smaller headings identify nested topic levels within a main heading.

If the default text size of your style sheet is 100 percent (something is always 100 percent of itself), headings are in the range of 140 percent, and subheadings are about 120 percent.

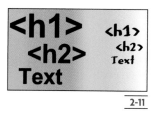

2-11

Specifying size using keywords

Web browsers recognize a number of keywords that specify a font size in relation to other font sizes. Using the browser's default normal size, the browser can display text as either smaller or larger incrementally depending on the keyword used, ranging from xx-small to xx-large.

I rarely use the keywords for defining font sizes. How large is large? How small is small? The values vary according to browser and browser version interpretation, and may not display your page as intended.

Which method is best to use? There's no answer to that question aside from "It depends."

In general, I use em or percentages when I am working with lots of text to visualize relationships among headings; I use px for sites that are usually viewed online and that contain mixed text/images. The ex method is best for pages having very small text because it allows for resizing according to a specified aspect ratio. I don't rely on keywords.

STRETCHING OR ADJUSTING FONT SIZES

Two other font style properties are available to help control the display of fonts on a Web browser page. You can specify that a Web browser scales the fonts used on a page horizontally, or control the perceived height of a font displayed regardless of the font shown on the Web page.

PRO TIP

If you haven't used percentages for defining values, give them a try. Percentage values are always based on the inherited value of the parent element. Change the default text size, and your headings and other navigational text items based on the default text size automatically resize as well. Simple.

PRO TIP

Neither the font-stretch nor the font-size-adjust properties can be specified in a shorthand Font style. Read about using a shorthand method for declaring values for your page's fonts later in the chapter.

Scaling fonts horizontally

Use the `font-stretch` property to condense or expand a displayed font horizontally on a Web page like the examples shown in figure 2-12. The `font-stretch` property is a quick way to expand the spacing between characters for page headings, for example, or condense horizontal spacing for other styles such as links on a page. All three headings/labels variations use the same-sized font. The main heading uses expanded text, the "Celtic" label uses default spacing, and the link's text uses a condensed version of the same font. The labels are distinctive enough to demonstrate the hierarchy used on the page.

2-12

The values for the property are condensed, expanded, or normal. For either condensed or expanded values, you can further define the amount of scaling using `ultra`, `extra`, and `semi` prefixes. Write the property and its values like this:

```
h2 {
font-stretch: extra-expanded;
}
```

You can also use `wider` or `narrower` values to set the scale of an element's style one increment wider or narrower than a parent element.

Using font size changes

A common trend these days is to use small fonts on a page, such as 8px or 9px. If your viewers' browsers

substitute your font with another from the `font-family` property's values or a system font, the substituted font may not be able to display the content clearly.

The ratio between the height of a font's lowercase letter x and the height of the font's size is its *aspect ratio*. The aspect ratios for some fonts commonly used on Web pages are listed in Table 2-2.

The aspect ratio value is the reason some fonts look a lot smaller than others, even if you have specified the same size of font. The higher the aspect ratio, the more legible the font displays on-screen when shown at a small size.

The `font-size-adjust` property specifies an aspect ratio value that is applied to whatever font is displayed in your user's browser.

Specifying a font aspect ratio is useful for your browser to determine the best substitute font to use in lieu of a font that isn't available.

NOTE

Although the `font size adjust` property has been available since CSS 2.1, it is still not widely supported. In the following steps you can see the difference between using the style in IE and Firefox browsers.

Table 2-2: Aspect Ratios for Some Common Fonts

Font Name	Aspect Ratio
Comic Sans	0.54
Georgia	0.50
Gill Sans	0.46
Myriad Web	0.48
Times New Roman	0.46
Trebuchet	0.53
Verdana	0.58

To use a font's aspect ratio in a style and determine the font size of a substitute font, follow these steps:

1. Assign font values to the `font-family` property on your style sheet. For example, write:

```
p.fineprint {
font-family: Verdana, "Gill Sans",
 sans-serif; font-size: 9px;
}
```

2. Write a style to declare the aspect ratio for the style; the style is written as:

```
p.fineprint {
font-size-adjust: 0.58;
}
```

3. Calculate the effect of applying the style to other fonts that may be substituted in a viewer's browser window. In the example written in step 1:

> The first listed font is Verdana, with an aspect ratio of 0.58.

> The second listed font is Gill Sans, with an aspect ratio of 0.46.

> The font size is 9px.

If a viewer has Verdana on their computer, the Web browser displays the font at 9px size. If the viewer doesn't have Verdana, Gill Sans is used, like the left example shown in figure 2-13. If the viewer is using the Firefox browser, the font is displayed at a calculated size like the right example shown in figure 2-13.

The displayed size is based on this calculation:

```
font size value * (aspect ratio of
 first font / aspect ratio of sub-
 stitute font)
```

In our example, the text using Gill Sans font is shown on-screen at a size of:

```
9px * (0.58/0.46) = 11.34px
```

SETTING THE HEIGHT OF LINES

In addition to the height of the text on a page, you can specify the space between two lines of text as the `line-height` property. I often use an expanded line height to identify a style for an item I want to emphasize in a page of text. Using different line heights is a technique commonly seen in word processing and page layouts, and can be readily transferred to Web pages as well.

An example of using `line-height` to apply spacing to a one-line paragraph in a text-heavy page is shown in figure 2-14.

PRO TIP

Instead of writing a style like my example, you could use any of a number of other styles and formats, such as a set of margins or a blockquote.

I find building a simple modification of the paragraph style using a `line-height` value quicker to write and easier to remember. To further emphasize a line, like that in figure 2-14, use bold or colored text.

A newly completed piece in Smalti glass, tile on fiberglass mesh, 23 x 18 inches.

A newly completed piece in Smalti glass, tile on fiberglass mesh, 23 x 18 inches.

2-13

commerical port. By the 10th Century it had its own police force, merchant and other classes, and currency.

In 1291 the Venetian Republic declared all glassmakers could operate their foundaries only on the island of Murano. The purpose wasn't to segregate the glassmakers for any nefarious reason. Instead, the decision was made based on the predominant building material of the homes in Venice at the time. Glassworks presented a fire hazard, and most buildings were made of wood.

Moving to the island had its advantages for the glassmakers.

They were immune from prosecution by the Venetian state, noted for being oppressive. Daughters of glassmakers were allowed to marry into aristocratic families by the end of the 14th Century.

Development of Modern Factories

2-14

DEFINING A LINE'S HEIGHT

Line-height is inherited and applies to all elements.

Write the height of a line using one of the relative values described in the previous section such as an em or percentage value.

You can also use a number to calculate the value of the line-height. For example, in a style written as:

```
p {
font-size: 10px;
line-height: 1.4;
}
```

the space between the lines of text would be 10 * 1.4 = 11.4px.

One line of text can use more than one line-height depending on the content and its styles. The `<span>` tags enclosing the final phrase in the last line shown in figure 2-15 use a style with a larger font size than the other `<blockquote>` text. The paragraph, with some of the text removed to save space, is written as:

```
<blockquote>...trip to Venice, and
had the opportunity to spend <span
class="phrases"> a day on the Island
of Murano. </span> </blockquote>
```

If you are looking at a page layout and something seems a bit off in terms of the spacing, consider whether there are multiple elements in a line.

NOTE

You can read about block and inline elements, the basic layout options on a Web page, in Chapter 5.

PRO TIP

Older browsers have problems with many styles, including line-height. For example, IE3 can't process line-height in any way, while Netscape resets line-height to normal if a border property is specified. Fortunately you can correct this error by declaring a left margin value for the element.

Opera applies spacing beneath text below the baseline rather than below the bottom of the font, pushing the bottom line down a few pixels. Correct the issue by adding padding for Opera.

*You are most likely to come across glass artisans at craft shows. For a glimpse into the past, and an opportunity to see where the standards against which all other products are measured, I took a recent trip to Venice, and had the opportunity to spend **a day on the island of Murano**.*

2-15

DEFINING ABSOLUTE FONT VALUES

Adjusting text size in styles displayed on a Web page also changes the amount of text shown on a printed page. Use an absolute value, such as point size, to define font sizes for printing.

Point size is a unit familiar to anyone working with print and refers to an imaginary box that extends from the top of an ascender, like the top of the *h* shown in figure 2-16, to the bottom of a descender, like the tails on the *p* and *q* shown in the figure.

2-16

The problem with using point size as a unit of measure is that Macintosh computers display points at a smaller size on-screen — about one-third smaller in size — than the same text shown on-screen on a Windows computer OS.

Absolute units such as in (inch), mm (millimeter), or cm (centimeter) can be used to define text size.

Real-world units of measurement are difficult to use in a browser. A browser might be able to show a 4-inch-tall string of text, but you won't see much beyond the text color using the same style sheet on a handheld device.

RELATIVE ADVANTAGES

There are a number of reasons to use relative or *liquid* sizing, using either the em or percentage values. For some designers, percentages are more intuitive, while for others the em value is more intuitive. Regardless of which unit of measure seems more straightforward, the values of using a relative sizing method for fonts include:

> The relative units can be configurable by user preferences, important for those who need to change the display size to compensate for visual problems.

> The relative units maintain proportion among element sizes. If a user applies custom style sheets or changes his or her browser text size, the elements' sizes change as well, maintaining the size relationships.

> The relative units work cross-platform and cross-media.

FONT STYLING SHORTCUTS

Instead of writing a sequence of properties and values for a style, build a single shorthand style. Some people need to keep the sequence of properties declared in the style systematic to prevent errors of omission and make troubleshooting easier. Others prefer to write a shortcut style freehand. Regardless of which method you prefer, keep these factors in mind:

> You can't include `font-stretch` or `font-size-adjust` properties in a shorthand style.

> You have to include at least the `font-size` and `font-family` properties.

> Other properties not included in the style are defined as normal by default.

For example, a style written as:

```
p {
font: 11px Garamond;
}
```

is the same thing as writing:

```
p {
font-weight: normal;
font-stretch: normal;
font-variant: normal;
font-style: normal;
font-size-adjust: none;
font-size: 11px;
font-family: Garamond;
}
```

NOTE

Line-height can be included in the font declaration as well, and is preceded by a / to differentiate the height from the font size. For example, write `12px/18px` to define the height of the font at 12px and the line height at 18px.

REDEFINING TAGS

Instead of using named styles for elements such as headings and blockquotes, style the appearance of the default element. By simply changing how the default styles appear, you save time trying to develop a logical naming system for the elements and remembering the names when writing and applying the styles. You also save troubleshooting should things go wrong, which can certainly happen. The previous section lists a style for a `<p>` tag. In the Web page to which the style is applied, any and all paragraphs use the new default style, except for those using a named style.

STYLING SYSTEM FONTS

Rather than specifying custom styles, or those for page tags, specify the system font. Going back to the source lets you identify a font to use for different properties, listed in Table 2-3.

Styles for system fonts are written the same way as other font styles once you define the system font as a value for the `font` property, such as:

```
{
font: status-bar;
font-size: 16px;
font-style: italic;
}
```

In this example, the status bar at the bottom of the browser window would show a 16px italic font.

Table 2-3: System Font Properties

Property	Specifies the Characteristics for
Caption	Fonts that use captioned controls, like buttons and drop-down lists
Icon	Fonts used by icon labels
Menu	Fonts used for drop-down menus
Message-Box	Fonts used by dialog boxes
Small-Caption	The font used for labeling small controls on the window
Status-Bar	Fonts used for a browser window's status bar
Inherit	Characteristics that are inherited from higher-level elements. If a property isn't specified in a style, it uses the `normal` value.

Q & A

I am starting a new style sheet. What are the key concepts to consider in the font styles?

Having dozens of styles that are used for text in your Web site can be unruly and confusing. Before you start, simplify what you need, or create different style sheets to attach to different parts of your site. For example, you could build and attach different style sheets for pages of a shopping cart, catalog, or text-based pages.

Keep in mind that:

> It's simpler to declare styles for parent elements and then let nested styles inherit the properties.

> Assigning a style to an existing tag, such as headings, is simpler to keep track of than writing discrete styles.

> For some designers, using shorthand to write styles saves time. For others, using shorthand styles costs time in troubleshooting.

> Develop a system for naming styles and declaring properties that works for you, and stick to it.

What user issues should I consider when I am writing styles?

A considerable number of people modify how their browsers display a page. To make the display more usable, consider these ideas:

> Using relative lengths lets your viewers control the text sizing in their Web browser if required.

> Since many users view content on browser windows displayed on large TV screens or small handheld devices, stay away from absolute values such as inches or centimeters.

> Italicized or bold fonts are more difficult to read than default font styles; sans-serif fonts are easier to read than many serif fonts.

Is there a rule for adjusting the height between lines? Why bother?

Line height is changed to make the appearance of a page easier to read. You don't want to get carried away though — increasing the line height too much makes it harder to read the page because the overabundance of white space is distracting.

Here are some factors that can influence how a line height change affects a page view:

> It's usually easier to read text over a background color when the line height is increased.

> Match the line height to the font's characteristics. For fonts having a small x-height and consequently a smaller appearance on the page, don't increase the line height dramatically.

> On a text-heavy page, experiment with increasing line height to improve readability.

> Headings don't usually need increased line heights because they usually don't have more than one line.

> Elements like text in table cells, preformatted text, and computer code don't need to use extravagant amounts of line height because it distracts from the content.

DESIGNING STYLISH TEXT

In the early days of Web design, page layout wasn't much of an issue because there was no way to lay out a page aside from applying several basic styles. Of course, if you simply had to have a piece of text formatted in a certain way you could create an image to place on the Web page. Fortunately, using big image files to display page text isn't done much anymore.

Instead, you can use styles to design the perfect pull-quote, indent the first line of a paragraph, or add a horizontal rule that coordinates with the rest of your Web site.

Text and fonts are not the same thing. As described in Chapter 2, *fonts* refer to the styles associated with the actual alphanumeric characters you display on a page; *text* refers to the appearance of words, lines, and paragraphs on the page.

A sure way to save time building a style sheet is to combine styles and specify that a style be applied to multiple elements; read how guest contributor Margaret Werdermann "stacks" style rules to help organize her clients' sites.

DISPLAYING TEXT

The first consideration is the appearance of the text itself. Styles associated with the text are based on colors, direction, and decoration.

SPECIFYING FONT AND BACKGROUND COLORS

Your perfectly designed color scheme isn't necessarily what your viewers see. Users can apply a style sheet or change their default preferences.

When you design your style sheet, specify a font color in your text style, and be sure to define a background color for the style as well. I make it a general practice to define a background for two reasons:

> Users can change the color in their style sheet or preferences to change your page's color scheme; if the background color isn't defined in your style

sheet, the text may disappear or not display well, like the lower example shown in figure 3-1. In the upper page, the default black text on a white background is shown.

> When a color is defined for text, the background color must also be declared to make the style sheet standards-compliant. If you create a style defining the text color, but don't specify a background color, when you validate the page the style triggers a warning, such as:

```
Line: 33 You have no background-
color with your color: p.product
```

APPLYING TEXT DECORATIONS

A number of different text decorations are possible using CSS. Some are widely used, while others are less common. Your choices (in alphabetical order) are as follows:

> The text-decoration: blink property was a big deal over a decade ago when it was first available, but the look belongs in the past with polyester. You see blinking text occasionally, but it is distracting and generally annoying.

> A property that isn't often used is the text-decoration: line-through attribute. It is useful for showing how subject material can be edited, or displaying a price cut on a catalog Web site like the example shown in figure 3-2.

Bask in the Sun

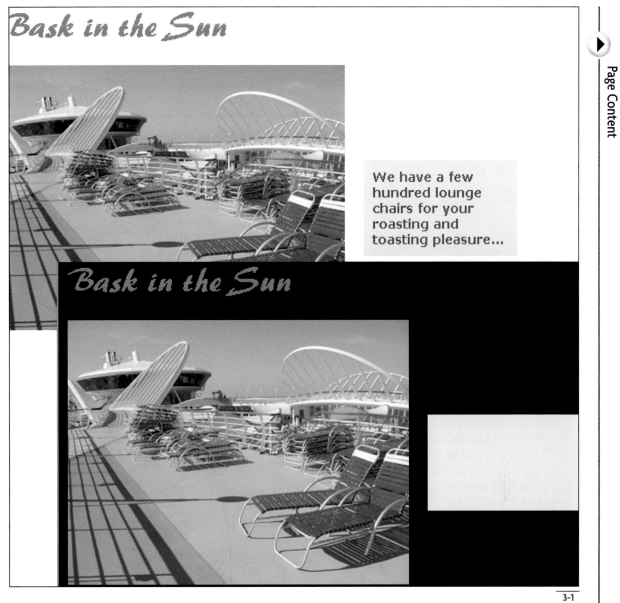

We have a few hundred lounge chairs for your roasting and toasting pleasure...

Bask in the Sun

3-1

3-3

> A `text-shadow` option can specify a drop shadow for a piece of text, but isn't widely supported by browsers other than Safari. You can define a shadow using JavaScript, by creating an image of the text, or by adding two copies of text to a page using absolute positioning and color variations to simulate text shadows.

> The most common text decoration property is `text-decoration: underline`. Underlining text as decoration confuses the viewer who is probably under the impression that the text is a link. Use bold or italic text for emphasis, and leave the underline as a visual cue for links.

> A hyperlink displayed on a Web page is underlined by default. Use the `text-decoration: none` property to remove the default underline.

> The `text-decoration: overline` decoration option isn't used often. It can look good used as a style for the `a:hover` selector of a link, like the example shown in figure 3-3.

PRO TIP

Don't expect consistent viewing of text shadows across browsers.

If you want to use a shadow, try the simulation described next. It has more chance of being viewed properly because it relies on positioning styles, which are more widely supported than styles using text shadow properties.

SIMULATING A SHADOW

The example shown in figure 3-4 uses two styles for the `<h1>` tags to create the appearance of a shadow. Follow these steps to build a shadow appearance:

1. Write or modify the style for the first version of the `<h1>` tag. In the example, the size, color, and font-family are defined in the style sheet.

2. Specify positioning properties (discussed in Chapter 6) to define the placement for the heading from the left and top margins. The example uses these rules:

```
left: 10px;
top: 10px;
position: absolute;
```

Ten seconds to liftoff...

4. Type two copies of the heading's text.

5. Assign the customized style to the second `<h1>` style. As shown in the figure, the text looks like it is shadowed on the page.

TRANSFORMING AND SPACING TEXT

Some of the text styles let you configure the layout of text on a page, both in how the text looks, and how it is spaced.

SPACING LETTERS AND WORDS

Use the `letter-spacing` property to increase or decrease the amount of white space between letters. The `letter-spacing` property can be defined using a specified length, such as pixels; you can also use a negative value to decrease spacing between letters.

In figure 3-5, for example, the text in the upper row uses default letter spacing, the middle shows the effect of increasing the spacing by 10px, and the lower row shows how using a negative value, in this case −1px, decreases the spacing between letters.

3-4

3. Write the second `<h1>` style. The second style includes margins and positioning properties again, as well as defining the `z-index` to place the shadow behind the heading (more on positioning in Chapter 6). For interest, the style defines a larger margin at the right and bottom sides and a background color, as you can see in the figure. The style is written as:

```
h1.shadow {
color: #F3F3F3;
z-index: -1;
left: 14px;
top: 14px;
position: absolute;
margin: 0px 120px 120px 0px;
background-color:#EEE8DD;
}
```

It does look like she's flying, doesn't it?

The   display   mannequin   is
perched   outside   the   door   of
a   children's   wear   boutique
on   the   boardwalk.

It was just the place to get out of the sun, but quite an expensive detour.

3-5

Specify the amount of white space between words using the `word-spacing` property. The default value is `normal`; increase or decrease the spacing between words by defining the length in the style like this:

```
p.expand {
word-spacing: 24px;
}
```

In figure 3-6, the upper line of text uses the default word spacing; the lower line of text shows the effect of applying the style.

Then it was back to the beach.

Then   it   was   back   to   the   beach.

3-6

NOTE

Chapter 2 describes condensing or expanding the content of a line; word spacing affects only the space between words.

CONTROLLING TEXT CAPITALIZATION

Do you ever work on projects where several people are involved in creating and editing content for a Web site? Do you have corporate or procedural style guides that define when content, such as headings, are to be capitalized?

The answer to both questions for many of us is yes. Keep the `text-transform` property in mind as you are working: you may be surprised how often you include it in your styles.

The `text-transform` property uses these values:

> `text-transform: uppercase` converts all text to which the style is applied to capital letters. If your content is regularly used by viewers working with screen readers, it's a good idea to use the style. For example, a screen reader may read a link labeled EMAIL US as the word EMAIL and define the word US as an acronym and pronounce the letters.

PRO TIP

To make it even easier for screen readers, use `<acronym>` tags to identify acronyms along with formatting the text using the `text-transform: uppercase` rule.

> `text-transform: lowercase` converts any string of text to which it is applied to lowercase text. It's a good option to use for styles applied to content that must be in lowercase, such as part or equipment numbers using alphanumeric strings.

> `text-transform: capitalize`, as you would expect, capitalizes the first letter of each word within the element to which the style is applied, such as headings. Although it takes a few seconds to type the property and value, knowing that each and every heading in a Web site that uses a specific heading style is always capitalized saves proofing and editing time.

DESIGNING PARAGRAPH LAYOUTS

One of the only times the average viewer pays attention to layout elements on a page is when there is something "off." The example shown in figure 3-7 has a few errors:

> The headings aren't visually appropriate in that they don't incrementally decrease in prominence from `<h1>` to `<h6>`, using instead a variety of indents and varying sizes and weights.

> The blockquote is indented unevenly with a wider margin at the left than the right. Whenever possible, I try to use default styles such as headings or blockquotes, and modify the characteristics of the default to suit my page.

ALIGNING PARAGRAPHS

The `text-align` attribute is an inherited attribute defining the horizontal placement of text within an element as center, left, right, auto, or justify.

Not all browsers display `text-align:justified` correctly, but instead left align the content.

INDENTING MULTIPLE LINES

Text using the `<blockquote>` tag's default style is indented on both left and right sides with margins of about 40px, and uses increased white space above and below the block.

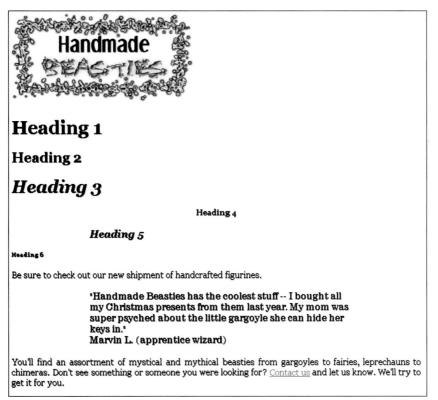

Heading 4

Be sure to check out our new shipment of handcrafted figurines.

> "Handmade Beasties has the coolest stuff -- I bought all my Christmas presents from them last year. My mom was super psyched about the little gargoyle she can hide her keys in."
> Marvin L. (apprentice wizard)

You'll find an assortment of mystical and mythical beasties from gargoyles to fairies, leprechauns to chimeras. Don't see something or someone you were looking for? Contact us and let us know. We'll try to get it for you.

3-7

Change the display of the default tag by adjusting its margins. Be careful not to go overboard, unless that is your design goal. In figure 3-8, the default `<blockquote>` tag's layout is used in the upper example. Contrast that with how awkward the page layout seems in the lower example, which uses 150px margins all around the text.

Be sure to check out our new shipment of handcrafted figurines.

> "Handmade Beasties has the coolest stuff -- I bought all my Christmas presents from them last year. My mom was super psyched about the little gargoyle she can hide her keys in."
> Marvin L. (apprentice wizard)

You'll find an assortment of mystical and mythical beasties from gargoyles to fairies, leprecha

Be sure to check out our new shipment of handcrafted figurines.

> "Handmade Beasties has the coolest stuff -- I bought all my Christmas presents from them last year. My mom was super psyched about the little gargoyle she can hide her keys in."
> Marvin L. (apprentice wizard)

You'll find an assortment of mystical and mythical beasties from gargoyles to fairies, leprechauns

3-8

DRAWING ATTENTION TO PHRASES

HTML 4 defined a number of phrase elements which are also used in XHTML. *Phrase elements* are tags used to identify a specific type of content. Use the tags as is or modify the default style to suit your Web page. You can write your own styles and assign them to `<span>` tags, which is what I usually do. The phrase elements and their appearances are shown in Table 3-1.

Table 3-1: Phrase Element Appearance

Phrase Element	Looks Like . . .
Emphasized text	*Emphasized text*
Strong text	**Strong text**
Definition term	*Definition term*
Computer code text	Computer code text
Sample text	Sample text
Keyboard text	Keyboard text
Variable	Variable
Citation	*Citation*

PRO TIP

Different browsers will show the default tags' styles differently or not distinguish them at all from the `<body>` tag. When you need control over an element's appearance, write your own styles to be sure you know what your viewers see on the browser window.

CUSTOMIZING HORIZONTAL RULES

Another device often used to separate content on a page is a horizontal rule. It's simple to modify the default appearance to suit the layout of your Web site.

On my Web site, for example, I use the default `<hr />` tag throughout, and coordinate it with my site's colors using this style:

```
hr {
    height: 4px;
    background-color: #C2B4B4;
    border-top: 1px solid #663333;
}
```

You can see examples of the coordinated content in figure 3-9. The upper part of the figure shows menu and content from the upper part of the page; the lower part shows the rule and contact information used at the bottom of every page on the site.

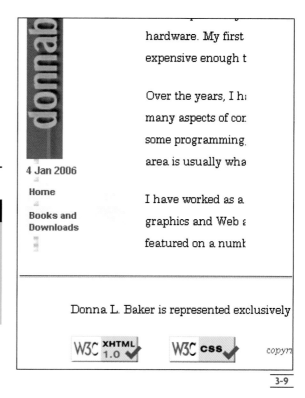

4 Jan 2006

Home

Books and Downloads

hardware. My first

expensive enough t

Over the years, I h:

many aspects of cor.

some programming.

area is usually wha

I have worked as a

graphics and Web ɛ

featured on a numt

Donna L. Baker is represented exclusively

W3C XHTML 1.0 ✓   W3C CSS ✓   copyri

3-9

CUSTOMIZING WITH PSEUDO-ELEMENTS

I am fond of pseudo-elements, as geeky as that sounds. They are a quick and convenient way to really customize the layout on a page.

Use pseudo-elements for creating drop caps to start a section of text, and to customize the first line of a block of text.

The syntax for pseudo-elements is written as:

```
selector:pseudo-element {property:
value}
```

Combine a CSS class with a pseudo-element, written as:

```
selector.class:pseudo-element
{property: value}
```

CREATING A DROP CAP USING A PSEUDO-ELEMENT

Write the style for a `first:letter` pseudo-element following these steps:

1. Decide how you want the style configured. In the example I am using, the style for the pseudo-element is written as:

```
p:first-letter {
font-size: 200%;
float: left;
color: #CC3366;
}
```

2. Type the text for the paragraph to which you want to apply the style.

3. Define the class for the tag, such as `<p class="first letter">`.

4. Test the page. As you can see in figure 3-10, the first letter of the paragraph is twice the size of the other letters, and a cherry red color.

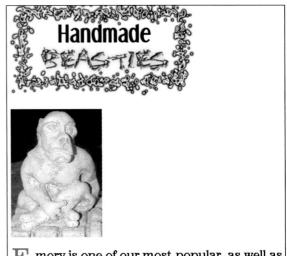

Handmade BEASTIES

E mory is one of our most popular, as well as of our favorites. His origins are French, and dates somewhere in the mid-1400's. Replicas ar

3-10

PRO TIP

The `float` style defines which side of an element the styled object will align so other content wraps around it. Read about using floats in Chapter 5.

PRO TIP

The first-letter pseudo-element can only be used with block-level elements, which makes sense because you are looking at customizing the first letter of an entity. If you want to use the style inline, drop in `<span>` tags.

CUSTOMIZING THE FIRST LINE OF A PARAGRAPH

Rather than styling the first letter, follow these steps to style the first line:

1. Write the style, such as in this example:

```
p:first-line {
color: #B34700;
font-family: Geneva, Arial,
 Helvetica, sans-serif;
}
```

2. Type the paragraph's text.

3. Apply the style to the tag, such as
   `<p class="first line">`.

4. Test the page. Figure 3-11 shows the results of applying the style written in step 1. The text for the first line uses a sans-serif font, and is dark orange in color.

Emory is one of our most popular, as well as one of our favorites. His origins are French, and he dates somewhere in the mid-1400's.

3-11

PRO TIP

Where the line breaks depends on the size of the browser window. If you want to have a specific segment of a line showing a different font, don't bother with a pseudo-element. Instead, write a style, and add `<span>` tags surrounding the subject text; specify the style as a class of the `<span>` tag.

MAKING COMBO STYLES

Whenever possible, I like to combine styles. If you plan carefully, you can combine styles made for pseudo-elements with CSS styles.

In the final example for "Handmade Beasties" shown in figure 3-12, both first letter and first line pseudo-elements are applied to the text.

Emory is one of our most popular, as well as one of our favorites. His origins are French, and he dates somewhere in the mid-1400's.

Replicas are available in a wide range of colors and finishes.

3-12

DEVELOPING STYLE SHEET NOMENCLATURE AND ORGANIZATION

If you think deciding how to name and keep track of styles is a problem only for newbies, think again. Education consultant Margaret Werdermann has a solution that works for her clients' Web sites.

I cannot tell a lie — I don't have some fabulous "secret-code-naming" convention for my CSS styles. Instead, I use very descriptive style names like `.vertDotLineCell` for a vertical dotted border used in a table cell and `.floatRight` for the rule I use on layers where I place graphics when I want them to hang on the right side of a page, or even `.forestGreenBkgd` for (you guessed it) a forest green background.

The truth is, I don't have time for secret-code-naming conventions. I need to be able to look at my CSS page and visualize not only what each rule does but also how it looks and where it fits in the site layout. I don't have the hex numbers memorized for every color known to man, for example, so I'll name a style `.goldText`. From that descriptive name, I know exactly what I'm looking at. This makes my job easier, and it makes it easy for anyone to pick up one of my style sheets and keep going where I left off.

I'm not completely unorganized, though. I do often follow a pattern when I'm naming CSS rules. For example, rules regarding background colors or images always end in the abbreviation "bkgd," and anything pertaining to font, color, or text-decoration ends with the word "text."

My style sheet files are also fairly well organized. The first rule on the sheet is always the BODY rule, followed by customized HTML tags like the paragraph tag (I usually pad it) and the H1 through H3 heading tags. I follow those with my own rules, keeping like rules together. For example, `.vertDotLineCell` would be right with `.horDotLineCell` (the horizontal version of the dotted table cell border).

Whenever possible, I like to "stack" related rules as well. Here's an example. Say I had a style called `navLink`. This is the style I'm going to use for text navigation links on my site. As a normal `<a href>` link, I want this text to be forest green. My CSS rule would look like this:

```
#navLink a {
   color: #046766;
}
```

Whenever it receives focus, or someone mouses over it, or it's already been visited, I want this text to turn gold. Doing this by the "brute force" method, I'd have to make up three more CSS rules:

```
#navLink a:focus {
   color: #FDCB37;
}
#navLink a:hover {
   color: # FDCB37;
}
#navLink a:visited {
   color: # FDCB37;
}
```

But, because I know that all three of those rules have exactly the same attribute value (gold text), I can stack them all into one rule instead, like this:

```
#navLink a:focus, #navLink a:hover,
 #navLink a:visited
   {color: # FDCB37;
   }
```

That means that if I change my mind and want navLink's `focus`, `hover`, and `visited` states to be teal instead of gold, I have to change only one attribute instead of three.

Better yet, I'm not limited to only stacking different states of the same rule — I can also stack similar rules. For example, if I want all of the links in my navigation pane and in my footer to start off forest green, I could make this stacked rule:

```
#navLink a, #footerLink a {
   color: #046766;
}
```

Again, by organizing my CSS file in this way, I have only one place to edit to make sweeping changes to a number of styles.

SPRINKLING CONFETTI

I like the look of a well-designed confetti menu, a term coined by W3C wizard Bert Bos. If you aren't familiar with the term, take a look at the example in figure 3-13. The menu is an integral part of the site's interface, with each link having a unique style.

NOTE

You can read the method and see a working example of the original confetti menu at www.w3.org/Style/Examples/007/maps.html. My example uses the basic premise of the original, but with a different appearance and different style structure.

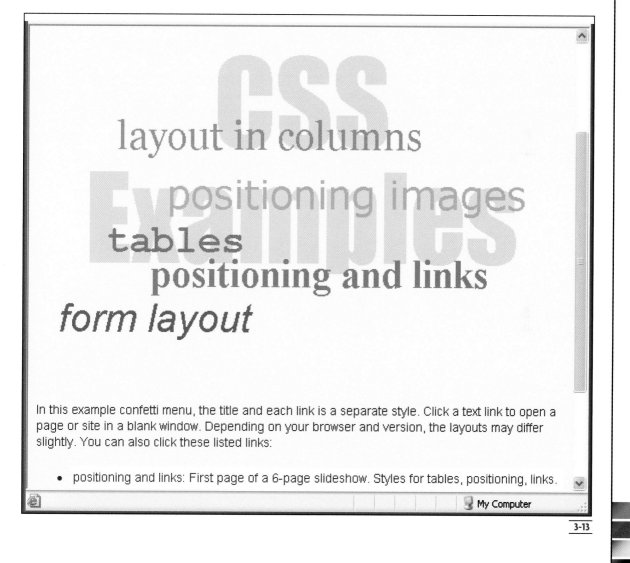

In this example confetti menu, the title and each link is a separate style. Click a text link to open a page or site in a blank window. Depending on your browser and version, the layouts may differ slightly. You can also click these listed links:

- positioning and links: First page of a 6-page slideshow. Styles for tables, positioning, links.

3-13

The menu appears complex, and it does require some planning. The method I use for constructing a confetti menu has several parts, including:

1. Writing the code for the page and adding the links from the menu items.

2. Writing styles for the overall page.

3. Creating styles for the menu's items.

4. Adding positioning styles and tweaking the layout.

CREATING THE INITIAL PAGE

The page containing the menu is straightforward and can contain any content you want. The example page includes:

> a page title and a graphic

> four text links that serve as the menu

Once your basic XHTML page is constructed, like the example shown in figure 3-14, check it for accuracy and test the links.

Product Examples

columns

balusters

plinths

pedestals

You could add more information below the menu, such as instructions for use.

3-14

PRO TIP

There are a number of ways to construct the menu to achieve the same appearance. My example uses paragraphs. You could also try a list, definition list, or even put the items into a table. Using <p> tags for each item is the simplest and least cumbersome to understand and manage.

More XHTML elements are required to make the menu work, including:

1. A `<div>` tag to hold the menu title and the menu links. The `<div>` tag's style defines the location for the menu on the page. In the sample, the tag is written as:

```
<div class="menu">
```

2. An `id` property to define each `<p>` tag. To prevent confusion, name the menu's static title differently than the links, such as:

```
<p id="title"> Product Samples</p>
```

3. An `<a>` tag for each link and its properties within the `<p>` tags.

The sample's code is written as:

```
<div class="menu">
<p id="title"> Product Examples</p>
<p id="p01"> <a href="eg_link.html"
 target="blank"> columns </a></p>
<p id="p02"> <a href="eg_link.html"
 target="blank"> balusters</a></p>
<p id="p03"> <a href="eg_link.html"
 target="blank"> plinths</a></p>
<p id="p04"> <a href="eg_link.html"
 target="blank"> pedestals</a></p>
</div>
```

NOTE

Read about using an `id` or `class` to identify styles in Chapter 1.

Learn to style paragraphs of different types in Chapter 4.

Chapter 10 describes navigation and links, including working with `<a>` tags.

APPLYING BASIC STYLES

Whether you choose to write and apply styles to the other content on the page at this point or after the menu items are styled is a matter of personal preference. I prefer to have the rest of the page styled beforehand for two reasons:

> I can see how adjusting my menu items affects other page content, if at all.

> I can incorporate some of the common properties into the parent page styles if possible.

To replicate the appearance of the example menu's page, follow these steps:

1. Write a style for the `<body>` tag. In the sample menu, the style written for the `<body>` tag defines the color; the font characteristics, which are applied to any text on the page not defined by special styles; and a background image. The example's style is written as:

```
body {
   background-color: white;
   font-family: Arial, Helvetica,
    sans-serif;
   font-size: 14px;
   line-height: 18px;
   color: #330066;
   background-image: url(bkgd.gif);
   background-repeat: no-repeat;
   background-position: center;
}
```

2. Define how the `<div>` tag will position the links on the Web page. In the sample page, the style for the menu's placement is specified with margins in pixel units. The margins are large at the right and bottom sides of the menu, and written as:

```
div.menu {
   margin-left: 0px;
   margin-right: 300px;
   margin-bottom: 100px;
   margin-top: 50px;
}
```

3. Next write a style for the menu's title. The sample page's menu is entitled "Product Examples." Its style is written as:

```
#title {
   font: 130px Impact, "Helvetica
    Narrow", sans-serif;
   text-align: right;
   color: #DDD;
}
```

4. Save the style sheet and check out the page shown in figure 3-15. You'll see things are quite a bit more interesting than the original page.

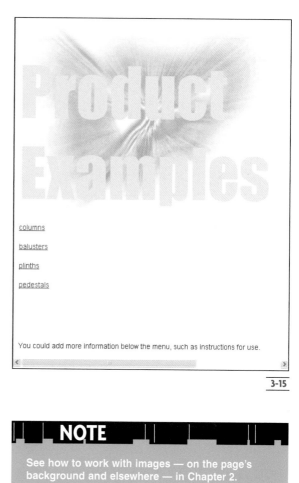

3-15

> **NOTE**
>
> See how to work with images — on the page's background and elsewhere — in Chapter 2.

STYLING THE MENU

Finally, it's time to add some pizzazz to the menu's links. In the sample project, each link uses a different font and font characteristics. Specify the appearance of each menu item by writing a style for both the `<p>` and `<a>` for each link. The four menu links in the sample project use these styles:

```
#p01, #p01 a {color: #81743F;
   background-color: transparent;
    font: bold 50px Georgia, serif;}
```

```
#p02, #p02 a {color: #666600;
  background-color: transparent;
    font: 50px Verdana, sans-serif;}
#p03, #p03 a {color: #333300;
  background-color: transparent;
    font: bold 50px Elephant, Times,
    serif;}
#p04, #p04 a {color: #999900;
  background-color: transparent;
    font: bold 50px Helvetica,
    sans-serif;}
```

Although the menu items look different, they are coordinated with the page's background, as you see in figure 3-16.

3-16

Although the menu items look interesting, they display the default underline used to identify a link. You can either add the property and value to each link's style, or write a single style that can be used throughout the page. In the sample project, the style is stored with the other basic page styles and written as:

```
a {text-decoration: none;}
```

As you see in figure 3-17, the links look more distinctive without the underline decoration. Read about underlines and other text decorations in Chapters 2 and 10.

3-17

POSITIONING THE LINKS

The final stage in the menu's construction is arranging the menu items. The links look all right in a list below the title and background image, but look quite spiffy when arranged over the image and title.

Chapter 1 described the box model, and demonstrated how the location on a page's box can be defined. In the sample project, the menu items are defined within the `<div>` tag's box. Here's how the links are positioned in the sample project:

> The positions for the styles are applied to the `<p>` tags for each link.

> Write a set of styles for the paragraph's positions separate from the other styling. You often have to make adjustments to the text appearance and the text position in relation to the other links, which is simple to do when the styles for appearance are separate from those for positioning.

> Decide how to organize the links on the page and define the location using whatever positioning method and unit of measure that are both comfortable for you to work with and meet the requirements for your site.

In the sample project, each style uses a set of margin values to position the paragraph containing the link over the image and menu title. The styles are written as:

```
#p01    {margin: -375px 0 0 130px;}
#p02    {margin: 20px 30px 0 0;}
#p03    {margin: 50px 0 20px 75px;}
#p04    {margin: 0 0 5px 200px;}
```

As you see in figure 3-18, the finished menu displays a coordinated, well-placed appearance on the Web page. The sample is shown in Internet Explorer 6 with the browser window maximized.

NOTE

Read about different positioning types, units of measure, and techniques in Chapters 5 and 6.

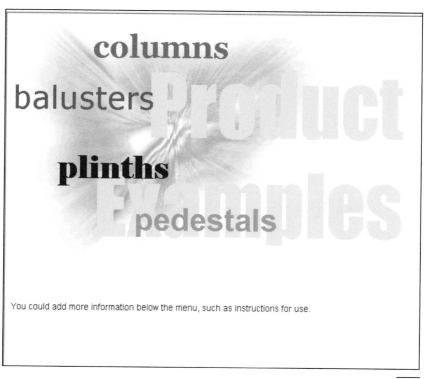

3-18

Testing the menu in different browsers shows some variation in the layout. For example, the page shown in figure 3-19 is how the menu looks in both Firefox 1.5 and Netscape 7. Notice that the background image is lower on the page, as is the title text. The menu items follow the same layout as the Internet Explorer example, but are also further down the page.

NOTE

Read about browser variations and how to manage differences in Chapter 11.

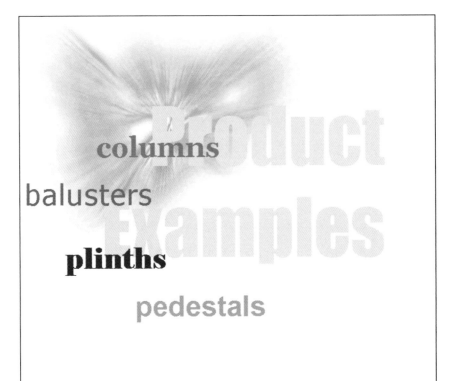

You could add more information below the menu, such as instructions for use.

3-19

Q & A

Why is spacing and indenting content important? Or is it more a matter of habit and conformity?

It's worth the time to configure styles to improve the flow on a page. Using properly laid-out text is more legible and visually sophisticated.

Your eyes look for straight lines. When type is indented like the exaggerated blockquote example shown in figure 3-8, the flow of text is disrupted.

The argument is that interrupting the flow is the point of using a blockquote, but that isn't really the case. The point of using the style is to draw attention to the content, not to interfere with how your eye tracks down the screen.

Do first-letter and first-line pseudo-elements use different properties?

There are some slight differences, depending on the characteristics of the elements themselves.

These properties apply to both first-letter and first-line pseudo-elements:

> font

> color

> background

> vertical-align (only if `float` is `none` for a first-line pseudo-element)

> float

> clear

> line-height

> text-decoration

> text-transform

The `first-letter` pseudo-element also uses `margin`, `padding`, and `border` properties; the `first-line` pseudo-element has `word-spacing`, `letter-spacing`, and `clear` properties.

IMAGES WITH STYLE, AND STYLES WITH IMAGES

Chapter 4

Unlike elements such as bulleted lists or blockquotes, images have styles applied to them, or are included as values in other styles' properties. The same image may display on a page as is, as part of a panoramic image or photo slideshow, or as a background for the page itself.

Images may be embellished on their own, such as with the addition of borders, or used as embellishment for other objects, such as table rows. And, speaking of borders, read how contributing Web expert Margaret Werdermann adds small borders with big impact.

Everyone has seen thumbnail galleries that link to larger images. For the most part these galleries are JavaScript-heavy. Instead, check out how to build a gallery using only CSS that works smoothly in most browsers.

CHOOSING AN IMAGE FORMAT

A number of image formats have been developed or adapted for use on the Web. Follow these steps when you are preparing an image for use on a Web page:

1. Size the image for the location on the page. You can resize an image by specifying its dimensions in the code, but resizing the image according to the size you intend to use on the Web page prevents unnecessary download time of an image that is too large.

2. Adjust the quality of the image as necessary. Balance the quality level against the size of the image.

3. Check the file size. The smaller and more compact the file, the faster it will download and display in a browser.

4. Save the image using the most appropriate file format.

Although an in-depth discussion of file formats and optimal uses of image types is far beyond the scope of these pages, the characteristics and advantages of Web image formats are listed in Table 4-1. I have separated the images into two subsets based on bit depth. GIF and PNG-8 images, which are both 8-bit formats, are best used for line drawings, images with large color blocks, or logos. 24-bit color, in the form of JPEG or PNG-24 images, is appropriate for a photo or images containing gradients or shading.

Table 4-1: Image Formats and Characteristics

8-bit Image Formats

Feature	GIF	PNG-8
Color	8-bit color, 256 colors	8-bit color, 256 colors
Dithering	Supported	Supported
Compression	Lossless compression	Lossless compression
Transparency	Supported	Supported
Background matting	Supported	Supported
Browser support	Widespread	Variable support for the format

Feature	JPEG	PNG-24
Colors	Over 16 million colors supported	Over 16 million colors supported
Image quality	Five quality levels from Low to Maximum	One quality level
Compression	Lossy; can specify quality	Lossless compression
Background transparency	Not supported	256 levels of background transparency
Download settings	Progressive download allows download in several passes	Specify interlacing to download in several passes
Browser support	Widespread	Not all browsers support format's features

KEEPING IT IN THE BACKGROUND

When the Web was fresh and new, using busy, overly colored tiled backgrounds was all the rage, and sometimes hard on the eyes, like the optical illusion shown in figure 4-1.

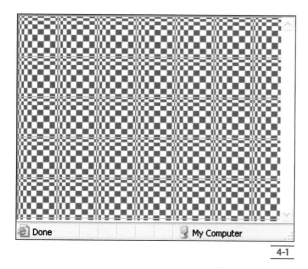

4-1

4-2

The other background format in vogue used enormous images as the page backgrounds; an example of this work of art is shown in figure 4-2 for those of you who don't remember "the old days"! After four or five minutes of download time you'd finally see the completed image, which sadly wasn't often as attractive as its size was large.

Thankfully, those days have passed. The careful use of backgrounds enhances the layout and appearance of a page tremendously.

Background options can look much different from the usual solid or tiled background depending on their styles.

> **NOTE**
>
> The same methods used to apply backgrounds to a page apply to page elements such as tables, blockquotes, or paragraphs.

CREATING A VISUAL GRADIENT

Try a gradient background instead of the same old tiled pattern or solid-colored background.

Follow these steps to build and apply a gradient background to a Web page:

1. Create the image file for the background in an image-editing or illustration program. Size the image at 1px wide by 1000px tall.

> **NOTE**
>
> If you must work with extremely long pages, increase the height of the image to prevent repeating the gradient. For most pages, an image that is 1000px in height is sufficient.

2. Use the program's gradient tool to select gradient colors and fill the canvas. Depending on the program you are using, you may have to select the blank image layer first.

3. Save the image as a JPG or PNG image. GIF files don't display a gradient's blend smoothly.

4. In your Web page or style sheet, create a style for the `<body>` tag that includes:

   > The URL reference for the image

   > The repeat frequency

5. Review the style. My style reads as follows (yours will vary according to the image file name):

   ```
   body {background-image:
     url("grad.jpg");}
   ```

6. Test the page and check out your oh-so-stylish gradient, shown in figure 4-3.

The Daily Bugle

(or: How we Learned to Live with a Howwwwling Beagles)

We live w

-- seven beagles. Our pack ranges in age from t Our kennel has enjoyed considerable success ir show ring.

Although this youngster has a good stance and i uneven coloring on her face makes her unsuitat

4-3

SPECIFYING BACKGROUND IMAGE LOCATIONS

You don't have to restrict the location of images in the background to an all-over tiled pattern or a single image. Instead of a uniform tiling, modify the style to define how, where, and whether the image is tiled.

Define where and how much of an image is shown on a page or in an element's background by:

> specifying the repeat, or lack thereof, like the single tile shown in the top corner of the page in figure 4-4.

> specifying the position.

> specifying the attachment.

4-4

Repeating background images

The default background image appearance tiles horizontally and vertically from the upper left of the element or page, written as:

```
{background-repeat: repeat;}
```

Instead of an all-over tiling, you can specify tiling horizontally on the x-axis or vertically on the y-axis alone.

Here's a quick way to add a vertical tiled image to a page:

1. Create the background tile. Make note of its dimensions for estimating positioning on the page.

2. Decide which page element will contain the style. In the example shown in figure 4-5, the <body> tag is styled.

4-5

3. Write the style for the element by defining the location for the tiling image, a color for the background of the page, the direction of the repeat, and the position for the image. For example:

```
body {
background: url("tile_dog.gif")
#F9F9F1 repeat-y 10%;
}
```

4. Adjust the background-position value to correspond with the layout of your page. Specify the value in percentage (as in the example), pixels, other units of measure, or descriptive locations.

5. Test the page in your browser.

Specifying image position

A tiled image can be used within a page element, such as the <blockquote> shown in figure 4-6. In the example, the tiling is along the x-axis, or horizontally, only. I used the descriptive value bottom to place the tiled image rather than a numeric value as for the page example shown in figure 4-5. The style is written as:

```
blockquote {
    background-image:url("bar_bkgd.
    jpg");
    background-repeat:repeat-x;
    background-position: bottom;
}
```

Glassmakers of Murano

You are most likely to come across glass artisans at craft shows. For a glimpse into the past, and an opportunity to see where the standards against which all other products are measured, I took a recent trip to Venice, and had the opportunity to spend a day on the Island of Murano.

4-6

When using a single axis, you can specify the position descriptively, such as `left`, `center`, or `right` for a horizontally placed tile or image, or `top`, `center`, or `bottom` for a vertically placed tile or image.

If you want to place the image tile in a location other than where the descriptive values allow, use a numeric value and unit of measure or percentage rather than a descriptive position.

The column of tiled images used in figure 4-5 uses a percentage value to move the images from the left edge of the window to a position 10 percent of the width away from the left side of the browser window.

Notice the column of images slides horizontally as you change the width of the browser window when the location is specified as a percentage in the style. If you specify a value such as pixels, the location remains static.

To fix, or not to fix?

We've all seen the pages where a static image is used as the background. Sometimes it's a good thing, while at other times, scroll as you will, you can't get away from that image!

The `background-attachment` property has only two values — either fixed or scroll. The position can be specified along with the attachment.

From a design perspective, a fixed image like the corporate logo shown in figure 4-7 is effectively used for branding purposes. Regardless of the information page the viewer is reading, the logo is a constant reminder of the page's source.

Proteus Nutriceuticals

Lorem ipsum dolor sit amet, consectetur adipisicing elit, sed do eiusmod tempor incididunt ut labore et dolore magna aliqua. Ut enim ad minim veniam, quis nostrud exercitation ullamco laboris nisi ut aliquip ex ea commodo consequat. Duis aute irure dolor in reprehenderit in voluptate velit esse cillum dolore eu fugiat nulla pariatur. Excepteur sint occaecat cupidatat non proident, sunt in culpa qui officia deserunt mollit anim id est laborum.

Sed ut perspiciatis unde omnis iste natus error sit voluptatem accusantium doloremque laudantium, totam rem aperiam, eaque ipsa quae ab illo inventore veritatis et quasi architecto beatae vitae dicta sunt explicabo. Nemo enim ipsam voluptatem quia voluptas sit aspernatur aut odit aut fugit, sed quia consequuntur magni dolores eos qui ratione voluptatem sequi nesciunt. Neque porro quisquam est, qui dolorem ipsum quia dolor sit amet, consectetur, adipisci velit, sed quia non numquam eius modi tempora incidunt ut labore et dolore magnam aliquam quaerat voluptatem.

Ut enim ad minima veniam, quis nostrum exercitationem ullam

4-7

Firefox Alternate Text Displays

With the exception of Mozilla Firefox, Web browsers display the `<alt>` text for an image in a mouseover comment, commonly referred to as a tooltip, regardless of whether there are tools involved!

Firefox displays the tag as it is actually designed. That is, it isn't supposed to show in a comment. Instead, it's used to show the alternative text only if the image isn't loaded.

Using a title attribute in the `<img>` tag displays the `<alt>` attribute as a mouseover comment.

The style for the page shown in figure 4-7 is written as:

```
body {
background-attachment: fixed;
    background-image:
     url(logo_proteus.jpg);
    background-repeat: no-repeat;
    background-position: left bottom;
}
```

NOTE

Check out Chapter 5 for information on using absolute positioning to define a Web page location precisely.

A background image is like a watermark. If you decide a fixed image is appropriate for your page or site, consider these pointers:

> Make sure the image's color is saturated enough to distinguish its features, but not too saturated that it overpowers the text on a page.

> Stay away from fixed images on pages containing multiple images because the background image distracts from the content of the page.

> Position the image on the page in an area that doesn't interfere with other page content.

A TIP FOR USING STYLES WITH TEMPLATES

*M*ost of this book deals strictly with CSS content, not with the program in which it is constructed. Read how online and Web education development expert Margaret Werdermann uses styles and templates in Dreamweaver.

I would never consider creating a Web site without using a combination of templates and cascading style sheets. The templates take care of the layout, and the style sheets take care of the format. This is what lets me sleep at night when I'm a day away from deployment and my clients change their minds about where they want the site's menu and what color the background should be (like *that has* never happened before!).

My favorite tip for combining CSS with templates is to use CSS to create really professional-looking graphic lines and borders on my templates. Here's how I create a CSS horizontal border using a Photoshop graphic along with a Dreamweaver CSS and template:

1. First, I create a full-size graphic border in Adobe Photoshop (another favorite program for this is Macromedia's Fireworks). I make it look just the way I want with gradients or shadows, or styles like bevel and emboss, and so on.

2. Then, I copy and save a very thin, vertical slice of the border — usually only 1 pixel wide (although the width varies if the border has some sort of pattern or texture that I want to capture).

3. My next step is to create a CSS rule in Dreamweaver with the following attributes:

```
background-image: url (x);
    /* enter the URL of the border
    slice here*/
background-repeat: repeat-x;
    /*if the border is vertical, the
    attribute's value is "repeat-y"
    */
height: enter the height of the bor-
  der slice;
    /* if the border was vertical,
    replace with a "width" attribute
    */
padding: 0px;
    /*this is important, as it will
    make sure the image repeats
    seamlessly */
```

4. Finally, I apply that CSS class to the appropriate `<div>` or table cell on my template, and the border magically appears.

Even though they may look graphic-intensive, the Web pages based on this template load quickly because that border is really only a seamless repeat of a 1K image slice. Best of all, if I've set up the page using relative widths — which I usually do, for accessibility reasons — the border automatically sizes to match the page width. In terms of visual impact versus bandwidth, it's like getting caviar for the price of a burger!

BUILDING A PANORAMIC IMAGE

In the old days, a large image or a composite image was handled in one of two ways: either as a single file, or divided into segments placed into table cells, like the example shown in figure 4-8. In the figure, I have shown orange borders to define each table cell.

4-8

Placing a sliced image into table cells was a good solution at the time, but inappropriate under current standards as the move to separate content and design continues.

Follow these steps to assemble a panoramic or large-scale image:

1. Construct your image, and then build and name the segments. For simplicity of calculations use same-sized segments. In my example, each segment of the image is 250px wide.

2. Insert the images into their appropriate page location. In the images' attributes, include the `<alt>` attribute, but not `<width>` or `<height>` attributes.

3. Surround the `<img>` tags with a `<div>` tag. Images are inline elements; using a `<div>` redefines them as a block element, allowing you to specify the layout on the page.

4. Create a style for the images, written as:

```
.layout {
width: 33%;
height: auto;
}
```

5. Include the `<style>` attribute for each `<img>` tag. The final code for my example reads as:

```
<div>
    <img src="hatter_01.jpg" alt=
    "site_banner01" class="layout"/>
    <img src="hatter_02.jpg" alt=
    "site_banner02" class="layout"/>
    <img src="hatter_03.jpg" alt=
    "site_banner03" class="layout"/>
</div>
```

6. Test the page. Resize the browser window. As you change the size of the window, notice the images resize themselves as well, like the Web browser window in figure 4-9.

![Web browser window showing "The Hattery -- on Pier 4 --"]

4-9

PRO TIP

Sometimes the effort to disassemble an image and build styles to reconstitute it on a page is more trouble than it's worth. Check to see if the image is optimized first. You might be able to decrease the image quality and file size, saving download time, and making the image practical as a single download.

CREATING AN IMAGE GALLERY USING STYLES

An image gallery is a display technique shared by artists, designers, photographers, and online sellers of all kinds.

By definition, an *image gallery* is a page displaying thumbnail images linked to full-size images. Like a composite or panoramic image, image galleries traditionally were built using tables. The appearance of a rollover was handled using alternate thumbnails and JavaScript. I recall having four or even five versions of the same image, depending on my level of enthusiasm for showing rollover states.

Instead of using tables, read how to construct an image gallery using CSS only. It takes some time to write and tweak the styles, but far less time than building multiple versions for each image. Not only that, but updating your image gallery is far less painful when you need only apply a style or two to each new image you add.

APPROACHING THE DESIGN

There are several steps in the planning and creation of the image gallery that include:

1. Prepare the images used for the gallery. You need one thumbnail-sized image, and one full-sized image for each gallery entry, like the examples shown in figure 4-10.

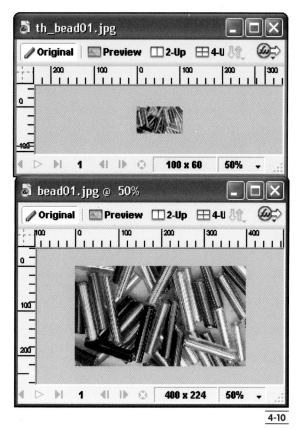

4-10

2. Design the styles for the gallery and the thumbnail links.

3. Add the `<div>` tag for the gallery structure to the page's XHTML code and assign the gallery style.

4. List the thumbnails, including the link, image source, text for the caption, and `<alt>` description of the images.

5. Specify additional elements needed to display the gallery properly both in Mozilla-based browsers and Internet Explorer.

To display properly in Internet Explorer, the gallery's XHTML code contains a `<div>` tag nested within a `<div>` tag. The external `<div>` tag defines the gallery structure, and the internal `<div>` tags define the individual thumbnails, their captions, and links to the full-sized images, like the example shown in figure 4-11.

4-11

DESIGNING WITH NESTED TAGS

To produce an image gallery usable in various browsers, follow these steps to design the style and write the tags for the gallery object:

1. Write a style for the gallery object that contains the thumbnails. Specify its characteristics such as width, margins, and position as desired. The example uses a simple style written as:

```
div.gallery {
    width: 80%;
    margin:10px;
}
```

2. Define a `<div>` tag for the box to hold the thumbnails. The example is written as:

```
<div class="gallery">
```

3. Write a style for the nested `<div>` tags that hold each thumbnail image. At a minimum, include these properties:

> A float specification to allow the objects to line up across the page

> A width for the thumbnail and its text

> A background color to set off each thumbnail and text unit.

The style so far is written as:

```
div.links {
    float:left;
    width: 80px;
    background:#F1F1D8;
}
```

4. Within the ⟨div⟩ tag defining the box for the gallery, insert each thumbnail item in separate nested ⟨div⟩ tags, and attach the style designed in step 3 to each item's ⟨div⟩ tag. Include these items in the tag:

> A single ⟨a⟩ tag containing both the image and text label

> Reference to the full-size image as the link

> Properties for the thumbnail image

> The text label for the thumbnail

The example at this point is shown in figure 4-12. Its layout is almost correct, but the appearance of the thumbnails and text needs some work. The example's tag is written as:

```
<div class="thumbnail">
<a href="bead01.jpg">
<img height="55" width="100"
    alt ="thumbnail of confetti bugle
    beads"
    src = "thumb01.jpg" />
Confetti Bugle Beads, 6mm
</a>
</div>
```

Just Beads

Your online source for beads. Just beads -- nothing but beads.

Glass Tubes

Confetti Bugle Beads, 6mm

Glass Tube Beads, 12mm

Lampwork Tube Beads, 14mm

4

FINISHING THE GALLERY'S STYLING

The thumbnail's appearance and text need some final styling. The additional styles you apply depend on the overall layout of the page, the site's style sheet design, and other styles already in use.

Uncluttering the images

In the example shown in figure 4-13, the images' default appearance is modified by removing the default link borders in the style sheet by writing:

```
image {border:none;}
```

Coordinating the text labels

Make the gallery look more like the other content on the site by applying a style to the text label. You don't have to write a separate class and style. Instead, include the properties within the `div.thumbnail` style. The example shown in figure 4-14 uses these properties:

```
text-align:center; text-decoration:
  none;
font-family:"Gill Sans MT", Arial,
  sans-serif;
font-size:12px; color:#880044;
```

4-13

4-14

Separating the thumbnails

The thumbnails and their labels can be separated further by using borders, or you can take advantage of the way Internet Explorer defines a box width.

Chapter 1 describes the box model, used to define the content of a page and the relationships among the components. Internet Explorer defines a box width differently than other browsers or the CSS standards in that it includes padding and borders within the box width rather than outside the box width.

Earlier in the chapter, I specified a width of 100px for the thumbnail images. This is where that width comes into play.

I first designed the styles with a width of 80px arbitrarily assigned to the `div.links a` style. Taking advantage of the IE interpretation of the box model, changing the width to 108px resizes the thumbnails and creates the illusion of 4px borders on either side of the thumbnail, as shown in figure 4-15.

The final tweak for the gallery objects is finishing the frame around the images. Instead of applying borders, add padding to the top and bottom of the objects, as shown in figure 4-16. Include these lines in the `div.links a` style:

```
padding-top: 4px;
padding-bottom: 4px;
```

> **NOTE**
>
> See Chapter 8 for in-depth information about working with borders.

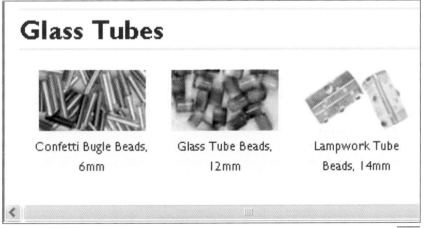

Glass Tubes

Confetti Bugle Beads, 6mm

Glass Tube Beads, 12mm

Lampwork Tube Beads, 14mm

4-15

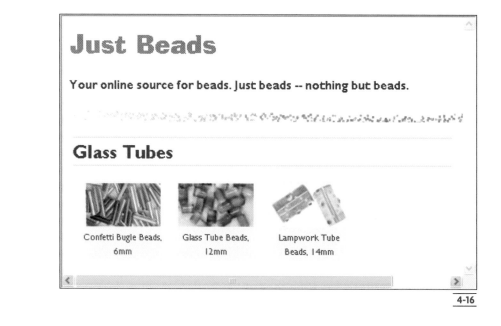

4-16

Rewriting the Gallery

The example gallery used thumbnails styled as single units, instead of dealing with the three component parts, including the image, text label, and the `<div>` tag.

CSS2 allows for elements other than the `<a>` tag to use the `hover` property; writing for browsers other than Internet Explorer can use `div.thumbnail a:hover` as a declaration.

Q & A

Why does a background image on a page disappear some of the time when viewed in Internet Explorer?

At times, image backgrounds and text disappear from the browser window for some unknown and unreproducible reason. Refreshing the window restores the content. For the most part, the problem occurs with background images and text next to a floating element (refer to Chapter 5 for information on floating properties).

Try either of these solutions:

> Attach the ruleset `position: relative` into any style applied to the disappearing object.

> Assign a width ruleset to the element in the page's style sheet.

LAYOUTS AND POSITIONING

Part

POSITIONING CONTENT USING CSS

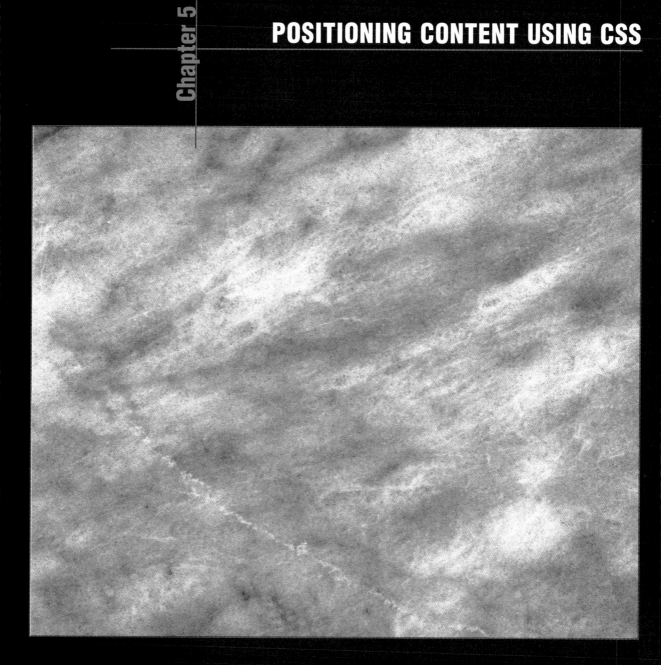

When you start out in Web design, you usually start with an understanding of how XHTML and HTML tags produce different layouts depending on the element. For example, we know what heading styles look like, that blockquotes are indented, and that an ordered list uses numbers.

Any tag used to define an element as a visual type (as opposed to one defining a structural element) has an inherent style. CSS lets you configure the layout, appearance, and position of content on a Web page in a number of ways. One integral difference in positioning relates to whether an element is displayed as a block object or as an inline object. As part of an element's style, you can specify how content is displayed, or whether or not it is even visible.

Styles let you specify positioning of elements on a page in three dimensions, either in relation to one another, or to the page itself. In addition to positioning content precisely on a page, you can also specify the spacing and distribution of elements on a page using objects defined by the box model, such as margins and padding.

To reinforce how XHTML and CSS work hand-in-hand, check out how Web designer and photographer Denyer uses the languages' features to construct and maintain his photo gallery site.

MANIPULATING BLOCK AND INLINE ELEMENT DISPLAYS

Nearly all HTML elements are either *block* or *inline* elements. Each category of element produces outcomes that are opposite to one another. In general, the differences relate to positioning and sizing on a line.

Understanding how block and inline elements work, how they differ, and what you can do to manipulate their appearances is a sure way to move beyond writing basic CSS.

DIFFERENCES BETWEEN TYPES

Block elements are the basic building blocks (pun intended) of a Web page. Examples of block elements include `<div>`, `<p>`, `<h1>`, `<hr />`, and `<li>`.

Block elements share these characteristics, shown in the example in figure 5-1:

> They always begin on a new line.

> The top and bottom margins, height, and line-height can be manipulated, like the margins and borders applied to the paragraph in the figure.

> The width of a block element defaults to 100% of its containing element — such as the paragraph element's width or the horizontal rule element's width — but it can be specified.

Examples of inline elements include `<a>`, `<span>`, `<img>`, and `<em>`. Inline elements share characteristics which are opposite to those shown by block elements. An example is shown in the image in figure 5-2, and shows these traits:

> The element always begins on the same line, like the link in the first paragraph.

> The top and bottom margins, height, and line-height aren't configurable.

> The width is based on the content and can't be specified.

Proteus Nutriceuticals

Lorem ipsum dolor sit amet, consectetur adipisicing elit, sed do eiusmod tempor incididunt ut labore et dolore magna aliqua. Ut enim ad minim veniam, quis nostrud exercitation ullamco laboris nisi ut aliquip ex ea commodo consequat. Duis aute irure dolor in reprehenderit in voluptate velit esse cillum dolore eu fugiat nulla pariatur. Excepteur sint occaecat cupidatat non proident, sunt in culpa qui officia deserunt mollit anim id est laborum.

Sed ut perspiciatis unde omnis iste natus error sit voluptatem accusantium doloremque laudantium, totam rem aperiam, eaque ipsa quae ab illo inventore veritatis et quasi architecto beatae vitae dicta sunt explicabo. Nemo enim ipsam voluptatem quia voluptas sit aspernatur aut odit aut fugit, sed quia consequuntur magni dolores eos qui ratione voluptatem sequi nesciunt. Neque porro quisquam est, qui dolorem ipsum quia dolor sit amet, consectetur, adipisci velit, sed quia non numquam eius modi tempora incidunt ut labore et dolore magnam aliquam quaerat voluptatem.

Ut enim ad minima veniam, quis nostrum exercitationem ullam corporis suscipit laboriosam, nisi ut aliquid ex ea commodi consequatur? Quis autem vel eum iure reprehenderit qui in ea voluptate velit esse quam nihil molestiae consequatur, vel illum qui dolorem eum fugiat quo voluptas nulla pariatur?

5-1

Sed ut perspiciatis unde omnis iste natus error sit voluptatem accusantium doloremque laudantium, totam rem aperiam, eaque ipsa quae ab illo inventore veritatis et quasi architecto beatae vitae dicta sunt explicabo. Nemo enim ipsam voluptatem quia voluptas sit aspernatur aut odit aut fugit, sed quia

consequuntur magni dolores eos qui ratione voluptatem sequi nesciunt. Neque porro quisquam est, qui dolorem ipsum quia dolor sit amet, consectetur, adipisci velit, sed quia non numquam eius modi tempora incidunt ut labore et dolore magnam aliquam quaerat voluptatem.

5-2

CHANGING HOW AN ELEMENT DISPLAYS

One very useful technique you should investigate — if you aren't already using it — is swapping an element's status to display an inline element as a block and vice versa. Display properties are not inherited.

An example of a `display:block` declaration is shown in figure 5-3. Notice that the icon image is disproportional, and that the image is shown at the left margin of the Web page. The appearance results from applying the style, written as:

```
.icon{
display: block;
width: 120px;
height: 55px;
}
```

The properties' declaration makes the inline element:

> Start on a new line

> Manipulate the height of an inline element

> Control the width of an inline element

Use the `display:inline` property to make a block element start on the same line as the existing content. You can also define a background color as wide as the text without having to specify a width.

Follow these steps to specify page content as inline:

1. Enclose the content within `<span>` tags.

2. Write and apply the style, for example:

```
.inside {
  display: inline;
  background-color: #F2E5DF;
  border: thin groove #CCCCCC;
}
```

3. Test the page. You'll see that regardless of the size of the page, the text appearance remains consistent, like the example shown in figure 5-4.

doloremque laudantium, tot
veritatis et quasi architecto
ipsam voluptatem quia volu
consequuntur magni dolores

sequi nesciunt. Neque porro
amet, consectetur, adipisci v
incidunt ut labore et dolore

5-3

Lorem ipsum dolor sit amet, consectetur adipisicing elit, sed do eiusmod tempor incididunt ut labore et dolore magna aliqua. Ut enim ad minim veniam, quis nostrud exercitation ullamco laboris nisi ut aliquip ex ea commodo consequat. Duis aute irure dolor in reprehenderit in voluptate velit esse cillum dolore eu fugiat nulla pariatur. Excepteur sint occaecat cupidatat non proident, sunt in culpa qui officia deserunt mollit anim id est laborum.

Sed ut perspiciatis unde omnis iste natus error sit voluptatem accusantium doloremque laudantium, totam rem aperiam, eaque ipsa quae ab illo inventore veritatis et quasi architecto beatae vitae dicta sunt explicabo. Nemo enim ipsam voluptatem quia voluptas sit aspernatur aut odit aut fugit, sed quia consequuntur magni dolores eos qui ratione voluptatem

5-4

Positioning Content Using CSS

5

Other Display Values

The `display` property specifies how and if an element is shown on a Web page.

Use `display:none` to hide an element. This ruleset is similar to the `visibility:hidden` ruleset, except that the hidden element doesn't take up space on the page.

There are several more `display` values; some are considered in the discussion on lists in Chapter 7; others are included in Chapter 8 with other information on tables.

The *run-in* value, as the name suggests, lets text using one tag, such as a heading, run in to text using another tag, like a `<p>` tag, without breaking the line or adding line space. The run-in value isn't widely supported.

PRO TIP

An easy way to add consistency to the visual design of your pages is to repeat elements.

The style shown in figure 5-4 uses the same background and border details as the top paragraph on the page for consistency.

ORGANIZING CONTENT ON A WEB PAGE

One property that I use a great deal is a *float*, which defines where an image or text appears in another element, like a page or a paragraph. In the example shown in figure 5-5, for example, the page uses a float to position the image within the blockquote area.

The Official SWiSHmax Bible, Wiley Publishing

This book is developed and comarketed with SWiSHzone. The 696-page book includes hundreds of sample projects and source files. The book's companion Web site includes all the sample projects, source files, as well as several additional appendixes of information on topics such as PHP and XML.

Several of the world's top SWiSHmax designers and developers have contributed chapters to the book. Brian Ayers, the brains behind swish-tutorials.com , served as Technical Editor.

Visit the book's page at Wiley Publishing . At the Wiley page you will find a description of

The Official SWISHmax Bible information page   Unknown Zone (Mixed)

5-5

Float properties are not inherited, which stands to reason because the property specifies where an object displays in relation to its parent element.

Specify a float as `float:left` or `float:right` to display the content at the left or right of its parent element. The `float:none` value states the obvious, in that there is no float, and the element sits where you placed it in the page's layout.

In figure 5-6 I have shown three similar images on a page that display in different locations — left, right, or left of the page — defined by their style's float values. In each case, the paragraphs use the same style.

There is a difference between using a `float-left` property and using a `float-none` or no `float` property at all.

Look carefully at the third image in figure 5-6. You see that the image uses a default page location as its placement. The text aligns with the bottom of the image, also a default display.

CLEARING SOME ROOM

Another property I use frequently is the `clear` property, which specifies where floating content is displayed in relation to the element to which it is applied.

 Ut enim ad minima veniam, quis nostrum exercitationem ullam corporis suscipit laboriosam, nisi ut aliquid ex ea commodi consequatur? Quis autem vel eum iure reprehenderit qui in ea voluptate velit esse quam nihil molestiae consequatur, vel illum qui dolorem eum fugiat quo voluptas nulla pariatur?

At vero eos et accusamus et iusto odio dignissimos ducimus qui blanditiis praesentium voluptatum deleniti atque corrupti quos dolores et quas molestias excepturi sint occaecati cupiditate non provident, similique sunt in culpa qui officia deserunt mollitia animi, id est laborum et dolorum fuga. Et harum quidem rerum facilis est et expedita distinctio. Nam libero tempore, cum soluta nobis est eligendi optio cumque nihil impedit quo minus id quod maxime placeat facere possimus, omnis voluptas assumenda est, omnis dolor repellendus.

Temporibus autem quibusdam et aut officiis debitis aut rerum necessitatibus saepe eveniet ut et voluptates repudiandae sint et molestiae non recusandae. Itaque earum rerum hic tenetur a sapiente delectus, ut aut

5-6

The clear property isn't inherited, and can use values that you might expect to use, like the thumbnail images shown in figure 5-7. The options are

> `clear:left` disallows any floating content to the left of the element (like the blue porcupine at the upper left of the sample).

> `clear:right` disallows any floating content to the right (like the green cow at the right of the sample page).

> `clear:both` disallows floating content on either side of the unsociable element to which it is applied (like the cool yellow cat toward the right of the sample page).

> `clear:none` allows content to float on both sides (like the coral lamb at the bottom center of the sample).

The Hare and the Porcupine Redux -- Part 1

Early last week I was talking to Mort, one of my neighbors. Mort is an old porcupine who lives in the woods across the road with twin sons. Here's the story.

Mort lived in quite comfortable digs in the woods with his twin sons. Their favorite food was apples. Sometimes, when they wanted to score brownie points, the little ones (cubs? pups?) raided

my garden for turnips, their Dad's second favorite.

I'd known their dad for a long time, and we had come to an understanding about my garden a couple of years ago. Or at least I thought we had. We discussed the problem over some delicious chokecherry wine one night on the back porch. I agreed that I would plant extra veg just for him,

and I would also harvest it and leave it by the garden gate.   Mort was a pretty lazy guy overall, and having someone do the dirty work for him was a sweet deal.

The old guy and I developed a friendly relationship over the years, but he never did get along with my dogs. Even when I offered all sorts of inducements to cease and desist, everything from bottles

of wine to cabbages, he simply couldn't resist.   He said once, "Jay, if you were a porcupine you would know that it is something out of your control. My kind needs to smack dogs in the kisser. We breathe, we eat, we .... in the woods, and we smack dogs in the kisser."

WRAPPING TEXT AROUND AN IMAGE

Did you know you could simulate a page layout you commonly see in printed publications where text curves around an image? All you need to do is specify `float` and `clear` properties in the image's style, and slice the image into horizontal strips.

Follow these steps to curve text around an image:

1. Cut your image into strips, as shown in figure 5-8. The height of a strip should be equal to the size of the font and the line height.

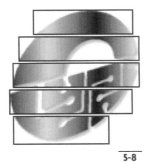

5-8

PRO TIP

The width of the strip should be the width of the content in the image. If you have the strips the same length, you won't have a curved outcome. Instead, the image looks like you used a single `float:left` ruleset, which is certainly a waste of your time and efforts.

2. Save each slice as a separate file. For ease of use, name the parts in sequence, such as logo01.jpg, logo02.jpg, and so on.

3. In your Web page or style sheet, write the style for the image. Include `float-left` and `clear:left` rulesets. If you like, specify margins surrounding the image elements as well, such as:

```
.logo {
  float:left;
  clear:left;
  margin: 0em .5em 0em 1em;
}
```

4. Insert the images into your Web page. Stack the images' tags as a group, like the example code shown in figure 5-9.

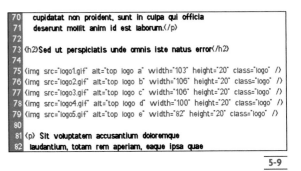

```
70  cupidatat non proident, sunt in culpa qui officia
71  deserunt mollit anim id est laborum.</p>
72
73  <h2>Sed ut perspiciatis unde omnis iste natus error</h2>
74
75  <img src="logo1.gif" alt="top logo a" width="103" height="20" class="logo" />
76  <img src="logo2.gif" alt="top logo b" width="106" height="20" class="logo" />
77  <img src="logo3.gif" alt="top logo c" width="106" height="20" class="logo" />
78  <img src="logo4.gif" alt="top logo d" width="100" height="20" class="logo" />
79  <img src="logo5.gif" alt="top logo e" width="82" height="20" class="logo" />
80
81  <p> Sit voluptatem accusantium doloremque
82  laudantium, totam rem aperiam, eaque ipsa quae
```

5-9

5. Test the page. As you see in figure 5-10, the text looks like it is floating around the curved edge of the logo.

Sit voluptatem accusantium doloremque laudantium, totam rem aperiam, eaque ipsa quae ab illo inventore veritatis et quasi architecto beatae vitae dicta sunt explicabo. Nemo enim ipsam voluptatem quia voluptas sit aspernatur aut odit aut fugit, sed quia consequuntur magni dolores eos qui

5-10

CLEARING OUT

For wrapping or positioning an element or other image on a page, it may not be immediately clear why you need to use a `clear` ruleset.

Another version of an example page used in this section is shown in figure 5-11. This is how the page looks without including `clear: left` in the image segments' style.

Sed ut perspiciatis unde omnis iste natus error

Sit voluptatem accusantium doloremque laudantium, totam rem aperiam, eaque ipsa quae ab illo inventore veritatis et quasi architecto beatae vitae

5-11

If you are using a single image or other element, using a `float` works fine alone. The image floats according to the value specified.

When there are several elements in sequence, like the image segments, you want each element to both:

> float to the left of the page

> prevent any other floating element from being displayed to its left

I'd known their dad for a long time, and we had come to an understanding about my garden a couple of years ago. Or at least I thought we had. We discussed the problem over some delicious chokecherry wine one night on the back porch.

I agreed that I would plant extra veg just for him, and I would also harvest it and leave it by the garden gate. Mort was a pretty lazy guy overall, and having someone do the dirty work for him was a sweet deal.

5-12

SPECIFYING ELEMENT POSITION

Beyond using a number of properties to classify the locations of an element and its relation to other content on the page, you can also specify position properties outright.

Use a position property to display an element in several positions, including:

> **Static.** The element is positioned using its normal location and flow. You don't need any additional properties. The two critters shown in figure 5-12 appear to be positioned in the same way, although the `position:static` ruleset is applied to the second (lower) image.

> **Relative.** An element is moved using a specified directional value.

> **Absolute.** An absolute value places an element at a precise location on the page by specifying directional properties.

> **Fixed.** The `position: fixed` ruleset is basically the same as the `position:absolute` ruleset, except that when the user scrolls the page, the element does not scroll with it. Instead, it stays in its defined location.

SPECIFYING A RELATIVE LOCATION

Using a relative location lets you quickly define how you want an element to appear relative to how it looks by default. I use relative positioning sometimes to define how I want a leading image to look in relation to its surrounding text.

Here's an example. In figure 5-13 two similar images are set on a page. In both cases they are defined with a `<span>` tag in the page's code.

I'd known their dad for a long time, and we had come to an understanding about my garden a couple of years ago. Or at least I thought we had. We discussed the problem over some delicious chokecherry wine one night on the back porch.

I agreed that I would plant extra veg just for him, and I would also harvest it and leave it by the garden gate. Mort was a pretty lazy guy overall, and having someone do the dirty work for him was a sweet deal.

5-13

NOTE

I have increased the text size in the browser window to show you the relationship of the image to the text more clearly.

I want the second image to move slightly on the page so it looks like it belongs to the text. I accomplished this feat following these steps:

1. Write a style for the position. The example uses this style:

```
.jay {position:relative;
  left:0.2em;
  right:0.7em;
  top:0.2em;
}
```

2. Attach the style to the `<span>` tag for the appropriate image.

3. Test the page. Change text sizes, the browser window size, and the browser to see what happens with the image position. In figure 5-14 you see the image of Jay moves down, to the right, and away from the left margin, as specified in the style.

4. If necessary, adjust the positional values in the style, and retest.

I agreed th just for him, and I leave it by the gard lazy guy overall, an

5-14

USING AN ABSOLUTE POSITION

If you assign a `position:absolute` ruleset to an element, its location is independent of any other object on the page. Instead, the location is based on the parent box coordinates, whether that is a table or a page.

NOTE

Read about the box model in Chapter 1.

Suppose I wanted to use the image of Jay in my previous example in a specific location, rather than at the start of a paragraph.

Here's how:

1. Write a style for the object based on the box coordinates. The example defines the position absolutely in relation to the page, and is written as:

```
.jay_bkgd {
  position:absolute;
  left:250px;
  top:150px;
}
```

2. Attach the style to the `<img>` tag.

3. Test the page. In figure 5-15 you see the bright pink image of Jay is positioned close to the top of the page and indented in from the left. It isn't spectacular at this point, and in fact looks like a browser display error.

5-15

One element that is certainly lacking is importance. The image is the same size as the other thumbnails, and doesn't offer anything interesting to the page layout.

If you use an absolutely positioned element, you can also define its height and width in the style. Notice how much larger the image is on the page in figure 5-16.

5-16

Unfortunately, the example also shows how the image overlays the text on the page, hiding the story. Adjusting the image's location three-dimensionally by changing how the page elements are layered produces the right look.

LAYERING TEXT AND IMAGES

In the introduction I mentioned that content can be displayed on three dimensions. The first two are used regularly: the x-axis extends horizontally across a page, with 0 at the extreme left of the page; and the y-axis extends vertically down a page, with 0 at the extreme top of the page.

The third dimension is the *z-index* property, which simulates the appearance of 3-D space. Use the property to specify the stacking order of elements on a page.

STACKING OBJECTS

Every Web page has a background layer with content stacked above the background. The higher the value, the higher the element's position in the stacking order, as illustrated in figure 5-17.

Underlying page —0—

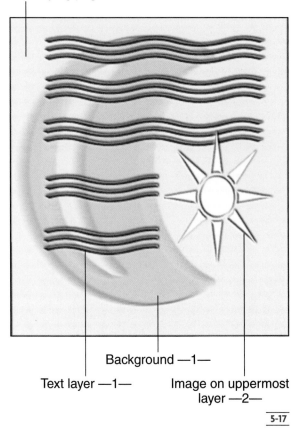

Background —1—

Text layer —1—

Image on uppermost layer —2—

5-17

The z-index property:

> is not an inherited property

> can use a negative number as its value

> works only on elements positioned with a ruleset such as position:absolute

> uses whole numbers as the property's value to define stacking order, or uses z-index: auto to define the stack using the parent values.

ORGANIZING CONTENT LAYERS

Figure 5-17 shows a page containing a number of images, including one using absolute positioning. In that figure, you see the image overlays the text on the page, which makes styling the page rather pointless.

Contrast that image with the example of the same page shown in figure 5-18. Now you see the image is behind the text.

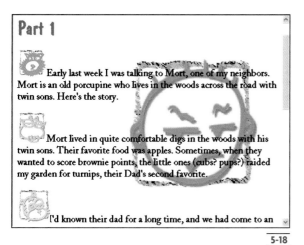

Part 1

Early last week I was talking to Mort, one of my neighbors. Mort is an old porcupine who lives in the woods across the road with twin sons. Here's the story.

Mort lived in quite comfortable digs in the woods with his twin sons. Their favorite food was apples. Sometimes, when they wanted to score brownie points, the little ones (cubs? pups?) raided my garden for turnips, their Dad's second favorite.

I'd known their dad for a long time, and we had come to an

5-18

The revised style for the image is written as:

```
.jay_bkgd {
  position:absolute;
  width:300px;
  height:300px;
  left:250px;
  top:150px;
  z-index:-1;
}
```

PRO TIP

If you are testing a page and can't see overlapping text, the browser type or version isn't supporting the style. Try wrapping the paragraphs in either a `<div>` or `<span>` tag and test again.

CONTROLLING THE VIEW OF BLOCK ELEMENTS

The positioning, if any, of block level elements on a page is under your control, allowing you to determine the appearance of content for your viewers.

You can control the view in these ways:

> Specify overflow values, used to define what is seen when an element is larger than the specified size for the element.

> Define a clipping property, used to control exactly which parts of an element are visible and which are invisible. Clipping works only with absolutely positioned elements.

> Specify whether the element is shown on the page at all using the `visible` property.

OVERFLOW

You don't have to show all of an element on a page in order for your viewers to be able to see it.

Suppose you have a page containing a lot of historical information about the development of your products. Some of the users visiting the page want complete details, while others are content with the basic information. You can use links to pages that contain further details, or add overflow styles.

There are a few `overflow` values; the one I use most often is the `overflow:auto` ruleset because the browser displays scrollbars when necessary, giving the user some control over the page.

The example shown in figure 5-19 illustrates the example I described at the start of this section.

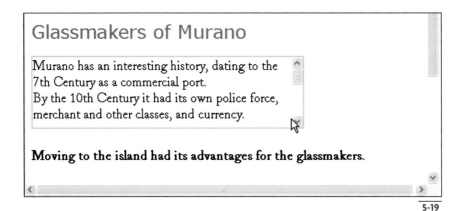

5-19

The style for the `<p>` includes a width and height for the overflow area. I also included border values to set off the box on the page.

```
p.history {
  width:400px;
  height:100px;
  overflow:auto;
  border:2px solid #c1c285;
}
```

The other overflow options include:

> `overflow:visible`, where all content is displayed even if it extends beyond the boundaries of the box. Figure 5-20 shows the same page as that shown in figure 5-19 with the overflow value now visible. The entire block of text appears on the page, even though the width and height use the same values as the original style.

> `overflow:hidden`, where the browser doesn't show the content outside the defined box boundaries.

> `overflow:scroll`, where the browser always displays a scrollbar, whether or not it is required.

Glassmakers of Murano

Murano has an interesting history, dating to the 7th Century as a commercial port.
By the 10th Century it had its own police force, merchant and other classes, and currency.

In 1291 the Venetian Republic declared all glassmakers could operate their foundaries only on the island of Murano. The purpose wasn't to segregate the glassmakers for any nefarious reason. Instead, the decision was made based on the predominant building material of the homes in Venice at the time. Glassworks presented a fire hazard, and most buildings were made of wood.

Moving to the island had its advantages for the

5-20

CLIPPING CONTENT INTO SHAPE

With clipping, you can control exactly which parts of an element are visible and which are invisible. Clipping works only on absolutely positioned elements, and you can specify only a rectangular shape.

I use clipping sometimes for effect. The example page in figure 5-21 uses two copies of a piece of artwork, each using different clipping values.

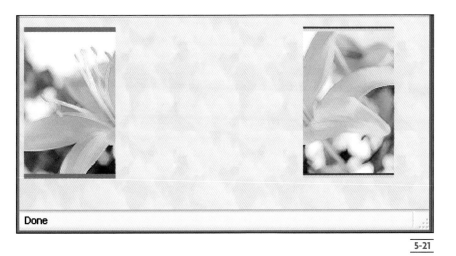

5-21

NOTE

By the way, the clipping styles I used in this example work fine in Firefox and Netscape; in Internet Explorer, only the first clipped image on the page displays.

PRO TIP

Like any other styles that use sides or locations, you can write the clip attribute as a single short-hand attribute. The sequence of values in the styles defines the clipping in a clockwise order; that is, top, right, bottom, and left.

Each image uses a separate class that includes height, width, and border values. In order for the left image on the browser page to show the clipped section of the flower in the browser window, the position and clip values are

```
.lily1 {
  position: absolute;
  left:5px;
  top:10px;
  clip:rect(0px 100px 200px 0px);
}
```

Similarly, the second image, shown at the right in figure 5-21 is clipped to show the right half of the image using these values:

```
.lily2
  {position:absolute;
  left:210px;
  top:10px;
  clip:rect(0px 100px 200px 200px);
}
```

HIDING ELEMENTS

One property often restricted to Dynamic HTML (DHTML) is visibility, usually associated with JavaScript that defines when an image is shown or hidden based on user actions.

I don't use visibility properties much anymore, and I suspect there are lots of us in the same position. Learning how to craft DHTML was important in its time, but for me, I suspect the novelty has worn off.

Invisible elements take up space on the page just as the spacer.gif files did in the early days of Web pages. In this situation, a blank image isn't used to define a space on a page, it's simply that an element uses the visibility:hidden ruleset.

The cursor in figure 5-22 indicates a bare space on the page, the location of one of the page's images whose style includes the visibility:hidden ruleset.

Early last week
neighbors. Mort is an old porcupi
the road with twin sons. Here's th

Mort lived in quite comf
twin sons. Their favorite food wa
wanted to score brownie points, t

5-22

You can write shorthand styles for these box components using the same shorthand assignments, but beware. Web browsers interpret the style and assign values to all four sides of the element, regardless of how many are defined in the property's value.

Check out the example styles and browser appearances to save some troubleshooting frustration:

> **Using a single value.** A shortcut style using a single value is written as:

```
.demo1 {
margin:25px;
}
```

When the style is applied, each side of the element is affected the same way, as you can see in figure 5-23.

Other visibility values include:

> **Visible.** The element is visible; usually used in conjunction with JavaScript or mouseover events to regulate when an object is seen.

> **Inherit.** The element inherits its visibility from its parent element.

> **Collapse.** The collapse value is mainly used with tables to remove a row or column without affecting the table. If used with other than table elements, the value displays as hidden. By the way, the value isn't supported by Netscape.

WRITING MARGIN AND PADDING SHORTHAND

Margins, padding, and borders are all components of the box model and can be applied to any block element.

5-23

> **Using two values.** A shortcut style using two values is written as:

```
.demo2 {
margin:50px 10px;
}
```

When the style is applied, the browser uses the first value for the horizontal sides of the element, that is, the top and bottom; the second value is applied to the vertical sides of the element. In figure 5-24 you see the differences in the margins.

5-25

5-24

> **Using three values.** A shortcut style using three values is written as:

```
.demo3{
margin:20px 10px 60px;
}
```

The browser still interprets the style's values systematically as you can see in figure 5-25. The first value is applied to the margin-top property, the second value to the margin-left and margin-right properties, and the third value to the margin-bottom property.

> **Using four values.** A shortcut style using four values is written as:

```
.demo4{
margin:50px 100px 20px 50px;
}
```

The browser applies the first value to the margin-top property. The remaining values are assigned clockwise, as you can see in the example shown in figure 5-26.

5-26

DEVELOPING THE DENYEREC GALLERY

*A*part of developing your own design skills is to examine and understand how other designers work. Here's an example, using the gallery and blog housing the Denyer photo collection, shown in figure 5-27. The site is a terrific example of how good design and practical considerations can readily coexist.

Denyerec.co.uk started out as a gallery project that grew to become a blog and gallery, using Wordpress (www.wordpress.org) to power the blog side of things.

My focus and observations with regard to the site included the following:

> I wanted minimum fuss in creating new row/column order without having to hack a great deal of code.

> I wanted the design to stay out of the way of the photos.

> The menu on the left is a semantic nested list, styled to clearly indicate subcategory status.

> I wanted the site to be easily indexed. Google and other search engines love it because the site is well-styled semantic HTML.

> Because the site is CSS-based, it can be easily restyled and the output customized. Attempting the same method using a table layout is an absolute nightmare.

From the perspective of the gallery, using CSS offered up two distinct benefits:

1. CSS allowed the layout to remain flexible and independent of the underlying PHP code that generates it.

2. As a secondary bonus, when Wordpress was integrated into the Web site, it was relatively easy to apply the styling from the gallery to the Wordpress template to maintain a continuous theme. On the surface it looks like the gallery was integrated into Wordpress but it's actually the other way round!

5-27
courtesy Denyer

PRO TIP

Using the gallery's styling in the Wordpress template is an example where using standard XHTML elements to mark up your pages is a bonus, because they will then integrate into any other standards-compliant system with the minimum of fuss.

Do you want your links to look the same across the entire Web site? Or how about the headings and copyright notices? A centralized CSS system makes these site wide integrations far easier to implement and maintain.

DEVELOPMENT OF THE GALLERY

When the gallery on www.denyerec.co.uk (direct link http://gallery.denyerec.co.uk) was first written, it was different from a lot of gallery systems available at the time. Rather than the old-fashioned table layout approach, the gallery was based exclusively on XHTML and CSS.

One of the principal benefits of the CSS-based method is that the arrangement of the menu, the information presented with each photograph, and the organization of the photo grid are all controlled through CSS rather than the underlying code. This means the PHP code is told to output 12 images, and the gallery's CSS does the rest. Any changes I want to make, from configuring the images in two rows of six to hiding a photo's date, can be controlled by changing the CSS.

Separating the visual display from the underlying code eases the programmer's workload considerably as well. If the programming team, or individual programmer — or just the left side of your brain! — only has to concentrate on producing clean, layout-free markup, it can make the programming job a lot easier. Separating the code from the appearance reduces the designers' need to keep trekking back to the programmer when they decide they'd rather have three rows of four instead of four rows of three.

STYLING THE GALLERY LAYOUT

When it came to laying out the gallery, I had a number of `<div>` elements housing the page's contents, including:

> An unordered list of categories

> An image collection

> Information about the gallery or selected photograph

> Separate `<div>` elements for the header and footer

With this rough sectioning decided on, the CSS could then be used to maneuver these components into the right positions using the `float` attribute.

PRO TIP

Floating content can sometimes cause confusion at first, and hunting down the usual suspects, typically but not exclusively restricted to bugs in Internet Explorer's box model, can cause some headaches.

On the other hand, floating does allow a layout to become more "liquid" than if elements of the page are positioned absolutely. In my gallery, for example, if there are fewer than 12 images, the floating thumbnails fill up the central `<div>` as required.

The ability to take a semantically marked-up document and apply styling independently of the markup is the greatest strength of CSS. What if you want the menu at the bottom? No problem; you don't have to edit the markup to do it. If you're working in a team or trying to decorate the output of third-party code, not having to edit the code is invaluable.

As a designer you have to edit CSS code, but at least in theory you don't have to rely on someone else — or your own programming skills — to modify the structure of the page.

I want to use a product's image as a background on its description page. In my experience, and based on some research I have done, the `position:fixed` **rule doesn't work in Internet Explorer, but I know most of my clients use that browser. What can I do?**

Rather than using the `position-fixed` ruleset, add your background image to the page's style. You'd have to substitute the URL for each background image you use and create different styles for different pages.

Alternatively, there is a workaround you can apply. In the `<body>` element's style, include these rulesets:

```
height:100%
overflow-y:auto
```

The problem with the workaround is that you can't use `position:absolute` or `position:relative` on the page, although you can use `float` properties.

Fortunately, IE 7 from beta 2 upwards will support `position: fixed`.

CONFIGURING PAGE LAYOUTS

Prior to the use of positioning styles, the only practical way to control the layout of a page was by organizing the content into tables. However, using structural elements to control the appearance of a page defeats the concept of separating content from design.

There are numerous ways to control page layouts using styles that you may have considered or experimented with. Hand-in-hand with separating function from design is the need to provide a Web site that is flexible enough to be modified according to a user's requirements and still maintain its appearance.

Should a page change relative to the size of the browser window, or should it use a consistent width and alignment? Like most design issues, the correct answer is that it depends on your requirements.

This chapter contains lots of "show and tell" materials to demonstrate the variation in page layouts and their intricacies.

If the vast number of options seems overwhelming, read how guest contributor Denyer creates a layout, letting the structure of the site guide its visual development.

CHOOSING A PAGE LAYOUT METHOD

Web design is the only form of visual design that gives the user so much control over how the material is displayed. On one hand, the degree of user control is a strong recommendation for using Web page delivery; on the other hand, it definitely requires a lot of testing and accommodation.

DESIGNING A PAGE WITH COLUMNS

Some pages use two columns; others use four columns. Some pages use a static layout; others use an elastic or fluid layout.

The layout of a page is based on three CSS concepts — position, float, and margins.

Designing and constructing a page layout uses the same course of action regardless of the particulars of the design.

Create the basic HTML structure using a sequence of <div> tags. The number of <div> elements depends on the column arrangement.

There are numerous ways you can identify the set of <div> tags for a page, but get in the habit of using a consistent naming convention for convenience. Here's one example:

```
<div id="wrap">
    <div id="header"></div>
    <div id="nav"></div>
    <div id="main"></div>
    <div id="sidebar"></div>
    <div id="footer"></div></div>
```

The layout of a basic page is shown in figure 6-1.

NOTE

Elements are identified by name and a background color.

6-1

TARGETING A LAYOUT OPTION

There isn't one "best" format to use for page design. How you choose to define the elements' styles differs according to the type of page layout you need.

My increasing preference is to use a hybrid layout, giving me the best of using percentages and relative font sizes to define elements' sizes. The layout types include:

> **Static.** A static layout uses fixed sizes for columns and contents.

> **Liquid.** A liquid layout maintains the relative sizes of a page's elements using percentages.

> **Elastic**. An elastic layout maintains the relationships among the page's elements by setting widths relative to the font size on the page.

> **Hybrid.** A hybrid layout combines both elastic and liquid elements.

DESIGNING A STATIC LAYOUT

A static layout uses fixed sizes and fixed relationships for the page's columns, like the two-column page layout with a header shown in figure 6-2.

Regardless of the size of the browser window or the monitor's resolution, the text and column sizes remain the same. In figure 6-3, you see that the same page shown in figure 6-2 leaves a lot of empty space on the screen when the monitor's resolution is increased.

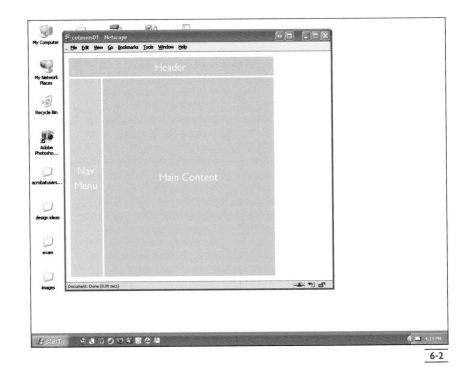

6-2

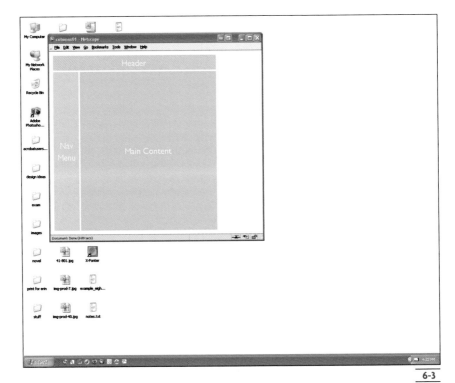

6-3

USING A LIQUID LAYOUT

A liquid layout maintains the relative sizes of a page's elements by using percentages. The example in figure 6-4 shows the percentages assigned to the components on the page.

6-4

A page designed using a liquid layout changes the size of the components as the browser window's size changes, either larger or smaller. The example in figure 6-5 maintains the same relationships among the components, even though the browser window size is much smaller.

6-5

MAINTAINING RELATIONSHIPS WITH AN ELASTIC LAYOUT

An elastic layout maintains the relationships among the page's elements by setting widths relative to the font size instead of the browser width using em lengths, like the sample page shown in figure 6-6.

6-6

In figure 6-7, increasing the font size in the browser window doesn't affect the relationships among the page's elements. Even though the font size is increased from medium to extra large, the page's layout integrity is maintained.

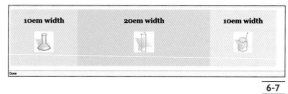

6-7

COMBINING LAYOUT TYPES

A hybrid layout combines both elastic and liquid elements. The length values are specified in em measurements, and the maximum widths allowed for elements are defined as percentages.

> **NOTE**
>
> You might see the term *jello layout* used to refer to a hybrid layout. It's quite descriptive, isn't it?

CENTERING A PAGE LAYOUT

Monitors have increased in size dramatically. I currently work with two 21-inch monitors, one in a traditional landscape view, and one rotated into portrait view. That's a lot of screen space, and plenty of opportunity for eye strain.

One of the issues with larger monitors is that the extra width allows for extremely long lines of text.

As shown in the upper part of figure 6-8, the longer the line of text, the harder it is to read. For that reason, many designs use a centered layout where text is allocated to a central area of the screen, and lines of text are shortened to a comfortable reading length, like that shown at the bottom of figure 6-8.

There are two ways to produce a centered design:

> Use auto margins to set a specified width column.

> Use negative margins and positioning.

CENTERING WITH AUTO MARGINS

The W3C model for visually formatting content says if the values of `margin-left` and `margin-right` are `auto`, the values are equal, as in this example:

```
div#container {
margin-left: auto;
margin-right: auto;
width: 80%;
}
```

As a result, the element is centered and uses 80 percent of the window width. Or is it? Sadly, a number of browsers don't recognize the `auto` margin value, including Netscape Navigator 4, and Internet Explorer 4, 5, 5.5, and 6 in *quirks mode,* a method of displaying a browser using intentionally buggy code. Read about this mode, and why you'd want to use it in Chapter 11.

You can make a page center the content regardless of browser version by adding two additional rulesets specifying text alignment. Follow these steps:

1. Write a style for the `<body>` tag specifying the text alignment for the page:

```
body {
text-align: center;
}
```

2. The new ruleset centers all text on the page. For any containers you need to align differently, add either of these rulesets:

```
text-align: left;
text-align: right;
```

3. Test the page. You see the contents of the `<div>` tag are centered on the page, like the example in figure 6-9.

6-9

ORGANIZING WITH NEGATIVE MARGINS

When you are designing with two or more columns on a page, consider using negative margin values to place the columns correctly. An example using negative margins to control the column locations is shown in figure 6-10.

To use negative margins for column placement on a page layout, follow these steps:

1. Define the page's layout, and the relationships among the columns. In the example, the top and bottom columns are independent of the central two columns. In the main body of the page, the wider left column holds site content, and the narrower right column houses the menu.

2. Define the styles for columns placed side-by-side, and specify the margin of one column as a negative value equal to the width of the other column. In the example page, the styles for the two columns use 15% and are written as:

```
#main {
   background-color: #99CC99;
   float:left;
   width:85%;
   height:220px;
   margin-right:-15%;
}

#rt_sidebar {
   background-color: #99CC33;
   width:15%;
```
```
   float:right;
   height:220px;
   padding-left:5px;
}
```

3. Define the style for the footer column including a `clear` property to force the column to display below the rest of the page. The example's style is written as:

```
#footer {
   background-color: #33CCFF;
   clear:both;
   height:50px;
}
```

PRO TIP

In the styles shown in this section, notice how the `float` rulesets are specified. The left column uses `float:left` and the right uses `float:right`. When you increase the width of the browser window, the right column floats away from the left, and any blank space uses the left column's background color.

If you specify widths and margins in pixel values, widening the browser window pulls the right column to the right; any blank space is white.

DESIGNING MULTIPLE COLUMNS

Whether you use two columns or five columns, the design is the same. Layout is based on divisions, block-level elements that default to using the full width of the screen with line breaks separating them from one another.

DESIGNING FEATURES

Keep these concepts in mind as you develop more complex pages:

> Float the columns one way or the other.

> In a multi-column layout, float all the columns to one side.

> The total specified widths of the columns can't equal more than 100 percent.

> For more layout control, use margins and padding.

The page shown in figure 6-11 is the same as in figure 6-10, but uses two additional columns in the center row of the page.

MODIFYING A LAYOUT

The styles in this version of the page are configured using pixel values. Dragging the browser window larger creates a white space between the third and fourth columns in the middle row, unlike the previous example that showed the background of the left column in the middle row. The styles include:

> The narrow left column written as:

```
#lt_main {
    float:left;
    width:100px;
    height:200px;
}
```

> The main wide column written as:

```
#main {
    float:left;
    width:225px;
    height:200px;
}
```

> The narrow third column written as:

```
#rt_main {
    float:left;
```

6-11

```
    width:125px;
    height:200px;
    margin-right:-150px;
}
```

> The narrow right column used for the menu writ-ten as:

```
#rt_sidebar {
    float:right;
    width:150px;
    height:200px;
}
```

NOTE

The four columns making up the central portion of the Web page contain borders and background colors that are excluded from the code samples.

MAKING IMAGES CHANGE SIZES

Designing columns on a page that resize propor-tionally adds to a page's versatility, allowing users to resize text as necessary for their comfort. One thing that often bugs me is when a designer doesn't take that extra step and style the images as well.

PRO TIP

<soapbox> If your intent is to make a page more accessible, then allowing images to resize is as important as allowing text to resize. An image tells a thousand words, but only if you can see it clearly. </soapbox>

TESTING TEXT SIZES

Text can get larger and smaller, but with the exception of Opera's zoom and scale function, no browsers let images rescale automatically.

Check out the example in figure 6-12. The page layout looks good at a fairly wide browser window size and default browser text size.

However, if you change the browser text size, the image proportions remain static. In figure 6-13, using small browser text displays the images at a dispropor-tionately large size.

PRO TIP

Plan ahead. When I design content for a site, I always try to make uniform sizes for as many images as possible. It's simpler for me to keep track that way.

Using uniform sizes lets you readily build a style for the image sizes, and saves time applying separate styles to each image.

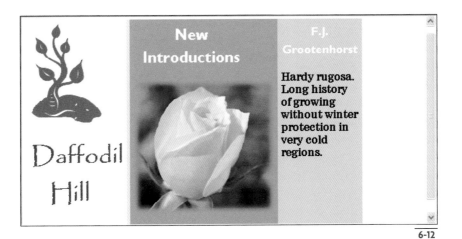

6-12

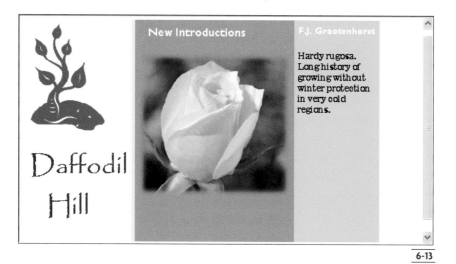

CONVERTING IMAGE MEASUREMENTS

In the example, the logo image's tag and attributes are written as:

```
<img src="hill.gif" width="110"
height="150" alt="Daffodil Hill
Nursery logo" />
```

The rose image's tag is written as:

```
<img class="flower" src="rose.jpg"
width="220" height="200" alt="F.J.
Grootenhorst" />
```

Use styles to scale images and maintain the content proportions. You can specify the proportions and relationships in different ways.

My preferred method is to use equivalent em values following these steps:

1. Convert the dimensions of your images to an equivalent em value by dividing the pixel size by 16.

2. Write a style for each image using the calculated em values. The style for the logo image is written as:

```
.logo {
  width: 6.9em;
  height: 9.3em;
}
```

The rose image's style is written as:

```
.flower {
  width: 13.75em;
  height: 12.5em;
}
```

3. Apply the style to each image tag.

4. Test the page. Increasing the text size, as shown in figure 6-14, proportionally increases the image sizes as well.

PRO TIP

Defining proportions for images works in ordinary circumstances, such as increasing the browser's text size to extra-large. In a browser like Firefox, where you can zoom in dramatically, at a certain magnification the visual integrity of the image is lost.

I don't get overly concerned because a user needing such a high magnification level probably uses a screen device for managing the view.

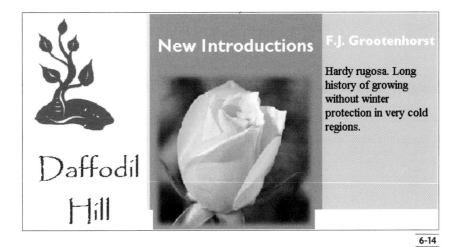

6-14

CREATING A LAYOUT

*M*any people think they can design a Web site. A
quick browse shows that not everyone designs
a Web site successfully. On the other hand, there are
certainly sites that are striking, like the example
shown in figure 6-15.

*It is my pleasure to offer you some design insights
from the award-winning principal of Sozu Design,
Denver. Here's what he has to say about designing a
layout for a site.*

Designing and building a Web site isn't for the faint of
heart. I have found there are a number of key principles to keep in mind, as well as a general path to follow in the design and production of Web materials.

APPLYING KEY PRINCIPLES

When I start new Web sites, I always keep a few key
points in mind, including:

> Start with blocks of related content. Don't position
content on a whim if at all possible. Try to place
related or ergonomically sensible things in sensible places.

> Don't buck convention for the sake of it. People
accept and expect certain things in certain places

to do certain things. For example, people expect a
picture of an envelope to correspond with e-mail
links; there is no point actively going against the
grain for stylistic reasons.

> Pay some attention to the aesthetic principles
taught and mastered by great artists from the
past. There's a reason they're called "Great
Masters." Things like the "golden section" and
"rule of thirds" apply equally well to Web design
as they do to classical artwork.

> Remember that the main power of CSS allows you
to window-dress information that is originally
stored in a computer-readable form. XHTML
specifically allows for the semantic markup of
data, and it's important not to lose sight of that.

> If you find yourself applying hack after hack,
sometimes it's best to just start over.

> The clients are always right. (No matter how
wrong they are!)

PRO TIP

CSS2.1 and CSS3 will make life a lot easier, but
don't expect to be using them any time soon.

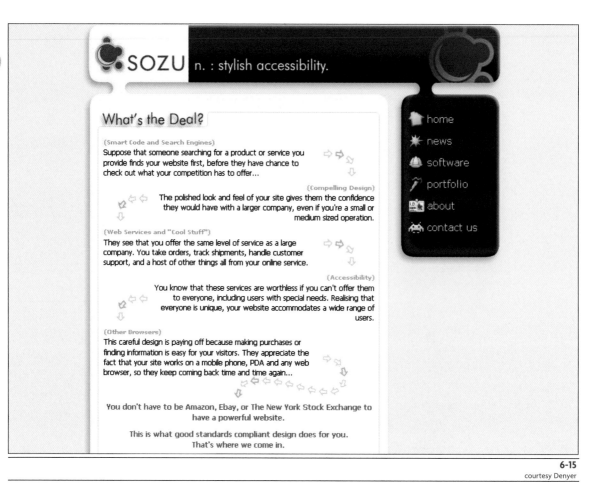

LAYING OUT THE DESIGN

When laying out a new design, I follow this method:

1. First up, establish the structure of the design. You need to know the answers to a multitude of questions, including these few examples: Where will the logo and strap line go? Is the menu system horizontal or vertical, or is there even a traditional menu? Does the copyright notice live in the page content, or does it float on its own at the foot of the page?

2. Rough out on paper the block elements that make up the pages' composition and the approximate locations where they live. For example, on http://gallery.denyerec.co.uk the header and footer sit as separate units. There is a central content area, and within this central area are three distinct areas. One area is for the menu, one for the thumbnails, and one for the extra information, as you can see in figure 6-16.

3. With the main areas defined, it is then a matter of pushing and pulling them into place and sizing them to fit both aesthetically and practically into the browser window.

6-16
courtesy Denyer

Drawing out blocks like "content," "header," "logo," "menu," and so forth on paper almost always leads directly to the `<div>` tags that make up the page layout. (And usually their names too!)

MANIPULATING THE COLOR SCHEME

It is possible to overhaul the color scheme in CSS alone, depending on the amount of graphical content in your Web site.

Using a program such as TopStyle Pro (From Bradbury Software) allows a designer to tweak and see results in real time. Previewing is a fantastic timesaver that also allows you to simply "try things out" and see if they work. Find out more about the program at www.bradsoft.com/topstyle.

Other programs such as Dreamweaver have similar features, but in my experience the less a program tries to do for you, the easier it is to get the results you want — and TopStyle Pro does just that.

For example, in support of the Grey Tuesday protest, held on February 24, 2004 to lobby against recording industry practices, it was quite simple to make www.denyerec.co.uk turn gray. All that was required was editing the colors in the CSS.

ACHIEVING PIXEL PERFECTION — OR NOT

Sometimes it isn't possible to achieve a pixel-perfect representation of your design in every browser. The more complex the design, the more likely it is that some concessions have to be made along the way.

I'm not implying that you shouldn't try your best to avoid cross-browser inconsistency, but in a production environment, a Web site that at least works in every browser and is actually online and usable is better than one still stuck on a designer's hard drive!

MATCHING COLUMN LENGTHS USING AN IMAGE

It's hard to make elements fill a page vertically because CSS prescribes that only the required space is used, like the examples seen in figure 6-17. If you have content that is 5px in height, the element containing it is 5px high; for an image that is 500px in height, its container is 500px, and so on.

6-17

CONSTRUCTING THE IMAGE

You can simply and quickly produce a layout that has columns of equal appearance regardless of their content by using a tiled image. This method works only for absolutely positioned layouts.

Follow these steps to produce the image:

1. Decide on the background appearance of the Web page and prepare any tiled or decorative elements.

2. Construct an image file like the example in figure 6-18 that:

   > Can be tiled vertically

   > Contains the colors you want to use for backgrounds for each column on the page

   > Includes visible borders as desired

   > Includes space and decorative elements as required by your layout

3. Save the image file. The image should be the width of the page you are building.

The Future of Column Layouts

The ideal line length is 8 to 12 words. The average computer screen showing 1024 x 768 pixels can show many times that in a single line.

Regardless of your careful planning, you know that your visitors may be using different font sizes or browsing without images, throwing off your entire design.

The CSS3 standards include a multi-column module extending the CSS box model. The module allows content to flow into multiple columns within one element, and lets the designer specify the columns' characteristics. As a bonus, the browser deals with text formatting to maintain balanced columns.

The new properties include:

> `column-count`, the number of columns

> `column-width`, the width of each column

> `column-gap`, use of left or right padding

> `column-rule`, use of a left or right border

Only Mozilla 1.8+ (Firefox 1.5+) supports some of the module at the time of this writing.

BUILDING THE PAGE

Once the tiling image is ready, it's time to write the style and build the page, following these steps:

1. Style the `<body>` tag using these properties:

   > Background color

   > URL for the tiling image

2. Specify the background repeat for the tiling image using the `repeat:repeat-y` ruleset. In this case, you want the image to tile vertically.

NOTE

Read about other background tiling options in Chapter 4.

3. Define the image's position horizontally on the page. The image should be centered by using `left:50%`. The example's style is written as:

```
body {
   background-image:url(bkgd_strip.
   jpg);
   background-color:#FFF;
   background-repeat:repeat-y;
   left:50%;
}
```

TESTING THE PAGE

Don't forget the edges of the page! Viewing your layout on a high resolution monitor is going to "shrink" the contents.

If the edges of the image are the same color as the background color you intend to use on the page, your layout appears seamless. In figure 6-19, although the high resolution window isn't filled with the background column image, you can't see where the image starts. Both vertical edges of the image are gradients that fade to white, matching the background.

PRO TIP

Using a background image requires an absolutely-positioned page. The advantage is that the main content follows the body tag, easy for indexing.

On the other side of the coin, you can't clear an absolutely positioned `<div>`, so you will need to ensure your content `<div>` is taller than your navigation `<div>`.

6-19

CHANGING CURSOR APPEARANCES

There are so many different ways you can jazz up a Web page, make it more functional for your users, and illustrate the content more clearly. One way is using different cursors.

We have all seen cursors that change their icon depending on where you have moved the cursor on the page.

Instead of using the default arrow cursor or the pointing hand to indicate a link, consider specifying a different value for the cursor property value to draw attention to specific elements on your page.

Common cursor appearances are shown in Table 6-1.

PRO TIP

You can use custom cursor images by defining the cursor file's location. Prevent errors by including a generic cursor in your string of cursor locations. That way, if none of the url-defined cursors can be located, the user still sees a cursor on the page.

For example: { cursor: url("eg_01. cur"),url("eg02.cur"), pointer}.

Layouts and Positioning

Table 6-1: Cursor Values and Appearances

Value	Appearance	How to Use It
Default	⌖	The default cursor is usually an arrow. If your computer uses a specific theme, the default cursor used in the theme is shown on the Web page, whether the cursor is a ray gun or a magic wand or a tree branch.
crosshair	+	The cursor displays cross hairs.
pointer hand	✋	The cursor shows a pointing hand to indicate a link or action. The value is named cursor:hand in IE, cursor:pointer in IE6 and Netscape 6, and both for cross-browser compatibility.
Move	✛	The cursor shows thick cross hairs with arrowheads, indicating the object can be moved.
text	I	The cursor shows the I-beam associated with a text input location.
wait	⧖	The cursor, an hourglass or a watch, indicates the program is processing or busy.
help	⌖?	The cursor shows a question mark or a balloon to indicate help is available.
Auto	Various	The browser sets the cursor based on default or user style settings.
inherit	Various	The parent element's computed cursor value is used.

Cursors in Motion

In addition to the set of cursors generally used on a page to indicate specific activity or content, there is another set of cursors used with dynamic content to resize or reposition a box object on the page.

The cursors are defined as locations, and their terms are named directionally. For example, e-resize is a cursor that indicates the edge of a box can be moved right, or east. Similarly, w-resize is a cursor that indicates the edge of a box can be moved left, or west. The set is rounded out with n-resize, where the edge is moved upward, or north, and s-resize, where the edge is moved downward, or south.

Not to be forgotten, you can also assign cursors to the corners. Again, the names are based on direction, and include:

> ne-resize, which moves the edge of a box up and right, or northeast

> nw-resize, which moves the edge of a box up and left, or northwest

> se-resize, which moves the edge of a box down and right, or southeast

> sw-resize, which moves the edge of a box down and left, or southwest

Q & A

I have a nice page layout, but it has a problem. I notice that sometimes a column disappears when the browser window resizes. What can I do about it?

The issue you are referring to is called a *column collapse*. You can prevent the problem by using a `min-width` ruleset.

The value can be specified as either a unit of measure, such as em or pixels, or a percentage, which defines the minimum width for the element as a percentage of its parent element.

For example:

```
#container {
min-width: 200px;
}
```

My client wants scrollbars for their Web site to coordinate with their corporate color palette. Is there anything special I need to know about them?

Styled scrollbars are supported only by Internet Explorer in versions 5.5 and newer. The scrollbar styles don't display in any other browsers, but don't have a negative impact on the displays in any other browsers. Because the styles aren't standard CSS, a page including scrollbar styles won't validate.

There is some controversy over where to place code for scrollbars. Some sources say in the `<html>` tag, while others say within the `<body>` tag is the correct location.

Both methods work. However, if you put the styles into the `<body>` of the page, IE6 works only in its quirks mode using an incorrect DTD, described in Chapter 11. When a page is built using a correct DTD, the scrollbars don't display the style characteristics because they aren't standard CSS.

But, based on the method IE uses to calculate inheritance, if you attach the styles to the `<html>` tag they are displayed on-screen.

There are numerous similar attributes in a scrollbar style, including:

> `scrollbar-3dlight-color`, which are the top and left edges of the scroll slider and the arrow button boxes.

> `scrollbar-arrow-color`, which is the color assigned to the arrow inside the arrow button boxes at the ends of the scrollbar.

> `scrollbar-base-color` is the background color applied to the scrollbar.

> `scrollbar-darkshadow-color` is the color displayed on the right and bottom edges of the slider and arrow button boxes.

> `scrollbar-face-color` is the color assigned to the flat surfaces such as the front-facing panel of the slider and alternating pixels of the track.

> `scrollbar-highlight-color` can be used in two ways. The highlight used for the 3-D effect usually uses white. The track uses a dithered appearance with alternating pixels displaying the `scrollbar-highlight-color`.

> `scrollbar-shadow-color` is the color assigned to the shadowed edges of the objects.

> `scrollbar-track-color` is the color attributed to the entire scrollbar track.

STRUCTURED PAGE ELEMENTS

Where would we be without lists? Personally, I would be the person standing in a supermarket aisle looking clueless, or wandering aimlessly through the plumbing supplies in the local hardware emporium, or overcome with choices in a gardening center or art gallery.

Lists are a simple way to organize information. If you write a list of items to buy at the supermarket, the list is generally an *unordered* list, or one where the sequence of items isn't hierarchical. On the other hand, if you are the type of person who makes a supermarket shopping list based on the route you travel through the store, then you are going to write an *ordered* list. You won't be putting dairy on your list until you have listed produce, for example, based on the product locations in the store.

This book has many examples of both types of lists. You see bulleted lists when I want to describe components or elements of a topic, and numbered lists when I am describing a process or method. As you see in this chapter, the lines can be blurred by using an unordered list that numbers the items.

The final type of list, a *definition* list, isn't included as part of the book's design; if you have seen a written screenplay or transcript of a legal proceeding, you have seen a definition list.

You are no doubt familiar with the basic list appearances on a Web page, and will certainly have used styles for configuring list appearances. In this chapter you see how to do other types of styling, such as using custom images, adding an image to a background rather than to the list item itself, arranging a list in columns, nesting lists, and styling the first item in a list differently from the remaining items.

And, if styling lists isn't enough, turn to guest contributor Faruk Ateş' tutorial at the end of the chapter to see how a sequence of elements, such as a sequence of images or a list, can be animated and controlled using CSS.

STYLING LISTS

There are only four list-specific styles for configuring both ordered and unordered lists. In addition, you can use many common properties such as borders, margins, font, color, and spacing styles.

Briefly, the properties include:

> `list-style-position` defines whether the marker is inside the box containing the list items, or outside the box.

> `list-style-type` specifies what type of marker is used for each list item. The two categories include a constant shape, used for an unordered list, and a sequence of numbers or characters, used for an ordered list like the example shown in figure 7-1.

1. Line a cookie sheet with plastic wrap.
2. Wash and core fruit.
3. Place fruit in blender and puree until smooth.
4. Add flavorings to the puree as it is blended if you like. Try cinnamon, cloves, allspice, nutmeg, lemon, mint, or honey.
5. Spread the puree on the prepared sheet and spread out to 1/8 to 1/4 inch thick, leaving 1 inch around the edges for the puree to spread in the pan.
6. Dry the fruit leather until it is rubbery and pliable, but not sticky.

7-1

> `list-style-image` specifies the URL for an image used as a custom marker for a list.

> `list-style` is the shorthand attribute used to set the other attributes in one statement.

ADJUSTING PADDING AND MARGINS

Sometimes the default indent of a list isn't right for your design. However, simply changing the margin or padding of the list won't work in all browsers.

For Opera and Internet Explorer browsers, specify a margin value to define the list's position. For Mozilla/Netscape browsers, use a padding value for positioning the list.

For best results in the greatest number of browsers and versions, get into the habit of automatically specifying both margin and padding values.

NOTE

The box model described in Chapter 1 shows the positioning elements in a box.

POSITIONING MARKERS

The list-style-position property places the list-item marker in the list in one of two locations:

> list-style-position:inside indents the marker and text, like the list in figure 7-2.

fruit sticks to waxed paper and tin foil.
- Puree the fruit with or without the skin. The skin adds fiber and sometimes extra color.
- Experiment with your fruit puree. Some types of fruit puree better when cooked first.
- Instead of a big pan-sized sheet, pour smaller individual servings on the cookie sheet.
- Peel and roll fruit leather while warm. After it cools it is harder to roll.
- Wrap each piece in plastic wrap so that the pieces don't stick together.

7-2

> list-style-position:outside places the marker to the left of the text, like the list shown in figure 7-3.

Here are some tips:
- Use plastic wrap to line the pans or nonstick spray; the fruit sticks to waxed paper and tin foil.
- Puree the fruit with or without the skin. The skin adds fiber and sometimes extra color.
- Experiment with your fruit puree. Some types of fruit puree better when cooked first.
- Instead of a big pan-sized sheet, pour smaller individual servings on the cookie sheet.
- Peel and roll fruit leather while warm. After it cools it is harder to roll.
- Wrap each piece in plastic wrap so that the pieces don't stick together.

7-3

PRO TIP

If both a list item and its parent have settings for the same attribute, the individual list item's attribute is displayed.

MARKER TYPES

CSS defines the object prefacing a list item as a *marker;* commonly these objects are also called *bullets.* Lists use a variety of bullet or alphanumeric characters to identify the items. The list-style-type property specifies the marker's appearance. Regularly used markers are listed in Table 7-1. You'll notice that some of the values in the list are numerical or alphabetical characters. When a marker value is assigned that uses a sequence, the list is an ordered list.

Table 7-1: Common Markers

Value	Looks Like . . .
none	Blank
disc	A filled circle
circle	Circle
square	Square
decimal	Number
decimal-leading-zero	Number padded by initial zeros, such as 01, 02, 03
lower-roman	Number using lowercase roman numerals, such as i, ii, iii
upper-roman	Number using uppercase roman numerals, such I, II, III
lower-alpha	Lowercase alphabet, such as a, b, c
upper-alpha	Uppercase alphabet, such as A, B, C

Structured Page Elements

125

More List-Item Markers

In Table 7-1, I listed examples of the most commonly used markers. The table is by no means all-inclusive. In addition to the Western numbers and letters you are familiar with, other options that can be used as list markers range from Greek to Latin, Hebrew to Armenian and Georgian.

Several Asian character sets can be used as well, including cjk-ideographic, and variations of hiragana and katakana markers.

CUSTOMIZING LIST MARKERS

Instead of using one of the named markers allowed in CSS, you can substitute any image you want. There are two approaches to producing the custom appearance: you can specify an image as part of the style, or embed the marker in the background of each item.

SIMPLY CUSTOMIZING MARKERS

The simplest method is to specify an image you want to use for the marker. The example shown in figure 7-4 uses this style:

```
ul {
    list-style-image:url("swirl.gif");
    list-style-type: circle
}
```

EMBEDDING MARKERS FOR CONSISTENCY

My preferred method for using custom bullets for a list is to place the image into the background of each list item.

Here's the style associated with this method, applied to the list items. The list is shown in figure 7-5.

```
#list li {
    background-repeat:no-repeat;
    background-position:0.3em;
    list-style-type:none;
    list-style-image:url(apple.jpg);
    margin-bottom:2px;
    padding-bottom:2px;
    padding-left:1em;
}
```

Adjusting Flavors

Combine two or more types of fruit. If you are stumped for ideas, think of juice combinations available in your supermarket, such as:

- apples with anything
- apricots or peaches with apples or plums
- citrus mixes
- melons, like cantaloupe and watermelon

7-4

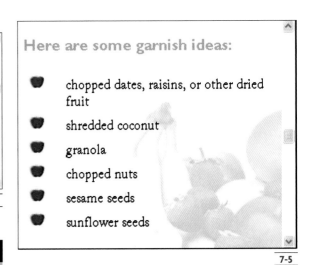

Here are some garnish ideas:

- chopped dates, raisins, or other dried fruit
- shredded coconut
- granola
- chopped nuts
- sesame seeds
- sunflower seeds

7-5

PRO TIP

Notice that the style for the list also includes a default marker, in this case, the circle. In the event the viewer can't access my image, the list is displayed using the named marker.

Changing a List's Indentation

A hanging indent is opposite to a traditional indent. Instead of the first line of a block being indented, the first line is outdented, with all other lines indented.

A list can be constructed without bullets, or displaying a custom character or image. The list's style needs to be adjusted to remove the bullet and display a hanging indent.

The style applied to the example shown in figure 7-6 is written as:

```
ul {
    list-style:none;
    margin-left:0;
    padding-left:1em;
    text-indent:-.5em;
}
```

Using a negative `text-indent` value moves the first line to the left to produce the indent.

Adding to the Mix

As the water evaporates from the puree, the product becomes more concentrated. Any spices or flavorings you have added also concentrate. For this reason, add very small amounts of flavorings to the wet puree. If you add too much spice or flavoring, add more fruit to the puree.

Garnish your fruit leather for extra color, texture, and flavor. Add the garnish after the puree has begun to dry but is still very sticky. Store leathers that contain nuts or coconut in the freezer.

7-6

NOTE

The appearance is the same whether you specify the left margin and padding as in my style, or reverse the values, that is, make the `padding-left` value 0, and the `margin-left` value 1em.

Using a Character for a Bullet

Instead of using a defined marker or an image, use a character by following these steps:

1. Write the style for the list without any marker, using the style shown earlier.

2. Add the list items to your page.

3. On the page's HTML, insert the character before each list item's contents, such as

```
<li> &#8211; item on list </li>
```

4. Test the page. As you can see in figure 7-7, the code and style generate an attractive list with the bullets defined as an en dash character.

Dehydrator Drying

Build or buy an electric dehydrator for the best results and the shortest drying time. Dehydrators come complete with racks for stacking food. The units are made up of:

- **a heat source**
- **a thermostat**
- **an air circulator**

7-7

Creating an Inline List

Sometimes you want to include content within a paragraph that is actually a list. For example, you might have a paragraph similar to the one shown in figure 7-8.

The key to producing fruit leather is to apply low heat for an extended period of time. You can use different methods such as sun, solar, or oven drying. There are also numerous dehydrator machines on the market.

7-8

XHTML doesn't allow a list within a paragraph. The only way to make *sun, solar,* and *oven* into a list is to include separate paragraph styles for the sentences before and after the list.

Follow these steps:

1. Write the text for the paragraph.

2. Design the style for the `<div>` containing the sentences surrounding the list's sentence. In the example, the style is written as:

```
#drying_list {
    margin:2em;
    width:80%;
    padding:5px;
    border:2px solid #669966;
}
```

3. Write the style for the two paragraphs preceding and following the list items. The example's style is written as:

```
#drying_list p {
    display:inline;
}
```

4. Finally, write the style for the list and list items. You don't want any margin or padding for the list items because they must appear to be part of a paragraph. The example's styles are written as:

```
#drying_list ul, #drying_list li {
    display:inline;
    margin:0;
    padding:0;
    color:#CC0066;
    font-weight:bold;
}
```

5. Apply the styles to the text on the page. The markup for the example is shown in List 7-1. Notice that the two paragraphs include all the words aside from the three list items themselves.

6. Test the page. As you can see in figure 7-9, the list items appear to be part of the overall paragraph, but are certainly differentiated visually.

The key to producing fruit leather is to apply low heat for an extended period of time. You can use different methods such as sun, solar, or oven drying. There are also numerous dehydrator machines on the market.

7-9

List 7-1: Markup for an Inline List

```
<div id="drying_list">
<p>The key to producing fruit leather
  is to apply low heat for an extended
  period of time. You can use different
  methods such as </p>
<ul>
    <li>sun, </li>
    <li>solar, </li>
    <li> or oven</li> </ul>
<p style="drying_list"> drying. There
  are also numerous dehydrator machines
  on the market. </p>
</div>
```

DIFFERENTIATING THE FIRST ITEM IN A LIST

A list, whether inline or not, sometimes uses a different character preceding the first item, or no character at all. In the previous example, you see I specified the three drying methods as list items that appear inline with other paragraph content. Instead, I could enhance their appearance further to draw more attention to the items.

I can reuse the `#drying_list` style for the `<div>` tag, and the `#drying_list p` style for the paragraphs before the list. I need three more styles for the list, list items, and the first list item. The styles used in the example are shown in List 7-2.

Displaying a List

Part of the discussion in Chapter 5 revolves around displaying content on a Web page. One of the `display` property values is the `display:list-item` ruleset. The `display` option specifies that an element using this ruleset looks similar to a `display:block` ruleset, with the addition of a `list-item` marker. Essentially it is the same as the `<li>` element described in this chapter. The ruleset is used with dynamic HTML to create expandable and collapsible elements responsive to JavaScript and browser events.

PRO TIP

You can use the styled inline list with a divider idea to configure a set of links that you want to display inline. My example visually looks much like a horizontal menu — read about building menus in Chapter 10.

NOTE

Horizontal lists are commonly used for menus and sets of links. Read about styling menus and links in Chapter 10.

The markup is very much the same as the previous example, except that the styles shown here are applied. The code for the first list item is written as `<li class="first">sun, </li>` to apply the borderless style to the first item.

In figure 7-10, you see how this version of the list appears on a Web page.

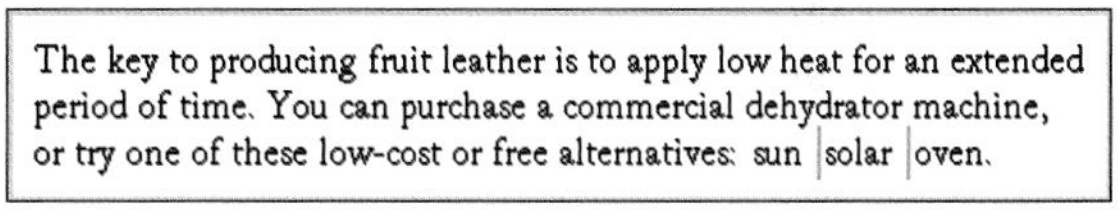

List 7-2: Styling an Inline List with a Divider

```
#divider ul {
    margin-left: 0;
    padding-left: 0;
    display: inline;
}
#divider ul li {
    margin-left:0;
    padding:2px;
    border-left:2px solid #669966;
    list-style:none;
    display:inline;
}
#divider ul li.first {
    margin-left:0;
    border-left:none;
    list-style:none;
    display:inline;
}
```

The key to producing fruit leather is to apply low heat for an extended period of time. You can purchase a commercial dehydrator machine, or try one of these low-cost or free alternatives: sun │solar │oven.

7-10

USING DEFINITION LISTS

Definition lists display both a term and definition pair, like what you may see in a glossary, or for a named item and a short description, like the example shown in figure 7-11.

The definition list shown in the figure is using the default configuration on the Web page. You'll notice the terms (`<dt>` tags) are aligned at the left of the browser window, and the definitions (`<dd>` tags) are indented.

Drying Methods

The key to producing fruit leather is to apply low heat for an extended period of time. You can use one of several methods, including:

Sun
  Dry produce in the sun over several days
Solar
  Concentrate the sun's rays to speed drying time
Oven
  Use your home oven at controlled temperature and time
Dehydrator
  Commercially-available machines designed specifically for drying

7-11

Like other list formats, the hierarchy for writing a definition list is based on nested elements. The `<dl>` tag is the parent; a definition list is written as:

```
<dl>
   <dt> First term </dt>
   <dd> First definition </dd>

   <dt> Second term </dt>
   <dd> Second definition </dd>
</dl>
```

The definition list's appearance can be modified using styles. For example, the same list shown in figure 7-11 looks considerably different with the attached styles shown in figure 7-12.

Drying Methods

The key to producing fruit leather is to apply low heat for an extended period of time. You can use one of several methods, including:

Sun
  Dry produce in the sun over several days
Solar
  Concentrate the sun's rays to speed drying time
Oven
  Use your home oven at controlled temperature and time
Dehydrator
  Commercially-available machines designed specifically for drying

Sun Drying

How well a product dries in the sun depends on the temperature and

7-12

As with other types of lists, attaching a style to the parent `<dl>` tag also affects the child `<dt>` and `<dd>` tags and their styles. In the example, I added a style for each of the three elements, written as:

```
/* definition list*/
dl {
border-left:2px groove #FF3300;
   margin-left:5px;
   padding-left:5px;
}

dt {
   margin-bottom:3px;
   margin-top:3px;
   color:#999900;
   font-weight:bold;
}

dd {
   font-style:italic;
}
```

PRO TIP

While most browsers indent contents within the `<dd>` tag, the tag defines the content type, and browsers can display it as they like. If you want to control the appearance, construct styles as with other types of lists.

Here's one final example of a definition list used for a specific purpose, shown in figure 7-13. You can mark up dialogs using a definition list, with each `<dt>` tag naming a person or character and each `<dd>` tag containing their words.

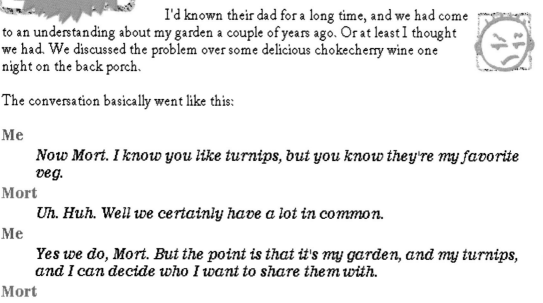

I'd known their dad for a long time, and we had come to an understanding about my garden a couple of years ago. Or at least I thought we had. We discussed the problem over some delicious chokecherry wine one night on the back porch.

The conversation basically went like this:

Me

Now Mort. I know you like turnips, but you know they're my favorite veg.

Mort

Uh. Huh. Well we certainly have a lot in common.

Me

Yes we do, Mort. But the point is that it's my garden, and my turnips, and I can decide who I want to share them with.

Mort

Uh huh. Being young boys and all I guess it slipped their minds.

Me

Well I would sure appreciate it if you could talk to those two again.

Mort

Uh huh. Any more of that wine left?

7-13

ARRANGING LISTS ON A PAGE

In addition to specifying how the list looks, where it is indented, and what sort of marker is used, you can also style a list to show in columns on a Web page.

The key to making a list show in columns is defining widths and using floats.

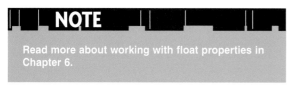

NOTE

Read more about working with float properties in Chapter 6.

SPECIFYING COLUMN APPEARANCES

Follow these steps to display a list in two columns on a Web page:

1. Define the list on your Web page; either an ordered or unordered list will work the same way. My example is an unordered list.

2. Decide on the width for the list, and write a style for the list such as this example:

```
ul {
  float:left;
  width:14em;
  margin:0 1em 0 0;
  padding:0 1em 0 0;
  list-style:none;
}
```

3. Next, write a style for the list items defining their width as half the width specified for the entire list. The example's style is written as:

```
li {
    float:left;
    width:7em;
    margin:0;
    padding:0;
}
```

4. Apply the styles to the page and test it in a browser. The example using the styles written in the steps is shown in figure 7-14.

Here are some garnish ideas:

Chopped dates or raisins	Shredded coconut
Granola	Chopped nuts
Sesame seeds	Sunflower seeds

7-14

PLACING A GRAPHIC BULLET IN THE LIST

Neither Internet Explorer for Windows nor Opera browsers show bullets or numbering when a list includes floated or width-defined list items. You must use a graphic marker inserted as an image into the style.

In the example shown in figure 7-14, the list is visually separated into two columns. There are a few modifications to make to the styles to include an image that serves as a bullet.

For the `<ul>` tag's style, increase the width to accommodate the graphics. The example changes the width from 14em to 18em.

The `<li>` tags' style needs a few additional properties, including:

> Adding padding to the left side to accommodate the image bullet

> Specifying the background image

> Including a background's position

> Specifying the repeat for the background image

The additional components for the example style are written as:

```
padding:0 0 0 1.5em;
background-image:url(grapes.jpg);
background-position:0 0 0 .3em;
background-repeat:no-repeat;
```

As you see in figure 7-15, the image is added as a bullet, and the two columns maintain a visually comfortable amount of spacing on the page.

Here are some garnish ideas:

Chopped dates or raisins	Shredded coconut
Granola	Chopped nuts
Sesame seeds	Sunflower seeds

7-15

WRAPPING ORDERED LIST COLUMNS

The method described here works fine for unordered lists, but it is a lot of work to use for an ordered list because you have to define separate styles for each `<li>` to assign separate images.

Don't waste your time. Instead, define a class for each column. In my example, I show how to assign classes to two columns. The same concept applies to as many columns as you need across the Web page.

Write the class styles and assign them to the list items by following these steps:

1. Design how you want the columns to lay out across the page.

2. Write the style for the `<ol>`. The example's style is written as:

```
ol {
  margin:0;
  padding:0;
  line-height:1em;
}
```

3. Write the basic style for the `<li>` like the example's style, which is written as:

```
li {
  margin:0;
  padding:0;
}
```

4. Write separate styles for the columns in your list. For each successive column, specify a left margin that includes the space for the preceding columns and some spacing. The styles in the example are written as:

```
.col1 {
  margin-left:3em;
}
.col2 {
  margin-left:25em;
}
```

5. Write a separate style defining the height for the second column. The style for the example is written as:

```
.wrap {
  margin-top:-4em;
}
```

6. Assign the class attributes to the `<li>` tags. In the example, the `<ol>` contains eight items so the list is split after item four. Assign the `.col1` style to the first four list items.

7. Assign the `.col2` style to the last four list items.

8. Assign the `.wrap` style to the fifth item, which is the top item of the second column. The code is written as:

```
<li class="col2 wrap">
  Spread the puree on...
</li>
```

9. Test the page. You see the list is split in two columns, shown in figure 7-16.

1. Line a cookie sheet with plastic wrap.
2. Wash and core fruit.
3. Place fruit in blender and puree until smooth.
4. Add flavorings to the puree as it is blended.

5. Spread the puree on the prepared sheet and spread out to 1/8 to 1/4 inch thick, leaving 1 inch around the edges for the puree to spread in the pan.
6. Dry the fruit leather until it is rubbery and pliable, but not sticky.
7. Remove the leather from the tray while warm.
8. Fruit leather can be left whole or cut into 4- to 6-inch pieces. Individually wrap the leather in plastic wrap or put it in an airtight bag or container. Freezing is best for long-term storage.

7-16

10. Make any further adjustments to the list as desired. Changes could include:

> Breaking the columns differently to have the content divided more evenly than my example.

> Tweaking the `.wrap` style's `margin-top` value to adjust the top of the second column. In the example, the line height is specified as `1em` in the `<ol>` style. To assign the negative top margin and pull the second column up to the top, multiply the line height by the em value, that is, `1 x 4 or 4em`.

LIST STYLING SHORTHAND

Like styles for elements such as fonts or borders, you can specify the values for the list in one declaration. Because the list-style properties are inherited, apply them to a parent element to have them displayed by child elements automatically. The condensed style applies to all three types of lists, as well as any element to which you have applied the `display: list-item` ruleset.

The three properties you can include in a shorthand declaration are

> `list-style-type` to specify the alphanumeric or graphic character applied in the list

> `list-style-position` to specify where the list markers are placed in relation to the text of the list and the page or container's borders

> `list-style-image` to specify an image for the list-item marker rather than an existing value

For example, the list shown in figure 7-17 uses a style written as:

```
#list01 {
inside upper-roman
}
```

Suggested Supplies

I. Casting resin

II. Casting epoxy

III. Release agent

IV. Pigments

7-17

In contrast, the list shown in figure 7-18 uses a style written as:

```
#list02 {
outside url(swirl.gif)disc
}
```

Pigment Types

opaque pigment

transparent pigment

pearlized pigment

admixtures

7-18

FACE: Faruk's Animated CSS Enhancements

With the rise of CSS-based design and progressive enhancements using JavaScript, the Web has started to become a more mature and interesting place, says Web designer, Faruk Ateş. This new dynamic has given free reign for innovation, and new ideas, concepts, and projects are being launched regularly. Here's what Faruk Ateş is doing with CSS.

While nearly everything these days seems to rely on JavaScript, at the heart of all these new technologies lies CSS and the power it has over markup. Clean, semantic markup styled with CSS has given you the freedom to play around with the page. Many people have taken this opportunity to create something that combines existing technologies into new tricks and techniques, and I am one of them.

In early 2005, I created a piece of JavaScript that looped through external CSS files in order to create a slideshow of sorts that showcased how a CSS-based design was made.

Some months later I wanted to do more with this stop-motion principle — real animation — but I knew that having a separate external CSS file for each step of the animation would not work. To make it easier, I developed an idea for letting JavaScript run through a series of classes on an element, with a numerical suffix that incremented each step. That would allow me to create one "frame" of animation in each CSS class definition, and all those CSS rules could be placed in a single file, solving my problem.

Eventually I sat down with friend and colleague Tim Hofman, and together we created a smoothly working, powerful JavaScript file doing all that and more: FACE was born.

One of the goals Tim and I set for FACE was that it would be easy to use for someone who had absolutely no knowledge of JavaScript whatsoever. It had to be Plug and Play, because we didn't want to force people to learn JavaScript programming just to use this method.

As a result, FACE can be used on any page simply by including the JavaScript file in the `<head>` section of the page, written as:

```
<script type="text/ javascript"
 src="/face.js">
</script>
```

With that in place, you can now add FACE-powered animations to any element on your page.

Understanding the FACE mechanism

Although you don't need to write your own JavaScript to understand our method, it's important to have an overview of the workings of the FACE mechanism.

Using FACE follows these steps:

1. A page is loaded with the `face.js` script included.

2. The script automatically checks for the presence of an `id` attribute on the page that has the value `enhance`.

3. If the FACE engine finds `id="enhance"` on the page, it starts up and moves to the next step: checking for the presence of the `Construct`.

The `Construct` is the name we've given to the class attribute that must be present on the same element that contains the `id="enhance"` attribute. In the `class` attribute, you configure the FACE engine and tell it everything it needs to know in order to run your animation for you.

Defining the configuration method

Before getting to the actual examples, let me explain why Tim and I chose this method of using the `class` attribute as a configuration tool for FACE.

As stated, we didn't want to force people to alter or change the JavaScript file in order to create different animations, thus excluding people who didn't know JavaScript. Additionally, changing the actual JavaScript code would mean changing the animation specifics sitewide, another undesirable option.

Including the configuration in the actual element that calls FACE to start up has several advantages, including:

> Any type of animation is allowed to be used on a page.

> Different types of animations are allowed on other pages of the site, using the same script.

> Upgrading to newer versions of FACE as they become available is as simple as replacing the JavaScript file.

RUNNING AN EXAMPLE

Using the class attribute presented us with a small problem: We had various configuration options to set, and effectively only one string to set them in. To solve this problem, we used a solution that embodies "nodes" within the class attribute's value.

Take a look at an example:

```
<ul id="enhance" class="C:slide:
 20:L:100:50">
  <li>Kittens</li>
  <li>Puppies</li>
  <li>Ducklings</li>
</ul>
```

In order to fully understand what is happening, I'll break up the Construct into these six nodes:

1. C

2. slide

3. 20

4. L

5. 100

6. 50

Each node in the Construct has a separate role:

> **Specifying node.** The first node in the Construct is the specifying node, and can be either C or S. It specifies whether the animation is to run on the element's Children (C) or on the element's Self (S). By specifying it on the element's Children, you can have the animation run through multiple elements in sequence.

> **Animation class node.** The second node is the animation class. Remember how I said that FACE runs through a series of classes, appended with an incrementing number? This is that class name. You can specify only alphanumeric class names, but for the sake of keeping things clear I recommend you use only letters and no numbers. In the previous example, we have the second node specify slide, which will make FACE run through the following classes: slide1, slide2, slide3, and so on.

> **Number of steps node.** The third node is very important because it specifies the number of steps. You don't want an infinitely running animation, so assigning a value to the node tells FACE when to stop. In our example, once FACE is done, we end up with slide20.

> **Trigger node.** The fourth node indicates when FACE is to trigger. At the time of writing, it allows for two values: MO for onMouseOver, and L for onLoad. The example uses L, which means the animation will run once the page has finished loading.

> **Animation speed node.** The fifth node indicates the speed of the animation in milliseconds. Combined with the number of steps, this allows you to create very slow or very fast animations, and of course, everything in-between.

> **Millisecond delay node.** The sixth node indicates the delay in milliseconds between the Child elements. If you set this to the same number as the fifth node, it means the second animation will start once the first one has finished, and so forth. Setting it to a lower value makes several animations run at the same time, one after another.

DESIGNING THE CSS

We're not there yet, though! We now have the system in place to run the animation, and we have specified how the animation should run and when it should trigger, but the most important step is yet to come: creating the CSS!

To have FACE work as a progressive enhancement, the JavaScript makes a call of its own for an external CSS file, but only when FACE is actually being loaded and executed on the page. This external CSS file is loaded by JavaScript as an include from the <head> of the page, written as:

```
<link rel="stylesheet"
  href="/face.css" type="text/css" />
```

Specify the CSS that makes up the actual animation in the face.css file.

For example, you could use the following:

```
.slide1 { text-indent: -19em; }
.slide2 { text-indent: -18em; }
.slide3 { text-indent: -17em; }
.slide4 { text-indent: -16em; }
...
.slide19 { text-indent: -1em;}
.slide20 { text-indent: 0}
```

FACE runs those 20 classes on the three list items in our example, at the speed of 100 milliseconds with a delay of 50 milliseconds between the list items.

Thanks to the CSS above, the text in the three list items slides into view and ends up in the right position once done. For other animations you can simply choose a different class name and add different CSS to the face.css file.

Is it better to use a reference to an image bullet's URL in the style or to embed the image in the list items' backgrounds?

There isn't one option that is always better than the other. Your choice may depend on:

> Your personal preference.

> Your level of familiarity with CSS; it's more complex to assign the image to a list item's background than to simply specify the image.

> The characteristics of the list and your image may influence which way you construct the style. If your style uses default values for the positioning and spacing, naming the image's URL lets you write a shorthand style for the list. On the other hand, if you are writing more complex styles to establish the correct layout, what's one more property?

I want to nest the individual pages on my site as lists within each item of a list of headings. Is there anything special I need to know?

Nesting is a good way to display a hierarchy on a Web page. Each successive nested list is indented from its parent list, producing the look we characteristically identify as a hierarchy.

You aren't really restricted in the number of nested lists you can have, aside from practicality and ease of use. You can use different markers for different levels of nested lists to help your viewers understand what they are seeing.

In a site map, for example, I might use three nested lists, but no more than that. Any more than three starts to become disorienting for the viewer — it's never a good idea to confuse your audience giving them directions through your site!

TABLE TUNE-UPS

Tables go back to the earliest days of Web design, when they were first used to house tabular data. As visual presentation capabilities developed, tables were used to organize other content visually on a page.

Chapter 5 describes how you can separate content from visual appearance and still maintain a tablelike structure using `<div>` tags and styles to display the columns. With the strength of CSS the tables are turning, so to speak, and tables are returning to their regularly scheduled function as data containers.

It's important to present table information visually and programmatically to all your viewers, including those using assistive devices. Tables are block elements, and you can apply a wide range of styles to configure their appearance. One common and highly configurable way to present table data clearly is through borders. Like other elements, borders can be specified for individual sides of a table, and you can use shorthand to write the styles to save time.

I sometimes use styles to color the backgrounds of alternate rows in a table to help users orient themselves to a table's content and not lose track of the data they are reading. Alternating colored backgrounds is a common device used in tables of all types. Because the Web is an active medium, why not apply a hover style to help your viewer even more? Hovers aren't restricted to links, and I like how they assist in orientation. In the discussion in this chapter, I show how to use mouse events to control the appearance of the table content.

Tables aren't only used for data presentation. In this chapter, see how a table is used for an attractive calendar on a Web page, and how an `<iframe>` can be used for accessing more detail for information on a table.

unless the table is configured properly — which to me includes the content needed to make the table accessible — it's just a jumble of colored lines and characters.

Tabular information belongs in a table because it is simpler to read and understand when presented in an orderly way. That fact must also apply to accessible browsers, screen readers, and other user agents like portable devices with small displays.

Here are the requirements and methods to achieve a usable table:

1. Identify row and column headers. Include `<td>` tags to identify data cells, and `<th>` tags to identify the headers.

2. If the table has two or more logical levels of headers, either row or column, associate data cells with their corresponding header cells. Group rows using `<thead>`, `<tfoot>`, and `<tbody>` cells, and `<col>` and `<colgroup>` to associate columns, as shown in figure 8-1.

Table 2: Base Temperature for Selected Crops and Insects

Crop or Insect	Base Temperature (° C)
Spinach	2.2
Lettuce	4.4
Wheat	4.7
General Plant Growth	5.0
Canola	5.0
Forages	5.0
Peas and Asparagus	5.5
Cabbage Maggot	6.0

8-1

MAKING TABULAR DATA ACCESSIBLE

I find it difficult to separate the styles for a table's component elements from the correct markup for said table. Not that the styles applied to a table are different than those used with other elements; it's that

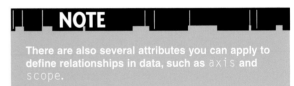

3. Test that the table makes sense when *linearized*, a technique where the table is converted to a series of paragraphs on a page, like the example shown in figure 8-2. If it doesn't, either revise the table or provide an alternative table.

Table 2: Base Temperature for Selected Crops and Insects

Crop or Insect Base Temperature (° C)

Spinach 2.2

Lettuce 4.4

Wheat 4.7

General Plant Growth 5.0

Canola 5.0

Forages 5.0

Peas and Asparagus 5.5

Cabbage Maggot 6.0

8-2

4. Communicate the content of the table using one or more of these `<table>` attributes:

> Use the `caption` attribute to describe the table in two or three sentences.

> Use the `title` attribute to describe the table in a few words.

> Use the `summary` attribute for the `<table>` element if the table is complex and needs more information on its structure.

CONFIGURING TABLE BORDERS AND SPACING

Tables can be configured using most of the visual configuration styles available. There are a few features and considerations to keep in mind when building the perfect table.

Here are examples of some differences you see in a table's appearance with slight changes in your style's property values. In all cases, the table uses the same layout, the same 2px border, background color, and default text appearance in the cells. The illustrated options are

> Using `cellspacing` for separation. In the example shown in figure 8-3, the table uses 6px cellspacing. You see the background color and cell borders are conjoined and define the cell, but the cells are separate from one another.

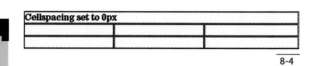

Cellspacing set to 6px

8-3

> Creating a grid formation. In the example shown in figure 8-4, the table uses 0px cellspacing. Interestingly, the table doesn't look as you might imagine it would. That is, some of the borders seem much wider than others. It's not an optical illusion — the borders are double the size.

Cellspacing set to 0px

8-4

> Collapsing the borders. The default border model separates the cells, and each cell has its own border regardless of the cellspacing. To get rid of the double borders as shown in figure 8-5, add a ruleset such as `border-collapse:collapse` to the table's style to create the final grid appearance.

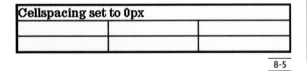

Cellspacing set to 0px

8-5

USING INHERITANCE TO SIMPLIFY STYLING

One CSS concept to consider carefully in a table is inheritance. Although inheritance is critical throughout your Web site's styles, it's perhaps easiest to see in action in a table.

You certainly don't have to repeat style information when dealing with inheritable properties. Here are some things to keep in mind when writing styles for tables:

> Decide on a naming convention before starting your site. A table can be named according to its content or its type. For example, a table named `products` is easy to figure out; so is a table named `calendar`.

> Look at commonalities in your table's elements and move up through the hierarchy to the level at which they first appear. For example, using a selector named `table.product td` lets you apply a style to all the `td` cells in the table without repeating any properties.

MAKING IMAGES AND TABLES COEXIST PEACEFULLY

Images have long been placed in tables as a means of organizing content. There are a number of considerations to keep in mind when configuring image appearances in a table.

If you place an image into a same-sized table cell, like the example in figure 8-6, you see the cell is filled with the image.

Shape is 80px wide by 60px high

8-6

If the table is part of a page using a strict DOCTYPE, an added space is seen below the image, like the example in figure 8-7. There isn't any difference in the page's markup or styles. Images are inline objects, and by default are aligned with the baseline of the cell, where the bottom of a row of text would fall.

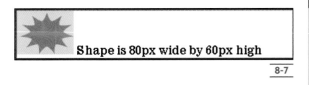

Shape is 80px wide by 60px high

8-7

To make images in tables behave properly and still have a standards-compliant page, here are some options to consider:

> Put images into their own table cells separate from other images or text and make them block-level elements.

> Make a single image in a table cell a block-level element.

> A cell having two or more images should be aligned with the bottom of the cell's box.

> Adjust the vertical alignment for an image in a cell with other images and text.

DISPLAYING TABLE ROWS IN ALTERNATING COLORS

When you are working with a table that displays a lot of similar information like a spreadsheet, one of the simplest ways to help viewers maintain their orientation is by using alternating colored backgrounds for the rows.

There are different ways you can style a table to show the rows' colors, such as:

> Writing two `<td>` tag styles for alternating colors

> Writing two `<tr>` classes and using inheritance

PRO TIP

If you want to apply a different background color to alternate rows in a table, directly classifying CSS styles to the `<tr>` tag does not work. You need to apply styles to the child `<td>` that follows the `<tr>`.

ALTERNATING COLORS WITH SEPARATE STYLES

On the surface, it seems like the best way to show alternating content is through two styles applied to either odd or even rows. It is the simplest method, but not very efficient.

In a simple table, where you are learning about more advanced table customizations, or where you aren't extremely sure of your CSS skills, follow these steps:

1. Write two styles for the alternating rows on the table. Here's an example:

```
td.odd {
    background-color: #E6E6CC;
    color:#3F3F3F;
}
td.even {
    background-color: #F9F9F9; color:
    black;
}
```

2. Apply the styles to your table's rows by assigning either odd or even styles to corresponding cells.

3. Test the page. As you see in figure 8-8, the table is simple to follow.

Agricultural Products Central Canada

Table 1: Number of Days Required for Selected Crops to Reach Maturity

Crop	>Days to Maturity
Barley	60 - 90
Canola - early Polish	73 - 83
Buckwheat	80 - 90
Yellow Mustard	80 - 90
Oats	85 - 88
Brown or Oriental Mustard	85 - 95
Flax	85 - 100
Lentils	85 - 100
Coriander	90 - 100
Field Peas	90 - 100
Navy Beans	90 - 100

8-8

Table 1: Number of Days Required for Selected Crops to Reach Maturity

Crop	Days to Maturity
Barley	60 - 90
Buckwheat	80 - 90
Canola - early Polish	73 - 83
Yellow Mustard	80 - 90
Oats	85 - 88
Flax	85 - 100
Lentils	85 - 100
Brown or Oriental Mustard	85 - 95
Coriander	90 - 100
Field Peas	90 - 100
Navy Beans	90 - 100
Wheat	90 - 100
Canola - late Argentine	92 - 102
Black Beans	95 - 105
Canary Grass Seed	95 - 105

8-9

That wasn't so bad, was it? Maybe you are wondering what is wrong with this method. As I mentioned, it's fine if you have a very short table. The downside is that adding the style repeatedly becomes boring after a while. It gets even more boring if you rearrange the content in the table and your stripe is out of sequence, like the table in figure 8-9.

PRO TIP

There is no simple way to provide alternating column colors using CSS. If you need a specific color or text alignment in a column, define the style for each <td> tag for each row of the column.

Tedious? Maybe, but it is accurate. And, until browsers offer more extensive CSS support, it's the only way to do it.

USING INHERITANCE FOR COLORING TABLES

To make the task simpler and more efficient, define two <tr> classes and the inheritance to their subordinate <td> tags by following these steps:

1. Write two complementary styles specifying a background and text color for the <tr> tags. Include the subordinate <td> tag in the selector, such as:

```
tr.bkgd0 td {
   background-color: #CC9999; color:
   black;
}
tr.bkgd1 td {
   background-color: #9999CC; color:
   black;
}
```

2. Apply the styles to the table. Regardless of the number of cells in a row, their background colors are uniformly modified, like the example table in figure 8-10.

3. Test the table.

Table 2: Base Temperature for Selected Crops and Insects

Crop or Insect	Base Temperature
Spinach	2.2
Lettuce	4.4
Wheat	4.7
General Plant Growth	5.0
Canola	5.0
Forages	5.0
Peas and Asparagus	5.5
Cabbage Maggot	6.0
Potatoes	7.0
Variegated Cutworm	7.0
Corn and Beans	10.0
Grasshoppers, Corn Borers	10.0
Pumpkins and Tomatoes	13.0
General Insect Development, House flies	15.0

8-10

PRO TIP

Simplify the task of assigning styles even further. Instead of building two separate styles, use one as the table's style, and then apply one other style to either the odd or even rows.

USING BORDER SHORTHAND STYLES

Like many other style categories, you can use shorthand styles for defining the appearance of borders. There are separate methods for writing a uniform border and a border with specific sides.

I find border style shorthand especially useful for a table using different border treatments because it lets me easily write and compare styles on the style sheet.

STYLING AN ENTIRE BORDER

The syntax for a border is:

```
border: border-width | border-style
   | color
```

For example, the style for the dotted pink border around the text shown in figure 8-11 is written as:

```
p { border: 2px dotted #FF99FF;}
```

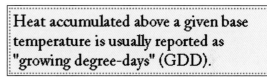

Heat accumulated above a given base temperature is usually reported as "growing degree-days" (GDD).

8-11

STYLING ONE SIDE AT A TIME

Often you work with borders that use different characteristics on different sides. You can still use a shortcut style for each border.

The syntax is the same as that for the overall border. The example shown in figure 8-12 frames the paragraph with a border on the left and bottom sides. The shorthand styles that produce the appearances are written as:

```
p {
   border-left: 3px dashed coral;
   border-bottom: 1px solid teal;
}
```

Heat accumulated above a given base temperature is usually reported as "growing degree-days" (GDD).

8-12

CHANGING A TABLE ROW'S BACKGROUND COLOR ON HOVER

You are no doubt aware of configuring the appearance of a link using pseudo-class styles, such as an `a:hover` style to show the users when their mouse is over a link.

In the interests of user-orientation, consider using styles to provide the same hover feature in a table when users position their mouse over a table row. In content-intensive tables it is a considerate feature to offer viewers.

The process works using two mouse event responses:

1. The user positions his or her mouse over a row on the table and the color changes, as you can see in the page shown in figure 8-13.

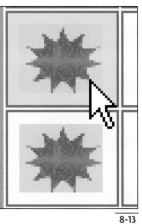

8-13

2. The user positions his or her mouse away from the row and the color reverts to the original.

Follow these steps to configure the rows on the table:

3. Create the two styles to use for defining the colors:

> The style `td.off` is the default table color.

> The style `td.on` is the hover color.

The styles in the example are written as:

```
td.off {
background-color: #CCCCCC;
}
td.on {
background-color: #999999;
}
```

4. Insert the styles and their events into each `<td>` tag in the table, written as:

```
<td class="off" onmouseover=
 "this.className='on'" onmouseout=
 "this.className='off'">
content for the row </td>
```

5. Test the page. As you move your mouse over the table's rows, watch for color changes, as seen in figure 8-14.

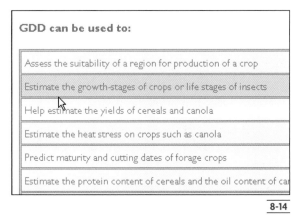

8-14

Losing Your Inheritance

Unfortunately, version 4 browsers applied the user's default settings to the table's text, regardless of any styles assigned to ancestor elements that should have been inheritable.

If you have to design tables that are likely to be viewed in version 4 browsers, list the table elements along with the ancestor's style such as `body`, `table`, `td {font-family: Arial Geneva sans-serif;}` to make sure the style is assigned to the child elements.

PRO TIP

Even though you intend to apply the hover appearance to links, named anchors on a page are also affected.

Prevent problems by using proper syntax such as: `a:link:hover {color:#339999;}` or `a:visited:hover color:#66CCCC;}`.

CONFIGURING SPECIALIZED TABLES

The sky is pretty much the limit when it comes to configuring how your tables appear on a Web page. Virtually anything that is tabular can be reproduced using XHTML and CSS.

There are two table topics that I want to touch on briefly because they are different from the usual, and have specialized styling requirements:

> A calendar that is shown on a Web page can use a raft of different configuration options, scripting, and styling, including my simple version.

> A table can present reams of data, and sometimes it is valuable to allow the user to see additional information about a particular value or label directly on the table's page. One way to manage this feat is by using inline frames.

DESIGNING A CALENDAR

One thing that I have seen online for the past several years, and for many years prior to that on the desktop, is the tidy little calendar table.

I use the regular link styling; if you prefer, you could use an image to identify visited or active days.

Follow these steps to construct and style a calendar table:

1. Write the style for the overall table. If you have no other tables on the page, use `table` as the selector. If you have more tables, or may have more tables, use an `id` selector instead, like this example style, shown in figure 8-15 and written as:

```
#calendar {
    width:140px;
    padding:0;
    margin:2px;
    font-family:Arial, Helvetica,
     sans-serif;
    text-align:center;
    color:#333333;
    border-right: 1px solid #DDDDDD;
    border-top: 1px solid #EEEDDD;
    background-color:#fff;
}
```

8-15

5. Write a style for the calendar navigation indicators to the left and right of the month's name, such as:

```
a.nav {
    color: #996600;
    text-decoration:none;
    font-weight: bolder;
}
```

6. Complete the markup by specifying the URL locations for the links.

7. Test the page. You'll see the changes in color depending on the link state, like the example shown in figure 8-16.

2. Specify the appearance of the table cells by defining a style for the `<td>` tag; the example is written as:

```
td {
    border-left: 1px dotted #A2ADBC;
    border-bottom: 1px dotted #CCCC99;
    width:20px;
    height:20px;
    text-align:center;
}
```

3. Write a style for the `link` and `visited` link pseudo-classes as in this example:

```
td a:link, td a:visited {
    color: #808000;
    text-decoration:none;
}
```

4. Write a style for the links' `hover` and `active` pseudo-classes such as:

```
td a:hover, td a:active {
    color: #ff8080;
    text-decoration:none;
    font-weight: bolder;
}
```

8-16

PLACING A FRAME INTO A TABLE

Whether you are using a table for displaying content, or a table containing multiple items such as tabular data, images, and links, there are times when you would like to make more information available to your viewers while still viewing the same page, like the example shown in figure 8-17.

Table 2: Base Temperature for Selected Crops and Insects

Crop or Insect	Base Temperature
Spinach	2.2
Lettuce	4.4
Wheat	4.7
General Plant Growth	5.0
Canola	5.0
Forages	5.0
Peas and Asparagus	5.5
Cabbage Maggot	6.0
Potatoes	7.0
Variegated Cutworm	7.0
Corn and Beans	10.0
Grasshoppers, Corn Borers	10.0
Pumpkins and Tomatoes	13.0
General Insect Development, House flies	15.0

```
Auxiliary Information
```

8-17

An inline frame adds an internal window that displays different pages within its boundaries. If you have ever built a Web site using frames, you are familiar with the concept, although an inline frame is considerably simpler to organize and manage than a frameset. Not only that, but inline frames don't have the same problems being indexed by search engines.

Here's an example of placing an inline frame along with a table to show extended information about data contained in the table.

Add the frame by following these steps:

1. Construct the table and add the data and other content as required.

2. Design and apply styles to define the table's appearance.

3. Include the code for the `<iframe>` in the table cell used to house the object and check it on the page. Specify the source file, height and width, alignment, and a name, such as:

```
<iframe src="growing_degree_days.txt"
 width="350"
height="120" name="#gdd">
```

4. Add any additional styles to the inline frame. It is an inline element, and can be styled as such.

5. Specify links using the `target` attribute and `iframe` name, such as:

```
<a href="growing_degree_days.txt"
 target="#GDD">
More Information</a>
```

6. Include alternate content for browsers that don't support `iframes` in the markup. You can use one or more links, text, or an image as the alternate content. The link shown in figure 8-18 opens the text file in a unique window.

Table 2: Base Temperature for Selected Crops and Insects

Crop or Insect	Base Temperature
Spinach	2.2
Lettuce	4.4
Wheat	4.7
General Plant Growth	5.0
Canola	5.0
Forages	5.0
Peas and Asparagus	5.5
Cabbage Maggot	6.0
Potatoes	7.0
Variegated Cutworm	7.0
Corn and Beans	10.0
Grasshoppers, Corn Borers	10.0
Pumpkins and Tomatoes	13.0
General Insect Development, House flies	15.0

More Information - Opens in New Window

Auxiliary Information

8-18

Q & A

Configuring the layout of a table using XHTML is simple because there are lots of tags I can use. What if I want to display a table layout in something like XML that doesn't use `<table>` tags?

In HTML, the default `display properties` values are taken from the HTML behavior or the style sheet. Other languages, such as XML, don't have defined display behaviors. Instead, you can use the properties listed in Table 8-1 for structuring content visually.

Table 8-1: Table-Based Display Properties

Value	The Element is Displayed As . . .
table	A block table with a line break before and after the table, like the `<table>` element. It contains `table-row` and `table-cell` properties that produce the appearance of table rows and columns.
inline-table	An inline table without line breaks before and after the table, like the `<table>` element.
table-row-group	A group of one or more rows, like the `<tbody>` element.
table-header-group	A group of one or more rows, like the `<thead>` element.
table-footer-group	A group of one or more rows, like the `<tfoot>` element.
table-row	A table row, like the `<tr>` element.
table-column-group	A group of one or more columns, like the `<colgroup>` element.
table-column	A column of cells like the `<col>` element; on a page you don't see anything, but it is used to hold style information, like properties attributed to a `<col>` tag.
table-cell	A table cell, like the `<td>` and `<th>` elements.
table-caption	A table caption, like the `<caption>` element.

I am trying to make the cells in my table display a mouseover hover color. The problem is that instead of only the cells changing, all the text on the page displays the hover activity. What's with that?

We usually use the `:hover`, `:active`, and `:focus` pseudo-classes with links, although they aren't restricted by CSS. Any element can be in any of the three states and can be styled based on those states.

Unless an element is defined in the `:hover` state style, the pseudo-class is applied to every instance of every hovering element. For example, writing

```
:hover {color:#339999;}
```

makes any text in paragraphs, tables, and headings display the text as a lovely shade of teal green. That may be a good thing, but a little effect goes a long way.

You can instead define the selector and assign the class to which the hover will apply, such as:

```
.nav:hover {color:#339999;}
```

The hover is then limited to the selector using the `nav` class. In a table, the style is applied to any table structure included in the class. For example:

```
<td class="nav">
<a href="one.html" class="nav">one</a> |
<a href="two.html" class="nav">two</a> |
</td>
```

In this example, the vertical bar characters and the links turn teal green when the mouse hovers over the cell.

For the control you seek, young Grasshopper, add an anchor element to the selector, such as:

```
a:hover {color:#339999;}
a.nav:hover {color:#339999;}
```

BUILDING INTERESTING FORMS

Forms are ubiquitous. How many forms have you used today? If you check your e-mail online, use a search engine, or place a bid at your favorite online auction, you are interacting with the active Web site via a form structure.

Some people, designers and nondesigners alike, find working with forms akin to an unpleasant dental experience — necessary, but not very high on the list of favorite activities. For others among us, building a form is the utmost in cool. Not only does the form present a design challenge in the way of integrating it with the rest of your Web site's look, but you have the extra added goodness of making the form work programmatically.

Regardless which side of the fence you are sitting on, forms are a big part of current Internet use. They are so important, in fact, that often their design alone is the basis by which a user decides to try what you are selling, or simply surfs away.

In this chapter, I have presented a range of situations where there are styling decisions to make regarding forms. Because forms are so extremely variable in their contents, dimensions, and type of fields, I have used a number of different examples to show you how to use styles for specific purposes, and how to follow through on a styling task.

CONSIDERING THE FORM AND USER'S NEEDS

What makes a good form? The answer to that question is variable, but there are some basic principles that apply across the board. The essence of a form, like that shown in the sample page in figure 9-1, is the same regardless of the complexity, styling, and content included.

9-1

Before delving into the design process, think about these ideas, and keep them in mind as you are developing:

> The appearance of a form should correspond with the appearance of the rest of your site. The sample page shown in figure 9-1 is minimal, undifferentiated, unlabeled form content. Contrast that with the sample page shown in figure 9-2 that uses the same colors, fonts, and images as other content on the example site.

> Styling a form requires some restraint: users expect to see certain form fields and structures on a form. Don't stray too far from what the viewer expects to see. The example shown in figure 9-3 is barely discernible as a form.

NOTE

Please be advised that I am not responsible in any way for eyestrain, headaches, nausea, and similar symptoms that may occur from looking at figure 9-3.

Sadly, the page is inspired by an actual form. By the time the form was crafted to the level you see in the figure I myself had to seek headache medication.

My apologies.

Customer Contact Form

Contact Details

Name

E-mail

Please comment on the service you received:

Would you like a customer service representative to call?

Yes ☐

No ☐

Please click "Submit" to send us your thoughts

Submit

9-2

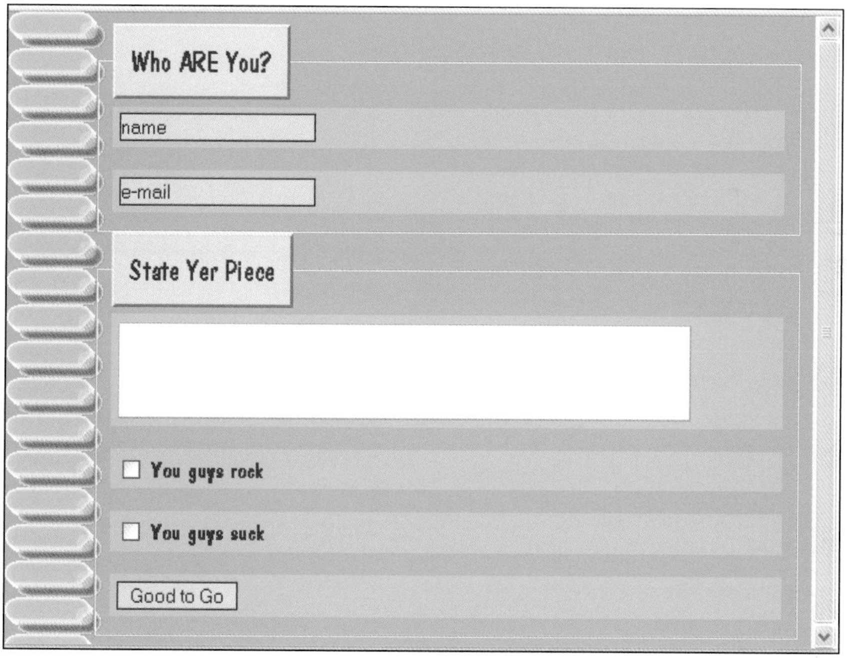

Who ARE You?

name

e-mail

State Yer Piece

☐ You guys rock

☐ You guys suck

Good to Go

9-3

> Different user agents have different responses to form elements and styles applied to them. For example, the CSS specifications don't even require that form elements have to be able to receive styles because forms are system-based, not browser-based.

> A functional layout is key to styling a form. Line up fields and labels, and use headings and directions as necessary.

> Make the form usable by as many viewers as possible. Be sure to include a variety of features and elements that support screen readers and other assistive devices.

REVIEWING FORM BASICS

Not everyone works with forms on a regular basis — some designers never work with forms at all. To make sure we are on the same page throughout the discussion, here's a quick rundown of form elements and their interrelationships:

> The parent element for a form is the `<form>` tag (no stretch of the imagination). All form content is enclosed within this tag.

> Nested within the form are one or more containers that hold a grouping of fields, called a `<fieldset>`. For example, the illustration in figure 9-4 shows three sections on the form, each a separate `<fieldset>`.

> Nested within each `<fieldset>` are the actual form elements or `<input>` fields.

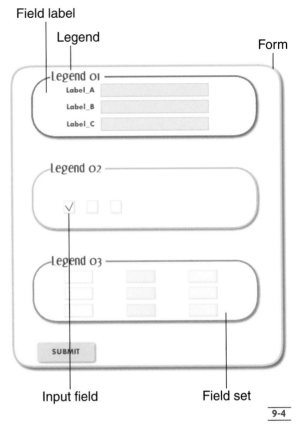

Field label
Legend
Form
Input field
Field set

9-4

One optional element is the `<legend>` tag, which assigns a title or caption to a fieldset grouping. Assigning the caption improves accessibility when the user is working with your site non-visually. It also helps orient your users to the form visually.

In figure 9-5, for example, removing the `<legend>` and `<fieldset>` elements makes the form appear less organized when compared to the same page shown previously in figure 9-2.

PRO TIP

Grouping controls and labels makes a form more accessible because it provides better tabbing navigation for both visual and speech-based user agents.

9-5

Styling a Simple Form

Aside from the usual types of styling, such as color, font, and so on, you have to configure layout styles for a form to align the labels and fields correctly.

Writing the code

To demonstrate the simplest way to make sure a form is in good alignment and styled properly, I am using the form stripped of most of its XHTML tags. I also stripped the styles, except one for the `<body>` tag to add a background and a bit of color, as you can see in figure 9-6.

9-6

PRO TIP

Your carefully crafted form layout will crumble in old browsers. Pre-CSS browsers don't use styles, obviously.

To create some semblance of structure, regardless of what your viewer is using to display your page, use `<br />` tags, as in my code example. This way each label and input field is on a separate line on the page.

157

The original XHTML is outlined in List 9-1.

List 9-1: Structure for a Simple Form

```
<form action="#">
    <label for="name">Name</label>
    <input id="name" name="name" />
<br />
    <label for="email">Email</label>
    <input id="email" name="email" />
<br />
    <label for="comment">Comment</label>
    <textarea rows="3" cols="30"
     id="comment" name="textarea">
    </textarea>
<br />
    <input type="submit" value="Submit"
     name="Submit"/>
<br />
</form>
```

PRO TIP

For the form's styles, you can write one style referencing the common properties and values in the form, such as the `display:block` ruleset as I have used.

If you are a bit unsure of yourself, or aren't accustomed to combining style content, write one separate style for each element, and duplicate the rulesets in each.

WRITING THE STYLES

Note in the page layout in figure 9-6 that there isn't any alignment for any of the elements, and that the fields are crammed together vertically.

Follow these steps to take care of the styling issues:

1. Write a style for both the `<label>` and the `<field>` tags. You want the style to:

   > Use a block display to control the location on the page.

   > Use a specified width and margins.

   > Use a float to control lateral placement on the page.

The page shown in figure 9-7 uses a style that includes the listed properties. The initial style is written as:

```
label, input {
    display:block;
    width:5em;
    float:left;
    margin-bottom:1em;
}
```

9-7

2. If you look closely at the form shown in figure 9-7, you'll see that each successive label is positioned laterally to the right and below the previous field. The labels need a separate style to align them correctly, written as:

```
label {
  text-align:right;
  width:5em;
  padding-right:1em;
}
```

The labels may be spaced further from the fields now, but the form's layout still doesn't display correctly, as you see in figure 9-8.

9-8

3. The style that defines how the content of the form lays out on the page is written for the `<br />` tag. List 9-1 showed that each field is followed by a line break. To take advantage of the break, write this style:

```
br {
  clear: left;
}
```

The style clears the `float` rulesets applied earlier. As you see in figure 9-9, the form finally looks good!

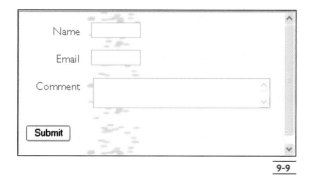

9-9

PRO TIP

You can declare the clear attribute on either the `<br />` tag's style or the `<label>` element's style. Using the latter doesn't work correctly in Opera browsers; using the former has a predictable outcome.

PRO TIP

If the `<input>` tag is specified in a style sheet, it will have an effect on the Submit button too, because the Submit button is also an `<input>` tag. If the Submit button needs to be changed, use an inline style, or a separate class defined in the stylesheet for the button.

STYLING BUTTON FIELDS

Some of the example pages I have used in this chapter don't differentiate the appearance of the Submit button from other types of input.

To configure a button separately from other fields on your form, follow these steps:

1. Decide if you want to use a separate style or create the style inline. When you have an attached style sheet and plan to use the button on several forms, by all means add a unique style. For a one-shot button, use an inline style.

2. Write the style for the button, such as this example:

```
.button01 {
  font-family:Verdana, Arial,
  Helvetica, sans-serif;
  color:#333366;
  border: 2px ridge #CC0066;
  background-color:#EEEEEE;
}
```

3. Attach the style to the appropriate tag in the code.

4. Test the page; click the button to see it in its depressed state, like the example shown in figure 9-10.

9-10

NOTE

Specifying an alternate border for the button may or may not show up in a browser: some browsers don't support button restyling.

LABELING FORM ELEMENTS

The `<label>` element defines a value for a form element that otherwise may not be identified. It's one of those form elements that are useful when you know your way around forms, but until then, it seems no different from adding a `<p>` tag.

The primary difference is that once a label is attached, you can assign other attributes to it designed to make the form more accessible.

A label for a form element is much the same as a label in your pantry — in both cases the content within the container is identified using a descriptive term. Just like the jar of salsa displays labels reading both "extra hot" and "thick and chunky," an input field on your form can be labeled using a simple term like "address" and another identifying the correlating form field name in a database such as "ClientAddress02."

A label is written like this:

```
<label for="email">Email </label>
<input type="text" id="email">
```

or like this:

```
<label>Email <input type="text"
    id="email"></label>
```

A label is designed to attach information to a control. If you use labels, when a user clicks on the label's text the *focus*, or active area on the page, is shifted to the label's associated field. For example, in figure 9-11, when the user clicks the label named "Email," the focus shifts to the corresponding field, indicated by the vertical bar.

Covering All the Bases

If you notice the XHTML in this chapter, you'll see that all form fields include both id and name rulesets, which I always use as a matter of course. Although on the surface they seem like duplicates, they serve different functions.

If your plan is to forward form content to a server, you need to use the name property, because browsers send only form fields having the name property. If you want the user to be able to click a label to bring focus to the associated field, you can provide this action only by using an id for the field.

A form field having only an id property isn't submitted to a server; a form field having only a name property isn't linked to its label.

9-11

STYLING A FORM USING FIELDSETS

Previously, I explained how to organize a simple form's layout using <br /> tags with a style attached to clear the float. That method works well to break the lines in a form.

In a more complex form, include <fieldset> tags to break the form into groupings of like fields or types of information.

CONFIGURING THE FIELDSET GROUPING

Figure 9-12 shows a partially styled example. The form is very similar in layout to the one shown in figure 9-2 because it uses the same content; I have changed the colors and background image for visual interest.

The form includes several fieldsets that group:

> Contact information

> Written comments

> Check boxes

> Submit instructions and the button

Fish Fingers

Tropical doo-dads for you and your home

Contact Details
Name _____
E-mail _____
Please comment on the service you received:
_____

Would you like a customer service representative to call?
Yes ☐
No ☐
Please click "Submit" to send us your thoughts
[Submit]

9-12

STYLING THE OVERALL FORM

To create the Web page form shown in the figure you have to:

1. Specify a `<body>` style to assign the background and text colors, as well as the font family and size.

NOTE

Read about the value of defining text properties in the `<body>` tag in the Q&A section of this chapter.

2. Define the styles for the `<h1>` and `<h2>` tags.

3. Write a style for the overall form. The style in the example includes background, border, and spacing properties, and is written as:

```
form {
  background-image:url(fish-bkgd.
   jpg);
  background-repeat:no-repeat;
```

```
  border:2px solid #FF8080;
  margin:2em;
  padding:2em;
}
```

4. Write a style for the legend elements. The example's style is written as:

```
legend {
  color:#003399;
  font-weight:bold;
  margin:.5em 0 .5em 0;
  padding:.5em 0 .5em 0;
}
```

NOTE

Depending on your form's appearance you may not need a `<legend>` style at all. Instead, the legend can simply inherit its characteristics from the `<body>` tag's style.

STYLING FORM ELEMENTS

The final two items to configure are the appearances of the label and the submit button. If you look at the form layout in figure 9-12, you'll notice the alignment of the labels isn't very attractive. Contrast that with the layout of the form in figure 9-13. The form now includes a `<label>` style written as:

```
label
{
width: 4em;
float: left;
text-align: right;
margin-right: 0.5em;
display: block;
}
```

The final element I styled in this example page is the Submit button. Its style applies a background color and custom border to the button, also shown in figure 9-13.

PRO TIP

The appearance of the `<fieldset>` element's border looks different depending on the browser you are using. For example, figure 9-13 shows the form in Firefox; note the square frames defining the fieldsets.

Figure 9-12 shows the form in Internet Explorer, which uses frames with rounded corners to define the fieldsets.

9-13

COLORING BACKGROUNDS AND TEXT

Be careful about assigning light-colored text to input boxes. There are numerous online assistants, like the Google Toolbar, that autofill fields in online forms for you.

The assistive agent automatically colors the backgrounds of the input boxes when the form page loads. If you use a light-colored text, such as the pale yellow shown in figure 9-14, you can barely see the content as it is inputted into the fields, also highlighted in yellow.

Name: ohn Jacobs

Email: ohn@

Comment: Hey pal, I can't read what I am typing!

Submit

9-14

Q & A

My layout looks great when I am designing and testing my form. When I see the page using some browsers, the whole design is out of balance. Is there anything I can do to prevent this from happening?

Browsers calculate the horizontal space used by `size` and `cols` attributes differently, which leads to different horizontal sizing and spacing for `textarea` and `input` fields.

Different browsers can calculate the horizontal space for different types of fields using different font family measurements. For example, a `text` field may be based on Times Roman font, and a `textarea` field based on Courier font.

The solution is quite simple. In the page's styles, write a style for the `<body>` tag specifying the `font-family` for the entire page. Then, when you use different types of fields, the sizing for all elements is based on a uniform measurement.

Many forms include dates. Is there a standard way to configure a date for a form?

Yes. Don't use dates like "06-03-02." This date could mean:

> The second day of March in 2006

> The sixth day of March in 2002

> The third day of June in 2002

The international standard organization (ISO) has defined an *international standard format* for dates as yyyy-mm-dd, where yyyy is the year, mm is the month, and dd is the day.

When you use this ISO format, you can expect most visitors to understand your dates.

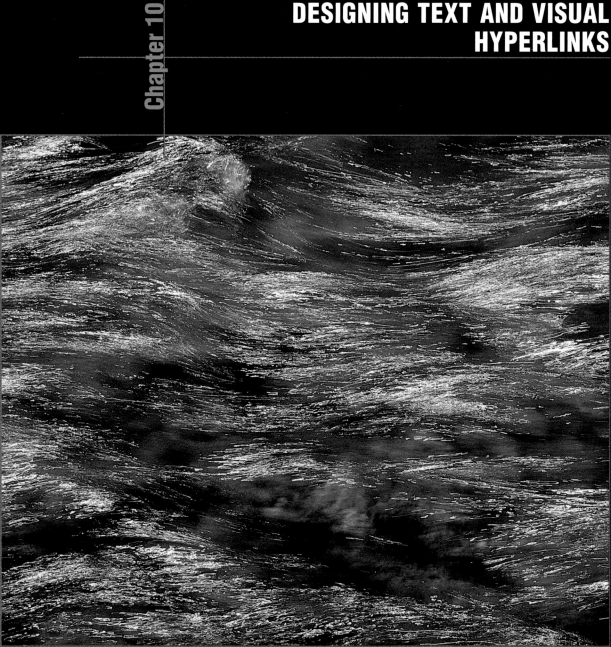

DESIGNING TEXT AND VISUAL HYPERLINKS

In the beginning we had text links. Originally, they came in bright blue and turned maroon the next time you revisited the page if they had been clicked on to reveal a linked page, and then followed to a new page. Being able to change the color was the first step in designing a page visually.

Next came visual links. Remember when using buttons as links was all the rage? So do I. The buttons were aligned in a row or column, and each looked like a conventional depressed button when you clicked it, and amazingly looked a different way when used with a `mouseOut` or similar action.

Historically, buttons were a good start. It was cool to be able to use such a common human-machine interface to control navigation, but it was much cooler when you could build a menu and craft an image map. The constraints of location were removed, and artistic interfaces flourished. Of course, links had to be modified as needed, and you had to upload modified images on a regular basis.

CSS can be used instead of text or image links, and can replace image maps. The principle advantages are that you build styles once, and can use multiple styles in the same page.

In this chapter, you'll also see how Web designer Chris Ware uses CSS and a single image to create a menu that simulates using multiple images.

CUSTOMIZING HYPERLINK TEXT

The default hyperlink appearances on a Web page aren't snappy or distinctive, as you can see in figure 10-1. The default appearances do the job of providing several bits of visual information, including differentiating the link's activity on the basis of color, and changing cursors to indicate a clickable object.

10-1

Using text decorations other than underlines requires several styles corresponding to the link's state and defined as `<a>` tag pseudo-classes, or *pseudo-class selectors,* as you can see listed in figure 10-2. In this CSS page snippet, notice I have specified styles for four selectors, and added color description comments for three styles; the fourth is merely removing the default underline from the link.

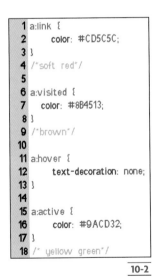

```
1  a:link {
2      color: #CD5C5C;
3  }
4  /*soft red*/
5
6  a:visited {
7      color: #8B4513;
8  }
9  /*brown*/
10
11 a:hover {
12     text-decoration: none;
13 }
14
15 a:active {
16     color: #9ACD32;
17 }
18 /* yellow green*/
```

10-2

Mr. Pink

Mr. Green

10-3

WRITING AND COMBINING PSEUDO-CLASS STYLES

Pseudo-classes, including those associated with links, are written on a stylesheet or XHTML page as:

```
selector:pseudo-class
  {property:value}
```

You can use more than one style for the same pseudo-class selector in the same page by following these steps:

1. Assign a class to each link in your page's code. For example:

```
<a class="pink"
  href="res_dogs1.html">Mr. Pink</a>
<a class="green"
  href="res_dogs2.html">Mr. Green</a>
```

2. In your style sheet, identify the pseudo-class for each style.

3. Specify the property to display and its value, such as the colors in this example:

```
a.pink:visited {color:#CC66CC}
a.green:visited {color:#336600}
```

Combining a CSS class with a pseudo-class gives you more design freedom.

On the Web page shown in figure 10-3, each hyperlink displays its custom color value using the styles and code listed in the steps.

Pseudo-class styles aren't case sensitive, but unlike other styles, the <a> pseudo-class selector styles have to be listed on your style sheet in a specific order to work.

The example in figure 10-2 shows the correct order. The a:hover state can't be defined before the a:link and a:visited states; the a:active state has to follow the a:hover state.

ASSIGNING STYLES

You can use numerous links in the same style sheet or on the same page. For example, on one page you may have your main site navigation links, a set of links leading to secondary pages, and still other links from specific content on the page. The key to multi-style success is using unique identifiers for each object.

On my Web site, for example, I use numerous class/pseudo-class combos to design the site. The page shown in figure 10-4, for example, uses one set of text link styles for the navigation menu at the left, and two more sets of styles for other links like the brown text shown at the right of the page.

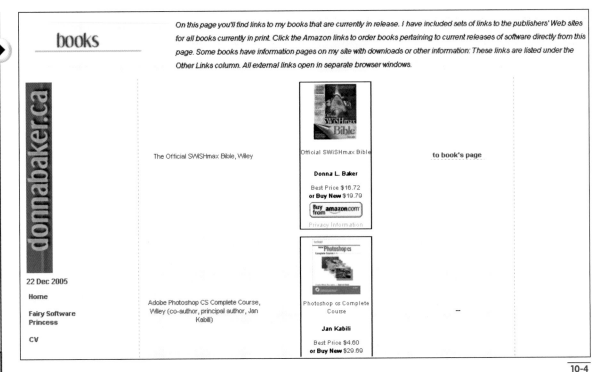

10-4

How you name classes many times relies on personal preference and habit. Just be sure to use names that make sense to you, and add comments for reference.

I often order a style sheet according to the content being styled, such as a menu or a table. For example, my Web site has a set of styles for the menu — links and otherwise — as well as positioning and other styles, all following a comment identifying what the group of styles is applied to. Others prefer to group styles according to type, such as all table tags and all image tags.

Change the characteristics of a text link as listed in Table 10-1. Some of the properties listed in the table are less commonly used in text links than others. For example, you aren't likely to use the `direction` property in a link written in languages other than those that flow from right to left. Refer to Chapter 2 for more detail about fonts, and to Chapter 3 for more information about text properties.

Figure 10-5 shows examples of several of the types of changes you can incorporate into a hyperlink's styles. Each link's customized property is reflected in its name.

Table 10-1: Common Text Link Properties

Property	Description
color	Specify text color; may be hexadecimal value, RGB, RGB percentage, or a named color.
direction	Specify the text direction, either left to right or right to left.
letter-spacing	Define the amount of space between letters in the text in length; include the unit of measure in the value.
text-align	Define how text in a tag is aligned, including left, right, center, and justify.
text-decoration	Adds lines above, below, or through text, or assigns the blink value.
text-indent	Indents the text based on a specified length or percentage value.
text-transform	Changes case for text, including capitalize, lowercase, and uppercase.
white-space	Defines how white space within the <a> tag is handled.
word-spacing	Specifies how much space is displayed between the words in the text link; includes the unit of measure in the value.

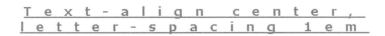

Text-align center, letter-spacing 1em

~~Text decoration line-through, indent 20px~~

White space nowrap, word-spacing 1em

10-5

Adding a rollover background

One commonly applied visual trigger is changing the background and text color in hyperlink images. Your Web page can display the same effects whether you are using a button image or text hyperlinks. The key is to use coordinating styles.

In the Web page shown in figure 10-6, for example, both text and image hyperlinks are used. Although the images for the links at the bottom of the page are created in an image processing program and the text links at the left of the page are styled using a style sheet, the page's color scheme is cohesive.

You have the most visual control over an image-based hyperlink. For example, a `mouseOver` may display a brighter version of the image with a lighter background and bolder text, and a hyperlink that has been clicked to visit the linked content may use a darker or paler version of the button. Building a rollover in this way needs a set of three images, like the examples shown in figure 10-7.

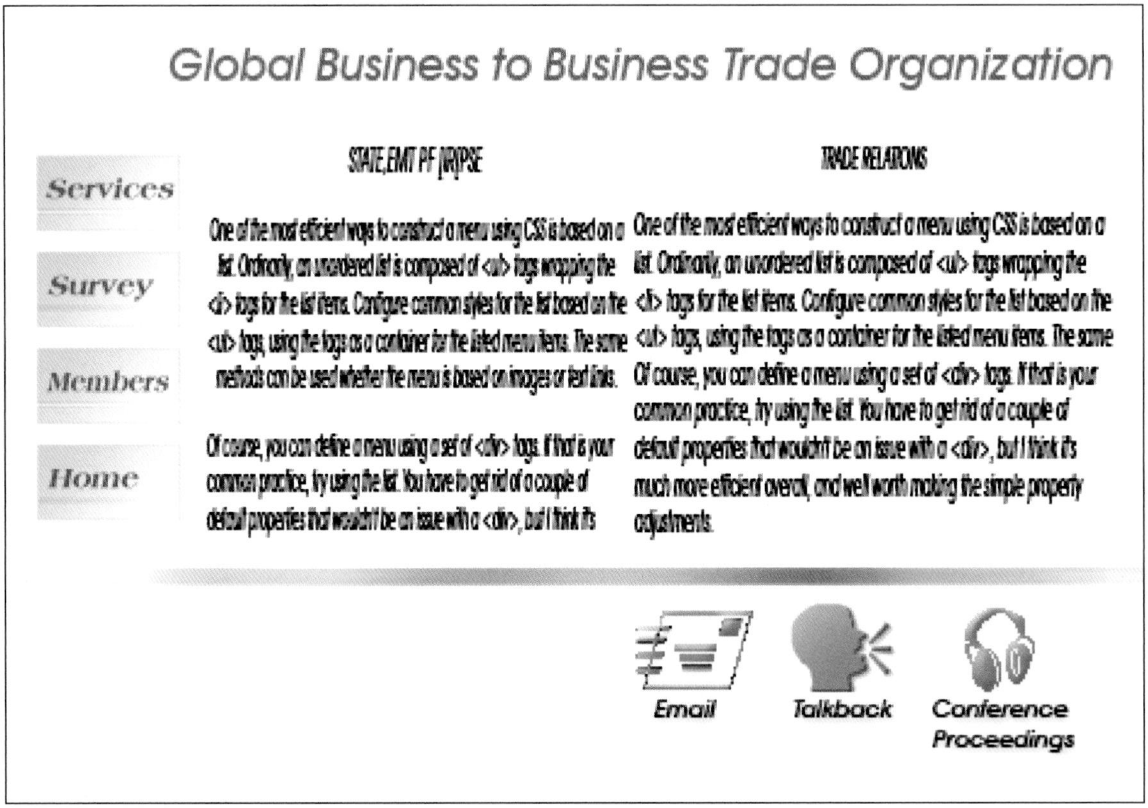

10-6

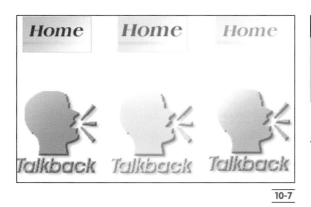

10-7

In figure 10-7, the left image in each row is the default appearance on the Web page, the middle is the button displayed on the mouseOver action, and the right button is displayed in response to the mouseOut action. Notice how the color schemes of the basic rectangular buttons coordinate with another button that displays a more graphic image; in this case, a link to the site's feedback and forums page. Although the colors aren't the same in both sets of buttons, they are well coordinated visually, and can easily coexist on the same Web page.

Instead of defining images as backgrounds in a hyperlink's styles, you can modify existing text hyperlinks to display custom background and rollover states. Making simple changes to the colors of text hyperlinks is an easy way to have your links coordinate with the rest of the color on your site — without having to create or import any images.

The example shown in figure 10-8 shows three states of a text hyperlink — from top to bottom — the default, visited, and hover states.

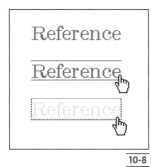

10-8

NOTE

In Figure 10-8, both the hover and visited states are shown as active. This is a composite image because only one state is active at any one time.

The text hyperlink's styles include:

> Different text colors for the default, hover, and visited states

> Text-decoration, overline, and underline styles used for the hover state

Change the appearance of a text hyperlink to include backgrounds by following these steps:

1. Configure the styles for the hyperlinks as desired, using any of the properties listed in Table 10-1. The text used for the examples is shown in List 10-1.

List 10-1: Styles for Text Hyperlinks

```
a:link {
    color: # CD5C5C;
    text-decoration: none;
} a:hover {
    color: #9ACD32;
    text-decoration: overline underline;
}
a:visited {
    color: #8B4513;
    text-decoration: none;
}
```

---

2. Add a style to the hyperlink states to define a background color. You can use a color for any or all states. In the example the three text hyperlinks are given a pale gray background using this style:

```
background-color: #EAEAEA;
```

3. Check the appearance of the hyperlink: The link text has a pale gray background the width and height of the block of letters. Although the links' backgrounds are colored, they would look better if the gray extended further from the text.

4. Adjust the area covered by the background color using a padding style. In the example shown in figure 10-9, the text hyperlinks are padded five pixels on each side using this style:

```
padding: 5px;
```

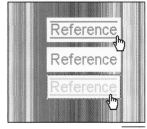

10-9

STYLING A MENU LIST

One of the most efficient ways to construct a menu using CSS is based on a list. Ordinarily, an unordered list is composed of `<ul>` tags wrapping the `<li>` tags defining the list items. Configure common styles for the list based on the `<ul>` tags, using the tags as a container for the listed menu items. The same methods can be used whether the menu is based on images or text links.

A menu can also be defined using `<def>` tags. Read about definition lists in Chapter 7.

PRO TIP

Of course, you can define a menu using a set of `<div>` tags; but if that is your common practice, try using the list. You have to get rid of a couple of default properties that wouldn't be an issue with a `<div>`, but I think it's much more efficient overall, and well worth making the simple property adjustments.

Creating a menu from a simple list involves several steps:

1. Write the XHTML for the list and the list items. For each list item:

    > Specify a link location for the `a href` property.

    > Uniquely identify each item using an `id` property and value.

2. Write and assign a style to configure the `<ul>` tag. The style should define common properties for all menu items, such as margins and borders.

3. Write styles for the list items. Each `<li>` in the list may have unique values for properties such as an image or location.

4. Write styles for the link states as described earlier in the chapter.

A sample menu is shown in figure 10-10 in its "before" state. You can see it is a simple list using the default circular bullet. Links are applied to the text, again using the default color scheme.

PRO TIP

You can make any nested list into a menu using JavaScript and defining a `makeMenu` function.

BUILDING MENU ITEM STYLES

Once the list is written and text links are applied, there are a few items to take care of. The exact order may vary according to what you have already written in your style sheet, but your tasks include:

> Deciding on a naming structure for the list and its items. When there is only one list on the page and it uses the global defaults, the `<ul>` tag doesn't necessarily need an `id` property and value assigned. The example uses `<ul id="nav">` to differentiate the navigation list from other lists that may be added to the page.

Attaching an `id` property to a `<ul>` tag is a good habit to develop, and saves time later if you decide to include another menu or list on the page.

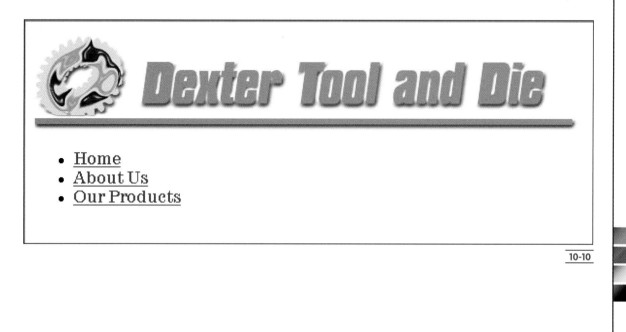

10-10

> Considering whether default properties or <body> properties can be inherited. In the example shown in figure 10-11, the <body> tag assigns a font-family to the page as written below:

```
body {
    font-family: Verdana, Arial,
    sans-serif;
}
```

> Writing the styles for the <ul> and <li> tags, again considering what properties can be inherited. There are no item-specific styles used in the example; figure 10-12 shows the results of attaching a style to the <ul> tag. In the figure, you can see that the bullets are removed from the list, and the text and background are styled. Each list item inherits its properties from the <ul> style, shown in the upper section of List 10-2.

10-11

Designing Text and Visual Hyperlinks

10

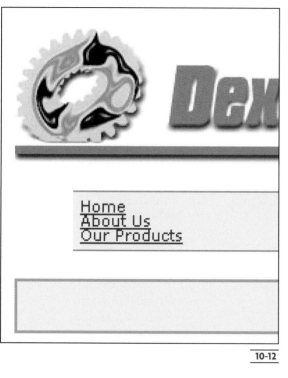

10-12

List 10-2: List Styles

Style for overall list

```
#nav {
    list-style: none;
    padding: 5px;
    font-size: 11px;
    line-height: 11px;
    background-color:#D9E4EA;
    border-bottom: 1px solid gray;
    border-top: 1px solid gray;
}
```

Link styles

```
#nav a {
    display: block;
    padding: 5px;
    text-decoration: none;
    text-align: center;
    font-weight: bold;
    color:#000;
}
#nav a:hover {
    color: # 0099FF;
}
```

> Finishing the text appearance by writing <a> styles, also included in List 10-2. Each list item's text and layout is modified, and a complementary hover color is assigned to the link text, as you can see in figure 10-13.

The menu looks good, and works correctly, but its position on the page isn't defined and the layout looks awkward.

Two different ways to take care of the menu positioning issue include:

> Positioning the list on the page

> Converting the list to a horizontal menu

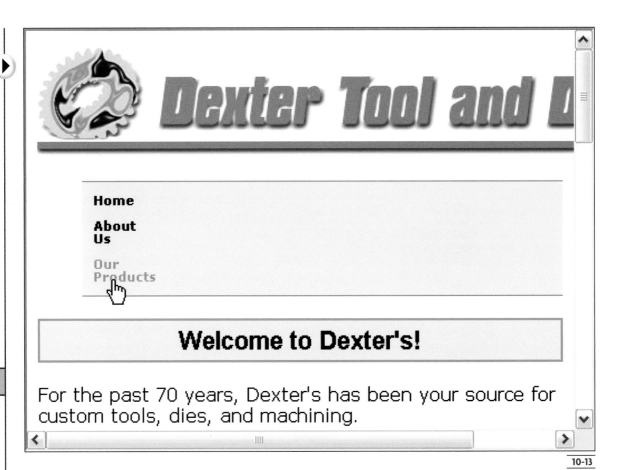

10-13

FIXING A MENU'S POSITION

In the past, menus were often built and displayed using a table. The content on the page might be included in the table as well to produce some degree of predictable positioning on the page. Instead of a table-based layout, you can simply add a `<div>` tag to surround the Web page's text content, and specify positioning for both the list and the content.

Follow these steps to use a `<div>` tag and some styles for proper positioning of a menu on a page:

1. Depending on the page design, you may want to include or exclude the `<h1>` tag from the `<div>` tag. In the example shown in figure 10-14, the heading is included within the `<div>` tag for the desired page layout.

2. Write the style for the `<div>` tag; the example style for `<div id="main">` is written as:

```
#main {
  color: #666666;
  background: #FFFFFF;
  margin-left: 15%;
  padding: 3%;
  border-left: 1px solid #339999;
}
```

3. Check the outcome of adding the style. Here's a breakdown of each property in the example and why it is selected:

   > The text is gray against a white background.

   > A large margin is added at the left which will accommodate the width of the list.

> Padding is added to separate the text of the page from the menu list.

> The narrow border at the left of the text divides the menu from the content visually.

4. Modify the original style for the `<ul>` tag to establish the menu's position on the page and coordinate with the rest of the content. The additional properties and their values used in the example are:

```
float: left;
margin: 0px;
width: 15%;
```

5. Check the list's positioning on the page after writing the style. In the example:

> Specifying a left float tells the browser where to place the list.

> Defining the margin's value at 0px moves the list to the absolute left of the page from its default style location, which is indented.

> The width of the list is specified as 15% of the total width of the page, which of course corresponds to the width of the border defined for the left of the `<div>` tag.

The new layout for the page is shown in figure 10-14. It's a layout that is pleasing to the eye, and distinctive enough to provide orientation to the user.

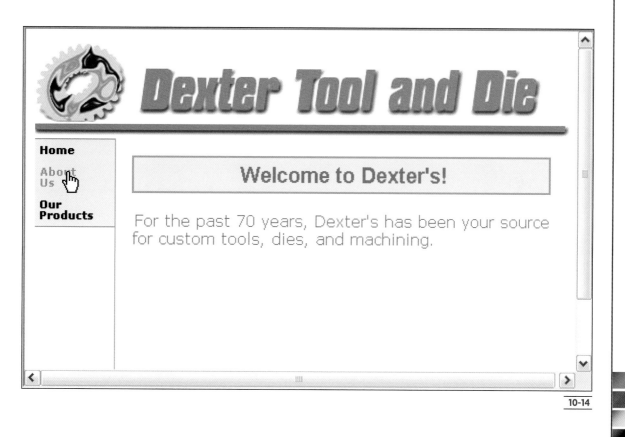

10-14

Menus are commonly displayed horizontally, usually under a banner or logo like the one used in the example. If you want to convert the layout of a page like that in the example from a vertical menu to a horizontal menu, you need to:

> Modify the page content style assigned to the `<div>` tag to use the full width of the page.

> Adjust the values for the `<ul>` style.

> Add a style to configure the layout for the `<li>` tags that arranges them on the page horizontally.

> Change the text alignment of the `<a>` tag's style.

The styles used to convert the example page's menu from vertical to horizontal are included in List 10-3.

List 10-3: Horizontal Menu List Styles

Style for `<div>` tag

```
#main {
    color: #666666;
    background: #FFFFFF;
    border-left: 1px solid #339999;
    margin: 0;
    padding-left: 2.5%; padding-top:
     25px;
    clear: left;
}
```

Style for `<ul>` tag

```
#nav {
    margin: 0;
    padding: 0;
    list-style: none;
    float: none;
    font-size: 11px;
    line-height: 22px;
}
```

Style for `<li>` tags

```
#menu {
    float: left;
    text-align: center;
    margin: 0; width: 33%;
    border: 1px dashed #339999;
}
```

Style for `<a>` tags

```
#nav a {
    text-decoration: none;
    text-align: center;
    font-weight: bold;
    color:#000;
}
```

The modified Web page is shown in figure 10-15. Here's an explanation of the changes and their outcomes:

> The content on the page is aligned at the left and uses padding to separate the text from the menu. The `float:left` property and value is replaced by the `clear:left` property and value to allow the text to be displayed correctly below the page banner and the menu list.

> The `<ul>` style is simplified. The `float:none` property and value replaces the `float:left` property and value. The `line-height` is increased to make the layout more visually pleasing and easier to read. The `border` is changed using several border properties in the `<li>` style.

> The layout of the list items is modified to fit across the browser window, with each `<li>` assigned 33% of the window's width.

> Finally, the `<a>` tag is modified by removing the `display` and `padding` properties and values.

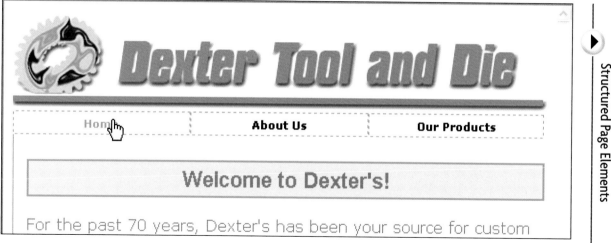

10-15

Writing Menu Styles

Using the way styles inherently nest themselves can save you both time and error. Consider these ideas when building a style sheet:

> Assign as many common style properties and values as you can to the style applied to the <ul> tag, which then styles the nested <li> tags.

> If you are using a single set of links on a page, assign common style properties for all <li> tags using a single style.

> If you are using two or more sets of links on a page, assign id names to each <ul> tag, and again follow the same method of assigning common properties to as many higher level tags as possible.

SIMULATING IMAGE BUTTON APPEARANCES

Simulating buttons using styles to create the appearance of rollovers works in much the same way as text links. In both cases, writing styles for an <a> tag's selectors, such as a:hover and a:active, creates the rollover look.

IMAGES VERSUS STYLE BACKGROUNDS

On a finished Web page you can't see the difference between an image inserted on a page using an <img> tag and an image used as a property of the <a> tag.

Figure 10-16 shows two very similar images. The left image of a cog is inserted on a page and then a hyperlink is attached to it. The right image looks and works the same, except it uses styles for the property of the <a> tag.

10-16

CRAFTING A SET OF LINKS

Include the image information in the styles for image-based links that display responses to mouse actions. In the sample page shown in figure 10-17, four images are used as links to pages on the site.

The images are defined as list items within a <ul> tag, such as:

```
<li><a href="10_ship1.html"
name="menu1" title="Enter the ship
through our beautiful mall area"
id="menu1"></a></li>
```

The stylesheet for the site uses a style for the generic <a> tag, as well as specific pseudo-class styles for each list item, like the set of styles shown in List 10-4.

List 10-4: Styling Images as Hyperlink Items

```
a {
    position:absolute;
    display:block;
    width:120px;
    height:90px;
    text-decoration: none;
}
#menu1{
    top: 20px;
    left: 20px;
    background: url(m_ship1.JPG) no-
    repeat;
}
#menu1:hover{
    background: url(pop_ship1.gif) no-
    repeat;
}
```

Enter the ship through our beautiful mall area

Cruises to Go:

10-17

DESCRIBING THE IMAGE

The problem with incorporating images as properties of a style is that they can't use <alt> text. If you look at figure 10-17, you'll see that the first image does in fact show text in a pop-up.

The text is a title property and value for the <a> tag associated with the image. Some browsers, such as Opera 2.1 and Navigator 6, don't recognize the title attribute. Some browsers, such as Safari 1.0, display the title in the status bar instead of as a tool tip.

DRESSING A SET OF MENU TABS

The sky is pretty much the limit when it comes to making a styled menu list look artistic. You can use an infinite range of background colors, images, colors, and so on.

USING A TAB APPEARANCE

One commonly used page layout component is a horizontal menu designed as a set of tabs. The tabs in their simplest form can be simply text with a background color. Moving a step up into a tablike appearance takes pairs of small images that round the corners of a text link, like the example shown in figure 10-18.

Home   Products   About us

10-18

CONSTRUCTING THE MENU AND STYLES

Building a tabbed menu uses the processes described earlier in the discussions on using lists as menus and creating horizontal menus. In order for the tab images and the text to align properly regardless of the amount of text in the link, assign the images to two separate styles by means of a `<span>` tag surrounding the text of the link, as detailed in figure 10-19. When the styles are applied, the left image and background color is applied by the list's `<a>` style; the right image is added by the `<span>` tag's style.

Text goes here

Background for text defines width of tab and padding at the left of text

Image for right side of tab and right padding specified in `<span>` tag's style

Image for left side of tab specified in same style as link and background

10-19

The steps involved in creating the tabbed appearance include:

1. Create a set of four small images. These images are

   > Left and right corner images in the background color you intend to use for the text link.

   > Left and right corner images in the color you intend to use for the hover color.

2. Construct the list and its links. The example assigns an `id="nav"` to the `<ul>` upon which the rest of the styles are based, and differentiates the list in the page from other lists you may include in the page's content. The example menu uses this XHTML:

```
<ul id="nav">
<li><a
href="#"><span>Home</span></a></li>
<li><a
href="#"><span>Products</span></a></
li>
<li><a href="#"><span>About
us</span></a></li> </ul>
```

3. Write the styles for the `<ul>` like those shown in List 10-5. The styles define the appearance of the list and the list items, as well as the appearances of the `<a>` and `<span>` tags' contents, including:

   > The basic appearance of the list and the list items, using the #nav and #nav li styles.

   > The `<a>` appearance for the list items, defining the text, color, background image, and padding.

   > Another `<a>` style for the `<span>` tags surrounding the link text. The `<span>` is used to house the right tab image, and define padding at the right of the tab image.

   > A style used by both the #nav a and #nav a span configurations that defines values for the display and float properties to orient the menu horizontally.

   > Two styles for the a:hover pseudo-class corresponding with #nav a and #nav a span styles to define the changes made when the mouse hovers over the tabs.

4. Test the page. The width of the tabs is equal to the length of the link's text string plus the left and right padding — a total of 40px in the example. Moving your mouse over a tab shows the equivalent layout using the hover colors, as shown in figure 10-20.

```
#nav a:hover span {
   background: url("hover_r.gif") no-
   repeat right top;
   padding-right: 20px;
}
```

List 10-5: Styling a Tabbed Menu

```
#nav{
   list-style: none;
   padding: 0;
   margin: 0;
}
#nav li {
   float: left;
   display: block;
   margin: 0;
   padding: 0;
}
#nav a {
   color: #FFFFCC;
   background: #5E2800
   url("left_tab.gif") no-repeat left
   top;
   text-decoration: none;
   padding-left: 20px;
   font-family: Arial, Helvetica, sans-
   serif;
   font-size: large;
}
#nav a span {
   background: url("right_tab.gif") no-
   repeat right top;
   padding-right: 20px;
}
#nav a, #nav a span {
   display: block;
   float: left;
}
#nav a:hover {
   color: #CCFF66;
   background: #99CC33
   url("hover_l.gif") no-repeat left
   top;
   text-decoration: none;
   padding-left: 20px;
}
```

NESTING MENU LISTS

With a few styles and a nested list, you can add another level of menu items to display when your viewers position their mouse over a menu item. Developing the nested list requires several processes when starting from a simple nested menu list.

These processes include:

> Insert the nested `<ul>` and its `<li>` links in your XHTML page.

> Write additional styles for the nested content.

> Assign id values to some of the page's elements to create the pop-up action and modify the styles to correspond with the new values.

ADDING THE SUBMENU

The example I am using for nesting is the same menu as the one used previously for the tabbed appearance, except that it has been changed to a simple vertical menu as you can see in figure 10-21.

In the code for the page, a list is nested within the existing list, and two additional <li> elements are added for the submenu's contents.

STYLING THE SUBMENU

The new submenu and the difference in the structure and representation of the lists on the page require specifying styles for the nested elements. The styles applied to the example shown in figure 10-22 are outlined in List 10-6.

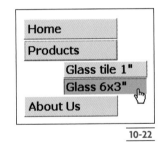

10-22

The styles' names identify the relationships among objects in your page, and tell the browser what to do when it encounters nested items. That is:

> The first style determines the layout when the browser comes across the <ul> that is nested within the original <ul>.

> The second style defines how the browser should treat a <li> nested within an existing <li>.

> The third style is again directed at the <ul> but in reference to how the browser displays the a:hover appearance.

Once you have configured the menu and submenu, there is virtually no end to what you can do to further configure the content by changing or modifying the styles.

DESIGNING SLIDING IMAGE MENUS

*I*n this tutorial, read how Web designer Chris Ware uses a single image and a style sheet to build a menu that looks like it uses several images and is easily configurable.

Cascading Style Sheets are an extremely valuable tool for all Web designers. It's amazing what can be accomplished using the power of CSS, especially when creating horizontal or vertical navigation menus. A simple unordered list can be altered using CSS to create many drastically different results.

List 10-6: Submenu Styles

```
#nav ul ul {
    margin-left: 60px;
    list-style: none;
}
#nav li li a {
    display: block;
    padding: 2px;
    width: 120px;
    color: #000;
    background-color: #D0C1AC;
}
#nav ul ul a:hover {
    color: #000;
    background-color: #A68962;
    text-decoration: none;
}
```

Any navigation object you can create using images and tables can be created using CSS, without the need for any JavaScript or image preloading. When compared to other types of menu creation methods, CSS-based menus are

> More search engine friendly.

> Accessible to a larger number of visitors.

> Smaller in overall file size, and use far less bandwidth than traditional image/table-based navigation.

> Easily changed in appearance in minutes by simply modifying the CSS style sheet.

CREATING THE BASIC PAGE AND STYLES

First up, create a CSS-controlled menu following these steps:

1. First, you need to create a list:

```
<div id="ourmenu">
  <ul>
    <li><a href="ourlink1.com"
    title="Link 1">Link 1</a></li>
    <li><a href="ourlink2.com"
    title="Link 2">Link 2</a></li>
    <li><a href="ourlink3.com"
    title="Link 3">Link 3</a></li>
  </ul>
</div>
```

2. Check the list in a browser. You see it appears as a simple vertical list with standard bullets, shown in figure 10-23.

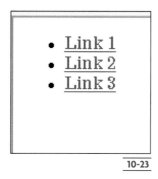

10-23

3. To define the type of bullet in our list, or in this case to do away with the bullet entirely, next create a style for the `<ul>` which removes the list bullets and makes the menu a specific width, shown in figure 10-24.

```
#ourmenu ul {
  width: 150px;
  list-style: none;
}
```

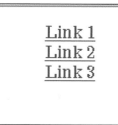

10-24

4. Next you add some additional styles and begin to really dress up the horizontal menu.

```
#ourmenu ul {
  width: 150px;
  list-style: none;
  margin: 0;
  padding: 0;
}

#ourmenu li a {
  height: 24px;
  padding-top: 6px;
  display: block;
  text-decoration: none;
  text-align: center;
  color: #FFF;
}
```

Now you have a pretty nice base for the navigation menu. Looking at the styles, you see that:

> The margin and padding is removed from the unordered list to do away with any unwanted spacing.

> In the second style, the `<li>` links are 24 pixels high with a 6-pixel padding applied to the top. The display property lets you define how a certain HTML element should be displayed.

> Using the ruleset `display: block` in the style means that the element is displayed as a block like paragraphs and headers have always been.

> I centered the menu text, colored it white, and removed the text-decoration property.

CREATING AND STYLING THE IMAGE

One image is used for all link states. Using CSS, I can tell the browser to "slide" the same single image up and down when the user either hovers over or clicks on the link.

First, you need to create an image with three different sections, like the example shown in figure 10-25. Each section of the image is 30 pixels high because the `<li>` link is 24 pixels high with 6 pixels of padding added to the top.

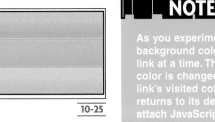

10-25

After creating the menu image I go back to the style sheet and add the following styles:

```
#ourmenu li a:link, #ourmenu li a:
visited {
  background: url(linkto/ourmenuimage
  .gif);
}

#ourmenu li a:hover {
  background-position:0 -30px;
}

#ourmenu li a:active {
  background-position:0 -60px;
}
```

Here's how the styles work:

> The first style makes the default background for the links the top part of the image, like Link 1 shown in figure 10-26.

> The second style moves the menu image up −30 pixels to display the middle section of the image when the user hovers over one of the links, like Link 2 in figure 10-26.

> Our final style moves the menu image up −60 pixels to display the bottom section of the image when the link is active, like Link 3 in figure 10-26.

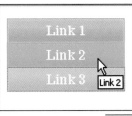

10-26

NOTE

As you experiment with the menu, notice that the background color change is applied to only one link at a time. That is, when you visit a link its color is changed; when you visit another link, that link's visited color is changed, and the original returns to its default appearance. Unless you attach JavaScript to the menu, it can't maintain a history of your actions.

This is a quick way to create a simple menu design using only one image and the power of CSS. The final style sheet for the navigation menu is shown in List 10-7.

List 10-7: Navigation Menu Using CSS and a Single Image

```
#ourmenu ul {
    width: 150px;
    list-style: none;
    margin: 0;
    padding: 0;
}

#ourmenu li a {
    height: 24px;
    padding-top: 6px;
    display: block;
    text-decoration: none;
    text-align: center;
    color: #FFF;
}

#ourmenu li a:link, #ourmenu li a:
    visited {
    background:
    url(linkto/ourmenuimage.gif);
}

#ourmenu li a:hover {
    background-position:0 -30px;
}

#ourmenu li a:active {
    background-position:0 -60px;
}
```

USING CSS WITH AN IMAGE MAP

You don't see as many image maps on Web pages as you once did. It's been nice to save the time downloading big, boggy image files that merely serve as links to other areas of a site, but they have their place. And, as the title of this section suggests, you can define the function of an image map using CSS. The image map works using invisible links placed on a background image.

Use a pair of <div> tags to hold the image and the links separately, nesting the links within the image's <div> tag. Although you can get by with one <div> tag, it's quicker to use two because the set of links can be changed or restyled as a group.

Apply these processes to create a CSS-based image map:

1. Prepare the images. The example used in this discussion uses a background image and two overlying a:hover images attached to the links' styles.

2. Write the code for the page. Add a <div> tag in the <body> of the page, and nest another <div> tag within the first in which to define the links. Assign an id to both tags. The example's tags are written as <div id="painting"> and <div id="menu">.

3. Define the links within the inner <div> tag, and assign each link an id. Although not strictly necessary with text links, giving each link its own id is the easiest way to use different background images. Enclose the text for the link within a tag that won't produce an obvious outcome on the page. Use a tag such as <i>, <b>, or the <em> tag used in the sample page, written as:

```
<div id="menu">
  <a href="nowhere_1.html"
  id="discs">
  <em>Discography</em></a>
  <a href="nowhere_2.html"
  id="tours">
<em>Tour Dates</em></a>
</div>
```

4. Place the image for the image map within the outer <div> tags by writing a style for the <div> tag's id property. In the browser window shown in figure 10-27, you see the background image as well as two text links using default styles. The style used for the example page is:

```
#painting {
  background-image:
url(map_bkgd.jpg);
  background-repeat: no-repeat;
  background-position: 0px 0px;
  position: absolute;
  height: 75px;
  width: 500px;
}
```

189

5. Write a style for the `div id="menu"` anchor by specifying the `<em>` tag to hide the link text. Although the text is hidden from view it is still an active link. The style is written as:

```
#menu a em {
   visibility: hidden;
}
```

6. Write styles for each link named using its `id` value, and specify the image to use for the `a:hover` as the visible link. In the sample, the links' styles include the position, height and width, and the background image. Include the `border:none` property and value to compensate for the IE problem with rollover images.

7. Test the page. In figure 10-28, notice the text is hidden and the image area is highlighted and named when the mouse moves over a link.

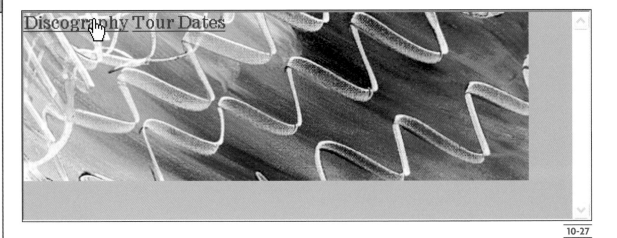

10-27

10-28

Q & A

Why bother writing complicated styles to display images in links instead of attaching a link to an image inserted on a page?

Using images as properties of a style advances the idea of separating content and style in a Web page. It's worth taking the time to make styles, and a good habit to develop.

As you assign more and more images to layout, you have simpler XHTML to handle. Of course, simplifying the pages lets you troubleshoot more quickly and efficiently since there's less to read. Assigning images to pseudo-classes of the `<a>` tag means you don't have to use any JavaScript control for the button to swap images and control behaviors.

What's the difference between assigning properties and values to a `<ul>` tag or to its enclosed `<li>` tags?

Basically, there isn't any difference. Like any style inheritance, it's simpler and less complicated to assign styles to higher-level tags. The higher in the hierarchy that you can assign a style, the less you have to repeat style content. For example, if you use a list for a menu, you could assign the `text-decoration` property and its value to either the list or its items and have the same outcome.

In many ways it is a matter of personal preference and the workflow you develop. For some people, especially those who haven't been working with CSS for too long, seeing the styles assigned to an individual element is less confusing than looking for inherited styles further up the hierarchy. When you have reached the point where you see an element as part of a bigger whole, the higher up the hierarchy you can assign a property, the fewer times a property has to be written. In some cases, it is also a matter of corporate policy; in which case follow the recommended guidelines.

Will the menus based on `a:hover` **pseudo-class selectors work in all browsers?**

Menus and link displays based on `a:hover` don't work in all the major browsers. Here are some issues you may encounter:

> JavaScript or server-side scripting may be required to check if a browser can use the styles.

> The menu works only in response to mouse actions unless you write some JavaScript for keyboard activations.

> The mouse response is based on the pseudo-class selector and not a mouse event, so moving the mouse away from the link removes the `a:hover` effect.

WORKFLOWS

TESTING PAGES AND DEALING WITH BROWSERS

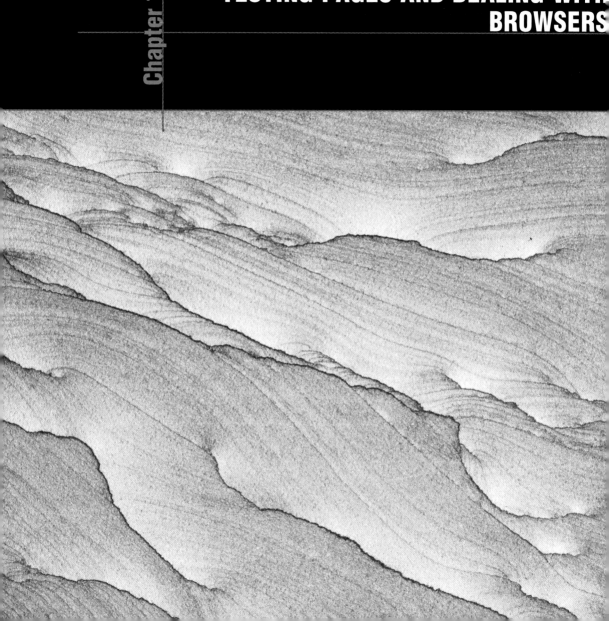

Support for XHTML tags isn't universal across browsers and operating systems, and certainly isn't universal across browser versions. Anything a browser can't understand it simply ignores, resulting in significantly different page appearances. Deciding what browsers and versions to support is essential to building, configuring, and maintaining your site's pages.

A browser is a translation program that reads a document written in XHTML and translates it into a formatted page. Each browser program interprets the translated code in slightly different ways, even if the browser complies with the World Wide Web Consortium (W3C) standards.

A Web site should be a powerful reflection of a company. If a Web site has browser display problems, unless a viewer has a specific need to plow through the errors, the odds are high he or she will simply leave the site.

In contrast, a site that is easy to view and navigate enhances the professionalism of a business or site. As a result, the viewer will probably stay longer, view more pages, and buy more of the product or service.

Making content accessible also means planning accessibility features from the start. Consider how Web designer and Apple developer Faruk Ateş designs and tests with accessibility in mind.

MAKING YOUR SITE COMPLIANT WITH W3C STANDARDS

Regardless of the type or purpose of the page, how it will be used, and what browsers are targeted, all pages should be validated, which saves time in the long run by ensuring you are starting with clean code.

HTML errors are the leading cause of browser display problems. Making sure your Web pages are error free by evaluating them with an HTML validator is one of the most important steps you can take to solve browser display problems.

In order to ensure your styles are complete and compliant with standards, run the style sheet through a CSS validator. You'll see if there are errors or incomplete rulesets that result in display errors.

NOTE

By the way, if there are additional types of code on your pages, such as Atom/RSS Feeds, or you would like to check links and page schemas, you can find a list of W3C tools at www.w3.org/QA/Tools.

PRO TIP

The W3C HTML Validator gives you a list of errors and warnings. Web design programs such as Dreamweaver show you a list of errors and warnings for a specified group of browsers. In both cases, you have to go through the list and make corrections.

Sometimes you just don't have time for long tweak-and-test sessions. Look for software that can both identify and help correct errors. For example, NetMechanic's HTML Toolbox identifies tags and attributes that aren't compatible with the three most recent versions of Netscape Navigator and Internet Explorer. Check out HTML Toolbox at www.netmechanic.com/maintain.htm.

VALIDATING THE PAGE'S CODE

My preferred validator is the W3C HTML Validator. Commercially available programs or components of other programs work as well. It's simply that I have used the W3C program since its inception, and I never need to update it.

To validate a page's XHTML using the W3C HTML validator, follow these steps:

1. Open the HTML Validator in your browser, located at http://validator.w3.org/.

2. Choose and define a source of the material for validation.

valid according to the `doctype` declaration on the page. An invalid page displays a red banner and defines the number of errors and warnings found, like the unfortunate example in figure 11-1 that contains 20 errors.

5. Follow the sequence of errors in the results page, and make corrections to your Web page. When the errors are corrected, upload the page again and validate it.

3. Click Check to launch the test process; wait a few seconds for the program to evaluate the file.

4. Results are shown in a new window. You can instantly see whether or not the page is valid based on the banner color. A page that is valid XHTML displays a green banner and tells you it's

6. Continue validating and editing until the page is clean XHTML. In some cases, it's a very complex task to follow through with a large number of corrections, in which case it might be simpler to manually debug the Web page.

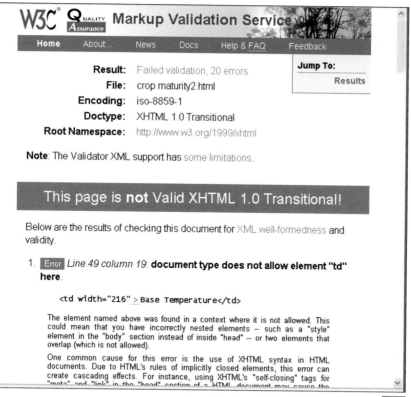

11-1

VALIDATING YOUR STYLES

Use the W3C CSS Validation service to check the integrity of your styles. As with the HTML Validator, the CSS Validator is a free service through the W3C that tests a style sheet against the chosen CSS standard. You can validate the styles in a standalone CSS file, within an XHTML document, or by directly inputting the text on the Web page — each format works the same way.

Follow these steps to validate your site's styles in a CSS file:

1. Open your browser to the CSS Validator, located at http://jigsaw.w3.org/css-validator/.

2. Click Browse and locate the file you want to check; click Open to dismiss the dialog box and load the file's name into the CSS Validator window, shown in figure 11-2.

W3C CSS Validation Service

| [HOME] | FEEDBACK | DOWNLOAD | DOCS | CREDITS |

Welcome to the W3C CSS Validation Service; a free service that checks Cascading Style Sheets (CSS) in (X)HTML documents or standalone for conformance to W3C recommendations.

Note: *If you want to validate your CSS style sheet embedded in an (X)HTML document, you should first check that the (X)HTML you use is valid.*

Validate Your Style Sheet

Validate your documents: by URI | by File Upload | by direct Input

Validate by URI
  Enter the URI of a document (HTML with CSS or CSS only) you would like validated:

  Address: [   ] [Check]

  Also available with extra options in the Advanced Interface.

Validate by File Upload
  Choose the document you would like validated (CSS files only):

  Local CSS file: [C:\ebooks\tutorialA.css] [Browse...] [Check]

  Also available with extra options in the Advanced File Upload Interface.

Validate by direct input
  Enter the CSS you would like validated:

11-2

3. If you want to specify how the testing is performed, click the Advanced Interface link to open a list of additional options, shown in figure 11-3. Choose other options, as required from their respective drop-down lists, and click Submit This CSS File for Validation.

NOTE

The name of the link varies according to the input method you are using. Validating by URI uses the Advanced File Upload Interface link; validating direct text input on the Web page offers the Advanced Direct Input Upload link.

PRO TIP

You can specify a number of parameters for the CSS Validator to consider when evaluating the page. You can specify the types of warnings you want to receive by choosing either Errors only or Errors and Warnings. The default Normal report contains both errors and warnings.

Specify the CSS version profile to use for validations from CSS1 to CSS3; the default is CSS version 2.

Finally, specify the medium to use for testing the page from a list that includes media ranging from aural to television; the default is all mediums.

W3C® CSS Validation Service

[HOME]   FEEDBACK   DOWNLOAD   DOCS   CREDITS

Welcome to the W3C CSS Validation Service; a free service that checks Cascading Style Sheets (CSS) in (X)HTML documents or standalone for conformance to W3C recommendations.

Validate Your Style Sheet

Validate by File Upload

Choose the document (CSS files only) you would like validated:

Local file: C:\1_css_wiley\Wiley CSS\smalti\tutorialA.css   [Browse...]

Warnings : [Normal report ▾]   Profile : [CSS version 2 ▾]   Medium : [all ▾]

[Submit this CSS file for validation]

Note: If you want to validate your CSS style sheet embedded in an (X)HTML document, you should first check that the (X)HTML you use is valid.

The W3C CSS Validator Team
$Date: 2005/09/01 11:51:21 $

W3C css   W3C XHTML 1.0

11-3

4. If you haven't used any advanced settings, click Check to Upload and Process the File. The button is located at the bottom of the page, a portion of which is shown in figure 11-2.

5. The results page replaces the original validation page, shown in figure 11-4.

6. Check out the results shown in the page. In my example, there are two errors, both of which are easy fixes.

7. Make the corrections as listed in the Validator Results page. In my example, one of my styles was written as `margin-right: 25`, and needs a length unit. The second error is a color number incorrectly written as `color:#66666`, with only five characters. To correct that error, I can either shorten the number to three numbers, or increase it to six hexadecimal numbers.

8. Test the page again. When you see the errors are cleared, your page is good to go from a visual perspective.

PRO TIP

Take full advantage of the information on the Validator Results page. The report lists the URI for the file and the line number, and specifies the style name as the Context followed by the error description. When working on a style sheet that is causing loss of sleep, I often save a copy of the report and use it as a checklist to make corrections.

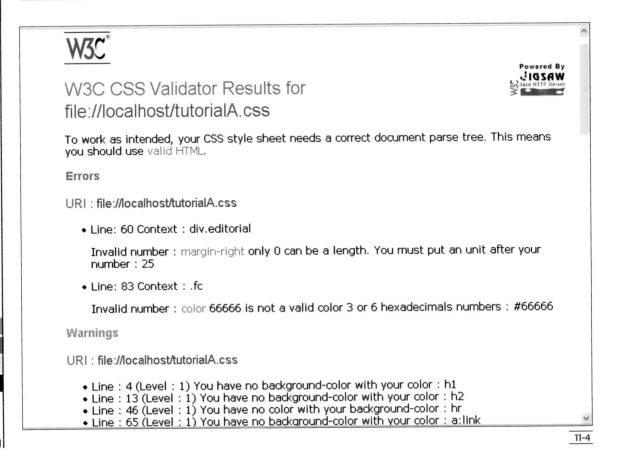

W3C CSS Validator Results for file://localhost/tutorialA.css

Powered By JIGSAW Java HTTP Server

To work as intended, your CSS style sheet needs a correct document parse tree. This means you should use valid HTML.

Errors

URI : file://localhost/tutorialA.css

- Line: 60 Context : div.editorial

  Invalid number : margin-right only 0 can be a length. You must put an unit after your number : 25

- Line: 83 Context : .fc

  Invalid number : color 66666 is not a valid color 3 or 6 hexadecimals numbers : #66666

Warnings

URI : file://localhost/tutorialA.css

- Line : 4 (Level : 1) You have no background-color with your color : h1
- Line : 13 (Level : 1) You have no background-color with your color : h2
- Line : 46 (Level : 1) You have no color with your background-color : hr
- Line : 65 (Level : 1) You have no background-color with your color : a:link

PRO TIP

Designers confronted by long lists of validation errors are prone to serious mishap and injury. These problems include falling into an exhausted heap on the floor and cracking their head against a hard surface, and howling in the night, setting their pet's teeth on edge and making it run for the nearest limb (unless the pet is a fish of course).

The key to avoiding a grocery list of errors and subsequent injury is to test the page as you are developing. I usually test a style sheet each time I finish a group of styles.

For example, if I write styles for a form, I test the style sheet against the CSS Validator, and then check it out in the target browsers. If I then write styles for a table, I validate and test the style sheet again, and so on. In my experience that's definitely the best way to prevent Web page development injuries.

> Check with your ISP to see what sort of tracking program they provide, such as Webalizer. Included in the reports generated by the program are the browsers used to access your site's pages.

> Conduct a survey of your visitors, asking them what versions and browser programs they are using to visit your site.

I am most likely to use both options. The tracking program gives you detailed, objective data. The online survey lets your visitors interact with your site and enhances the level of professionalism the site generates.

Once you have read the reports or collected the data, you can see quickly what browsers you should focus on in your style sheet development.

UTILIZING AUDIENCE INFORMATION

A common issue most designers face is deciding what browsers and versions to consider in their style sheets. You don't want to waste your time building versions of style sheets for browsers nobody uses to visit your site, but you don't want the site to seem unprofessional either.

FINDING VISITOR DATA

There are different approaches you can take to find out about the viewers reading your pages, either singly or in combination:

TARGETING CONTENT WITH LASER-LIKE PRECISION

You don't have to apply different style sheets to your entire site. Instead, target your site's content more precisely by checking which pages are viewed with different browsers. For example:

> Suppose your site contains information about color profiles. You're likely to find a large number of the visitors to that tutorial's pages are using Safari browser because color management is a common design issue, and many designers work with Macs.

> On the other hand, a tutorial on choosing Web page color for use on a television-based browser is sure to be visited by those using a TV-based browser — make the specific pages compliant for their purposes.

PRO TIP

Before investing time and effort into making multiple style sheet versions, decide if the number of viewers using different browsers justifies supporting them.

APPROACHING MULTI-BROWSER STYLE SHEET DESIGN

There are three approaches you can follow to design a collection of style sheets for different browsers:

> Build one style sheet that is usable by all browsers.

> Build one style sheet containing common styles used in all browsers and then create specific sheets for the individual browsers to account for individual differences.

> Make a separate style sheet for each browser.

PRO TIP

Which one are you?

On some days, my preference is to use standardized styles as simply and attractively as possible with the least amount of browser-compatibility kerfuffle. That's a good day.

On another sort of day, I want to use the latest and greatest, design for specific browsers only, post a huge "Best Viewed in Browser X" on the front page of the site, and call it a day.

USING ONE STYLE SHEET FOR ALL BROWSERS

Using one style sheet that works the same on all browsers is the simplest route to take. It is also the most limited in terms of style options, because you can't use style properties such as `margin top` or `line height`.

Some designers see the restrictions as limiting, while others find it an interesting challenge.

PRO TIP

You don't have to allow access to all styles by all browsers. In fact, sometimes the only way to make a page display properly is to hide some CSS rules or even the entire style sheet.

There are a number of CSS hacks and workarounds that can be used to make pages display correctly. You find a smattering of examples throughout the book, such as Internet Explorer issues in Chapter 12.

STARTING FROM A COMMON STYLE SHEET

Another way to accommodate multiple browsers is by using one style sheet that contains common styles, and additional style sheets that contain browser-specific styles.

Using generic and specific style sheets isn't as simple as you might think. You can't, for example, put all the rulesets for a category of styles such as fonts or text in the generic style sheet, and then write styles for other categories such as margins or tables in specific style sheets.

Instead, the generic style sheet becomes much more complex. Virtually any style that is included in the generic style sheet has to have qualifiers that specify exclusions from the rule. For example, margin values specified in the generic style sheet need to list excluded margin values on browsers a and b.

USING ONE STYLE SHEET FOR ONE BROWSER

It is both simple and time consuming to use different versions of your site for different browsers because you in effect are maintaining several sites and browser programs, rather than designing with standards.

If you decide to use separate style sheets for each browser, you need a JavaScript that serves one sheet to users based on their browser. Numerous online references describe and offer sample scripts you can use.

TIPS FOR DEVELOPING A SITE'S STYLES

The proper care and feeding of your Web site involves a lot of decision making. There are a few factors to consider that can be tremendous time-savers. These tips aren't necessarily things that may come immediately to mind, but they can take a lot of time to troubleshoot.

STAYING IN STANDARDS MODE

Did you know a browser has two rendering modes used for displaying a Web page? The two modes include:

> Standards mode, which works as closely as possible to the W3C specifications

> Quirks mode, which is intentionally buggy, and is provided by browser developers to let Web site developers continue to maintain older sites

Each time a browser version is released it complies with more and more of the W3C standards. Consequently, more and more pages break that relied on the code interpretations provided by earlier browser versions. The average user, unless able to view a site displaying in Quirks mode, won't be able to see the page as the designers intended.

A browser identifies a page as standards-compliant on the basis of its `<doctype>` declaration, such as:

```
<!DOCTYPE html PUBLIC "-//W3C//
DTD XHTML 1.0 Transitional//EN"
"http://www.w3.org/TR/xhtml1/
DTD/xhtml1-transitional.dtd">
```

The tag on the first line of the page's code tells the browser about the markup language used on the page. If the page defines a declared `doctype`, the browser switches to Standards mode.

NOTE

The `doctype` is also the tag that tells the HTML Validator how to test the page's standards compliance.

PRO TIP

When you are using `doctypes` and Standards mode, be sure the `<doctype>` tag is placed at the start of the document. If there is other content preceding it, IE switches to Quirks mode, which can be very difficult to troubleshoot.

DEALING WITH DEFAULT STYLING

Standards specify what is required for a compliant Web page but don't necessarily define values for the attributes. For example, the `<table>` tag supports `cellspacing` to define the space between elements of the table. However, the standards don't specify a default value for the attribute, and the outcome might look different depending on the browser displaying the page, like the two examples shown in figure 11-5.

In order to have the page display the same in two browsers, you have to explicitly define the `cellspacing` value.

Your pages maintain a certain look even if there are no styles applied based on default browser styles. You will see headings displayed at different sizes, links underlined and colored, and blockquotes padded, like the example shown in figure 11-6.

One problem area described in detail in Chapters 6, 7, and 8 deals with padding and margins. Some browsers recognize and use margins; others use padding.

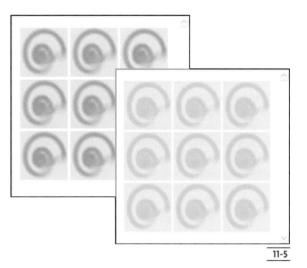

11-5

A newly completed piece in Smalti glass, tile on fiberglass mesh, 23 x 18 inches.

> "The glass is cool, with an almost buttery texture, and markedly different coloring on each side..."

In this issue:

Poured by hand using methods developed hundreds of years ago, true Smalti tile is produced only on the island of Murano, in the city of Venice. Read more about the history of the glass.

Smalti does have its peculiarities. Since it is handpoured, the thickness of the tile varies depending on which part of the mold the pieces are taken from. Read about tile characteristics.

11-6

The example page in figure 11-7 shows how Internet Explorer specifies a margin for the `<ul>` tag. You see the bullets are indented from the left margin, and the text is further indented from the bullets.

Contrast the layout in Internet Explorer shown in figure 11-7 with the list shown in figure 11-8. This page shows how Firefox pads the `<ul>` content, which is separated from the heading by more space than the Internet Explorer interpretation. Also note that the default bullets used in Firefox are larger.

For cross-browser consistency, you have to set either the padding or margin to 0 and the other property to the desired value. My preference is to reset only the elements that have differences, and leave the rest of the page's styles at their defaults.

Some folks prefer to be rid of default browser styles altogether, although that is a rather broad stroke to apply to a style sheet.

Reset all the margins to their defaults using a rule at the top of your site's CSS file. Using a universal selector forces the browser to apply the rule to all elements on the page, and is written as `* { margin: 0; padding: 0; }`, `*`.

PRO TIP

One of this book's Guest Contributors, Faruk Ateş, has developed a CSS template to use as a universal starting point. The contents are added to the page's `<head>`. Read about the template named initial.css in his blogged article "Starting with CSS: revisited" at http://kurafire.net/log/archive/2005/07/26/starting-css-revisited.

Petersen Electronics

custom vehicle monitoring and security controls

At Petersen Electronics we make it our business to offer a full range of custom and stock monitoring and security equipment **for all makes of domestic and import vehicles.**

How many categories do you or your business fit?

- customized vehicles, including boats and RVs
- sports cars
- vintage and antique vehicles of all types
- job-specific vans or trucks

11-7

makes of domestic and import vehicles.

How many categories do you or your business fit?

- customized vehicles, including boats and RVs
- sports cars
- vintage and antique vehicles of all types
- job-specific vans or trucks

11-8

COMPENSATING FOR A LACK OF CSS SUPPORT

A browser that doesn't support CSS obviously won't have problems with interpreting styles for display. On the other hand, the display doesn't have much pizzazz either: It's hard to get excited about black text on a gray background, like the dreary example in figure 11-9.

For these users, you can include some basic properties in the page's code to give the pages some style, and still let CSS-compliant browsers do their thing.

The key is understanding that a style overrides an HTML formatting attribute. Specifying colors for the background, text, and link colors on the `<body>` tag takes care of the absence of page styling, like the improved example shown in figure 11-10.

The problem is that the page loses its W3C compliance because adding visual attributes added to the `<body>` tag has been disallowed, or deprecated in XHTML.

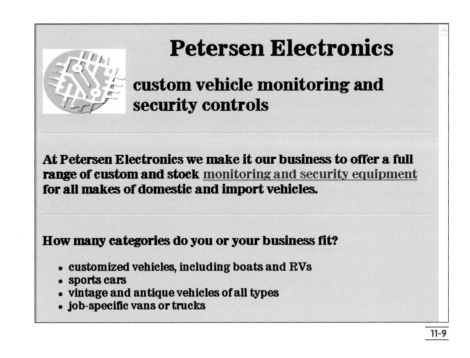

11-9

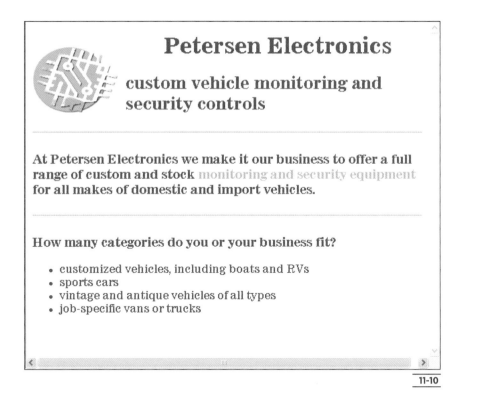

11-10

> **Available fonts.** The reason you write a `font-family` ruleset is to define a sequence of acceptable fonts for display of the page's content. Fonts are a computer resource, and vary from system to system depending on the owner's font library. The fonts also vary between PC and Mac systems. Avoid the problem by simplifying your font choices to use more common fonts.

SOLVING PC VERSUS MAC ISSUES

If you view a page on both a PC and a Mac using the same version of the same browser, it should display the same, right? In practice that's rarely the case due to:

> **Font size.** A Mac renders a typeface at a smaller pixel size than the PC. If you use CSS to define font sizes in pixels, the differences are minimized.

TESTING PAGES FOR SPECIFIC CIRCUMSTANCES

There are design considerations far beyond choosing among browsers and versions and how to construct styles for them. Designing styles and Web pages that are accessible are equally important to consider in your site's planning, development, testing, and evaluation.

A number of design issues revolve around *accessibility,* a way to make Web content usable for people with visual, motor, auditory, and other disabilities. Chapter 12, for example, touches on using special style sheets for assistive devices such as screen readers.

> **NOTE**
>
> The two largest accessibility initiatives to date are the W3C Web Accessibility Initiative, located online at www.w3.org/wai, and Section 508 of the Federal Rehabilitation Act, an American government initiative you can read about at www.section508.gov.

TESTING IN A TEXT-ONLY BROWSER

Many people prefer to turn off images when they are browsing, especially if they are looking for specific content, find image displays hard on the eyes, or are using a slow modem.

> **NOTE**
>
> The page used for the example is exported from a Publisher 2003 file with the content defined as images by default. The page also includes countless proprietary styles, and none of the images have alt text attributes, even though the page's code is a whopping 1,548 lines.

Take a look at the browser window shown in figure 11-11. This is what a viewer sees if visiting the page using a text-only browser. How's that for useless?

The same page, shown in figure 11-12, contains a considerable amount of information.

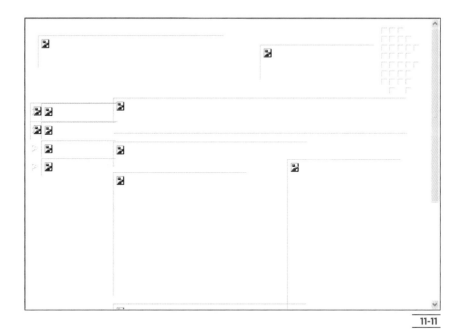

11-11

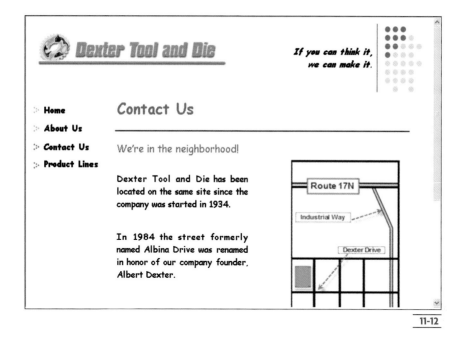

11-12

The page shown in these two figures is a rather extreme example, but differences in what you see with text-only or text/image browsers certainly can happen.

TESTING FOR SCREEN READER USE

A screen reader recites text that appears on the screen, as well as non-textual information like image descriptions and button labels.

Screen readers start reading at the top left of the browser window. For proper orientation, be sure to include tags such as labels for the form fields, like the labels including "Name," "Username," and so on shown in the sample page in figure 11-13.

You can read more about using accessible fields in forms in Chapter 9. Read about making other elements, such as tables, more screen-reader-friendly in Chapter 8. See Chapter 12 for the skinny on different types of style sheet mediums, like screen readers that specify voice characteristics.

PRO TIP

Evaluate the readability of your page's content (or any other text for that matter) using an online tool such as the Gunning-Fog Index or the Flesch-Kincaid Readability Test. The score assigned to your sample text determines how easy it is for your viewers to read your page.

Check out the Wikipedia entry on readability for links to the Gunning-Fog and other readability tests at www.wikipedia.org/wiki/Readability.

TESTING HIGH-CONTRAST COLOR SCHEMES

We most commonly think of pages of black text on light backgrounds. For those with vision impairments, it's often much easier to read a page by displaying a high-contrast color scheme, which shows light text on a dark background.

Figure 11-14 shows a typical Web page. The color palette is attractive, and suits the subject matter.

Contrast that page with the one shown in figure 11-15, which uses a high-contrast color scheme.

11-13

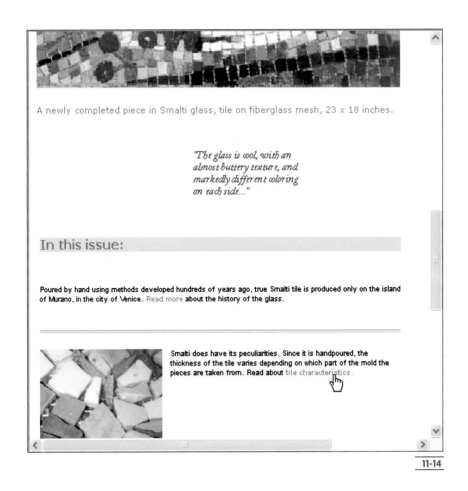

A newly completed piece in Smalti glass, tile on fiberglass mesh, 23 x 18 inches.

"The glass is cool, with an almost buttery texture, and markedly different coloring on each side..."

In this issue:

Poured by hand using methods developed hundreds of years ago, true Smalti tile is produced only on the island of Murano, in the city of Venice. Read more about the history of the glass.

Smalti does have its peculiarities. Since it is handpoured, the thickness of the tile varies depending on which part of the mold the pieces are taken from. Read about tile characteristics.

11-14

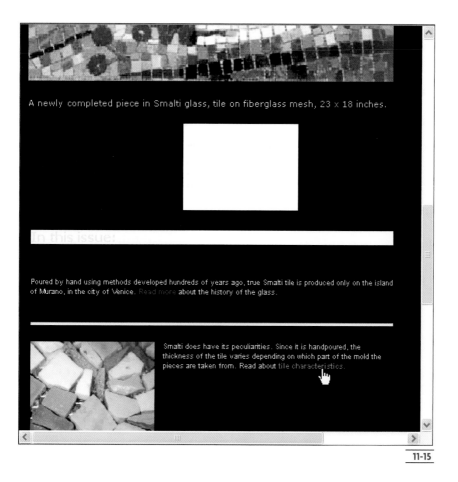

A newly completed piece in Smalti glass, tile on fiberglass mesh, 23 x 18 inches.

In this issue:

Poured by hand using methods developed hundreds of years ago, true Smalti tile is produced only on the island of Murano, in the city of Venice. Read more about the history of the glass.

Smalti does have its peculiarities. Since it is handpoured, the thickness of the tile varies depending on which part of the mold the pieces are taken from. Read about tile characteristics.

11-15

Can you see what's wrong with this picture? Several styles need to be changed in order to suit the high-contrast view, including:

> **blockquote.** The blockquote in a regular color scheme uses dark red text on very light-gray background. In a high-contrast scheme, the colors shift to bright yellow on a white background.

> **heading.** The heading that reads "In this issue:" is again barely legible. The green text in the original is converted to yellow, and the pale olive background fades to white.

> **horizontal rule.** The regular display shows a horizontal rule that coordinates with the site's color scheme. On the high-contrast page, the rule is pure white, which might be distracting to the average viewer.

> **text link.** The high-contrast version of the page converts the link text to a bright blue from the styled olive green. The active link, shown in bright pink, is suitable for the high-contrast scheme.

PRO TIP

Testing high-contrast color schemes isn't for the weak of stomach. People with color-sensitive eyes find the contrast causes a great deal of optical illusion and color vibration.

As one of those unfortunates, I can't avoid the situation, so I try to tone down the contrast a bit. Rather than using the default violent green or yellow against a black background, I attach my own style sheet that simply includes yellow #FFFF99 for the text, or choose a slightly paler yellow from the browser's Colors settings.

ACCESSIBILITY PLANS

The Web has become an incredibly mainstream medium, but accessibility on the Web is still a tricky, complicated, and (sadly) often overlooked issue. With so many potential problems we need to take care of, it is easy to forget some issues, or feel unable to find a satisfying balance. Web designers like Faruk Ateş are working to balance practical development with accessibility requirements. In Faruk's case, he has developed an Accessibility Plan to help you find that balance when developing a Web site. Read how his plan came into being and how it works.

My Accessibility Plan is basically a list of things to check against that takes the official Web Content Accessibility Group's guidelines to a more practical and business-compatible level.

NOTE

Refer to the Web Content Accessibility Group's guidelines for more detail at www.w3.org/TR/ WAI-WEBCONTENT.

Before getting there, however, it is important to keep in mind that with the existing technology, a completely accessible site is just about a myth. What matters is not that we do everything "by the book," but that we make every bit of content available to as many people as possible.

Conversely, it's important that accessibility never be overlooked or ignored. Even when you have a very specific target audience in mind, you will never know what unexpected audiences might make use of your site.

CONSIDERING ACCESSIBILITY ISSUES DURING DEVELOPMENT

So what do you need to do to keep your site accessible? To get an idea of what accessibility is and how accessibility problems creep up and are solved, it helps to ask yourself some basic questions during development that include:

1. If a visitor uses a screen reader, can he or she access all content easily?

2. If visitors have JavaScript disabled, can they still make full use of the site?

3. If visitors have motor skill difficulties, is it easy for them to navigate and find what they need?

As you can see, accessibility often comes down to a lot of hypothetical situations. What if this, what if that — with so many different types of disabilities, it is easy to see why accessibility can make one tired just thinking about it. But all is not lost!

PRO TIP

The basic principles of Web Accessibility are easy to learn and remember. You can also see it as an interesting challenge, making the problem less tedious and perhaps even fun.

USING AN ACCESSIBILITY CHECKLIST

Here is a list of tips that can help you make your sites more accessible:

> **Always use a descriptive `alt` attribute on images.** Blind users have no idea what an image looks like, so put the information in the `alt` attribute. This is particularly important when you use images for navigation.

> **Don't rely on mouse navigation.** You'd be surprised at how many people use JavaScript in ways that enforce the use of a mouse. Particularly with forms, using JavaScript can be a big accessibility hurdle.

> **Check things out of context.** Taking elements out of context applies in different ways. For a blind user, the visual context of a page is invisible, and all they can "see" is the linear structure that's being read to them. Another example is the "click here" link — when taken out of its context, what is the link for? "Click here" doesn't tell me that it's

a link to the PDF document with technical specifications, for example. A `title` attribute on a link is a noble attempt, but very few people who would need them actually use them.

> **Does it work with JavaScript disabled? Does it work with JavaScript enabled?** There are plenty of users on the Web who have JavaScript disabled or who use an old browser or a cell phone browser that doesn't support JavaScript. Don't rely on it for things to work. Similarly, don't assume that your JavaScript works when it works in your browser. Internet Explorer, Firefox, Opera, and Safari all handle JavaScript slightly differently, and your script may not work entirely in all browsers, if at all. A partially working piece of JavaScript can be a great usability problem, too.

> **Use markup for its intended purpose.** For example, don't use a `<blockquote>` element to indent some text; use it instead when you have a block of quoted text in the page. Related to this, do not use deprecated elements such as `<font>`.

> **Allow text to be scaled.** Make sure your users can increase or decrease the size of text on your page. To accommodate IE users, stay away from the "px" unit in CSS font sizes. In addition to allowing text to be scalable, make sure your site design is still usable when the text is scaled up a notch or two.

> **Use proper visual contrasts.** Beyond just making sure the content itself has a strong contrast to its background, also look at the contrast between links and non-linking text. Are your links easy to distinguish in a large body of text?

> **Use labels in forms.** Forms help make our sites more interactive by nature, so make sure the form experience is as smooth and accessible as possible through the proper use of labels.

TRYING AN ACCESSIBILITY EXERCISE

To get a good feel of what accessibility is like, try this exercise using a screen reader. This is by no means an all-encompassing test for accessibility, but it gives you a good idea of the caveats and problems that people can and will run into.

NOTE

If you don't have a screen reader, use Fangs, a screen reader plug-in for Firefox. The plug-in is available at www.standards-schmandards.com/fangs.

Follow these steps to experience how a screen reader interprets your Web site:

1. Open your browser and load your site into the browser window.

2. Turn off your screen.

3. Try to navigate through the pages of your site, fill in forms, and so on, all without turning your screen back on.

In the end, testing is the most important tool for creating accessible pages. You can't do a perfect job of making a Web site totally accessible, but you can come close by focusing on all the little details.

At all times, keep in mind that Web Accessibility is constantly in motion. Some ways to keep advancing your own knowledge and skills include:

> Getting some actual screen reader users involved.

> Paying close attention to feedback.

> Reading case studies.

The Web is hip and exciting; our company is hip and exciting — we'd like to use the latest and greatest on our site to show we are as current as the technology. Do you have any thoughts on that?

Why, yes I do indeed, Sparky: Overall, it's a bad idea. Cutting-edge features, while they can produce an air of hipness, can also be difficult to display properly in a browser, can take a long time to download, and can exist simply to exist without adding anything of significance to a Web site.

You can use the odd feature, like a simple Flash opening for your site, but please keep it short, and make sure you give the viewer the option to skip the intro.

The hallmark of a mature Web designer isn't that he or she uses each and every new technology that comes along, regardless of whether or not it is useful or compatible with the rest of a site. Instead, a mature Web designer applies design elements judiciously, and can produce sites that are both interesting and functional.

Interestingly, if you look at some of the largest and busiest sites on the Internet, like eBay and Amazon, you see the pages contain HTML, CSS, and JavaScript. What you don't see are elements like dynamic HTML or Java.

There are cases, of course, where only cutting-edge design is acceptable. If your business deals with training others to use design technologies such as Flash, you have to use it on your site to demonstrate the abilities of your company to deliver what you describe. Even then, make sure users have some control over what they are viewing, and rather than one huge feast for the eyes and ears, break the content into byte-sized portions (pun intended) for easier download, display, and viewer control.

Isn't there a quick way to decide what browsers are worth supporting and which aren't worth the effort?

Designing, developing, and testing a multitude of browser versions for a Web site takes a great deal of time.

A general rule of thumb is to design pages that work in the last two versions of the major browsers. Although some users will be viewing with older browsers, the numbers don't usually justify the time required to support those browsers.

My site deals with software produced by a single company, which also has a proprietary browser. Is there any reason for me to produce style sheet versions for other browsers?

It's probably safe to assume that few viewers will visit your site with Netscape 2. On the other hand, you are probably going to be visited by users working with an assortment of browsers, regardless of the site's contents.

Don't be lulled into thinking that if your site focuses on a specific market, such as Microsoft products or information, all visitors are viewing the pages using Internet Explorer. Personally, I visit Microsoft sites regularly using Firefox as my default browser — and I doubt I am the only person in the world who does that.

DESIGNING STYLE SHEETS FOR PRINT AND OTHER MEDIA

CSS allows you to define different style sheets to be used depending on what type of user agent your viewers use to see your pages. The most common types of output are on-screen display and printing on paper, but there are numerous other options for which you can design styles.

Some CSS properties are only designed for a certain media. For example the `speak` and `volume` properties pertain only to *aural* user agents, or those that use speech such as screen readers. Other properties can be used for different media types. For example, you can use `font-size` or `border` properties for on-screen, print, and TV media types.

Some processes described in this chapter can be used in a variety of media-specific styles, ranging from hiding content to defining widths for page elements.

Several types of media are more commonly used than others. See how to create styles for print, aural, handheld, and TV media.

And what of the future? Read how Web designer Faruk Ateş describes the continuing development of the Web as an organic structure.

SPECIFYING MEDIA TYPES

The key to configuring content for multiple media types involves two at-rules. The `@import` rule imports an external style sheet based on the values you assign in the page's styles; the `@media` rule groups a set of style rules in a single style sheet to apply only to one or more particular media types.

The choice of at-rule depends mainly on personal preference and the characteristics of the pages you are working with.

I use both methods, depending on the complexity of the content:

> If I am using a simple on-screen page and only need a few changes to make a print version, such as changing the font size or removing a background, it's easier to use the `@media` rule in the same style sheet.

> If the original page is complex like the example page shown in figure 12-1, and uses multiple columns and assorted margins, padding, and borders, it's simpler to build a separate style sheet to keep track of what applies to what media form.

12-1

UNDERSTANDING MEDIA TYPES

The CSS media types name a set of CSS properties that pertain to a display of content by different types of user agents. The different types of media and the type of user agent to which they refer are listed in Table 12-1.

APPLYING IMPORTED STYLE RULES

You can allow your users to import styles from other style sheets using the @import rule.

Follow these steps to use the @import rules:

1. Place the @import rule in the `<head>` of the page before listing other styles; on a style sheet, place the @import rule before other rule sets.

2. Include either the URL of the style sheet you are referencing or a string as part of the rule's syntax. Both of the following examples reference the same style sheet, and both are correct:

> Including a "url()" such as:

```
@import url("MMMedia.css");
```

> Including a string, such as:

```
import "MMMedia.css";
```

3. Specify media-dependent @import rules by defining the media types after the URL. Separate more than one media type using commas. Both of the following examples are correct:

> @import url("MMMedia_print.css") print;

> @import url("MMMedia_tv.css") tv, projection;

> ## NOTE
>
> The style sheet import is unconditional if you don't specify one or more media types, or specify all.
>
> It isn't required syntax to include the media type; it's merely good form and saves the user time waiting for style sheets that can't be used.

Table 12-1: CSS Media Types

CSS Type Name	Type of Media
all	The CSS works with all devices.
aural	The styles are intended for use by speech synthesizers.
braille	These styles are used for braille tactile feedback devices.
embossed	Paged braille printers use these CSS styles.
handheld	Devices like handhelds and telephones that have a small screen and limited bandwidth use this set of CSS styles.
print	Use the print CSS styles for printing Web pages as well as other sorts of paged media, such as projector slides or documents shown in print preview mode.
projection	The projection CSS styles are used for projected presentations or printing to transparencies.
screen	Screen CSS styles target color computer monitors.
tty	The tty CSS styles are used by some types of media that are based on a fixed-pitch character grid such as teletypes or terminals.
tv	CSS styles for TV are designed to address low-resolution color and sound devices that offer limited scrolling.

APPLYING IMPORTED MEDIA RULES

Rather than attaching separate style sheets to your page, use the `@media` rule to group styles that apply only to one or more designated media types within the same style sheet. The `@media` rule is well suited for simple page layouts.

Follow these steps to use the `@media` rules:

1. Decide how you want to modify the page for a different media format. For example, to change an on-screen page to a print page, you might change font size and background color, and remove background images. The page shown in figure 12-2 is having font and color changes made for the page's print version.

2. Open the style sheet for the page, or view the `<style>` code in the `<head>` element of the page.

3. Decide which styles pertain to which type of media. The styles for my example page include several that would be better modified for print, including the `background-color`, and `font-size` in the table rows.

4. Add the at-rules to the styles section of the page and separate the styles. The styles written for the example page are revised for the multiple media versions as shown in List 12-1.

List 12-1: Separating Styles for Different Media Formats

```
@media screen {
body {
    background-color:#F2F5AD;
    font-family:Arial, Helvetica, sans-
      serif;
    color:#3F3F3F;}
}
tr.bkgd0 td {
    background-color: #F1F1F1;
    color: black;
    font-family: "Gill Sans MT", Arial,
      sans-serif;
    font-size: 12px;
}
tr.bkgd1 td {
    background-color: #FFFFEE;
    color: black;
    font-family: "Gill Sans MT", Arial,
      sans-serif;
    font-size: 12px;
}
```

```
@media print {
body {
    background-color:#FFFFFF;
    font-family:times,serif;
    color:#000000;
}
}
tr.bkgd0 td{
    font-size:12pt;
}
```

Agricultural Products Central Canada

Table 1: Number of Days Required for Selected Crops to Reach Maturity

Crop	Days to Maturity
Barley	60 - 90
Buckwheat	80 - 90
Canola - early Polish	73 - 83
Yellow Mustard	80 - 90
Oats	85 - 88
Flax	85 - 100
Lentils	85 - 100
Brown or Oriental Mustard	85 - 95
Coriander	90 - 100
Field Peas	90 - 100
Navy Beans	90 - 100
Wheat	90 - 100
Canola - late Argentine	92 - 102
Black Beans	95 - 105
Canary Grass Seed	95 - 105

12-2

```
tr.bkgd1 td{font-size:12pt;
}
```

```
@media screen,print }
{
tr.bkgd0 td {
    background-color: #F1F1F1;
    color: black;
}
}
tr.bkgd1 td {
    background-color: #FFFFEE;
    color: black;
}
```

NOTE

An at-rule consists of everything up to and including the next semicolon (;) or the next block, whichever comes first. If you look through the code listing, notice how the braces are opened after the at-rule, and then closed after the first style is written.

5. Test each media type. The print version of the Web page shown in figure 12-3 is the same page shown on-screen in figure 12-2.

Growing Degree Days

Agricultural Products Central Canada

Table 1: Number of Days Required for Selected Crops to Reach Maturity

Crop	Days to Maturity
Barley	60 - 90
Buckwheat	80 - 90
Canola - early Polish	73 - 83
Yellow Mustard	80 - 90
Oats	85 - 88
Flax	85 - 100
Lentils	85 - 100
Brown or Oriental Mustard	85 - 95
Coriander	90 - 100
Field Peas	90 - 100
Navy Beans	90 - 100
Wheat	90 - 100
Canola - late Argentine	92 - 102
Black Beans	95 - 105
Canary Grass Seed	95 - 105
Fababeans	105 - 115
Corn (Grain)	110 - 120
Potatoes	110 - 140

12-3

PRO TIP

There is no single correct way to separate styles; I usually type the at-rule on the page, and drag each style into its proper location, or copy and paste the content to each at-rule's section when they apply to more than one media type.

MAKING TEXT INVISIBLE

Why bother going to the trouble of adding text to a page, only to make it invisible? There are particular situations where a cloak of invisibility is the right way to go. Circumstances where you should consider using invisible text include:

> When using print or handheld versions of CSS files to control how much content is seen on a page

> When assigning labels for screen readers that you don't want to show visually based on your page or site design

HIDING CONTENT

In the page's or site's CSS, follow these steps to hide content:

1. Open the style sheet for the specific media type, either handheld or printed media.

2. Evaluate the page and decide what elements you want to hide. In the page shown in figure 12-4, I decided to hide the background image as well as the small images scattered throughout the text.

3. Write the style for the element or elements you want to hide, and include the display:none ruleset for the defined media type.

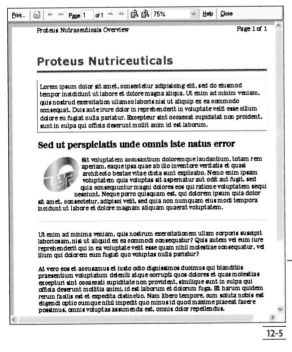

12-4

4. Save the file and test the page in the appropriate device. On the media page you see the layout excludes the graphic elements that use the `display:none` ruleset. In figure 12-5, for example, the sample page excludes most of the graphics shown in figure 12-4.

12-5

HIDING CONTENT IN A SCREEN READER

Many screen readers won't respond to the `display: hide` ruleset by reading the associated text aloud; instead, they ignore the text containing the rule altogether. Because one of the most common uses of hidden content is increasing information accessible to screen readers, hiding the text isn't serving its purpose.

Define a position for the text rather than using the `display` property. For example, to hide content you can write:

```
position: absolute; right: 5000px;
```

The text to which the style is assigned is positioned 5000px to the right of the left edge of the screen, making it invisible for all practical purposes. You can assign the style in any direction, and using any value larger than the page's dimensions, as illustrated in figure 12-6. That is, defining its position as `left: -8000px` also renders the content invisible from a practical standpoint.

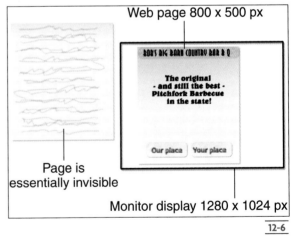

Web page 800 x 500 px

Page is essentially invisible

Monitor display 1280 x 1024 px

12-6

SPECIFYING PAGE WIDTHS

Several CSS properties come into play when designing style sheets for alternate types of media.

DEFINING THE MINIMUM WIDTH OF A PAGE

One CSS property that is especially useful for printing pages is `min-width`, which lets you specify a minimum width for an element on a Web page.

Specifying Page Width for Internet Explorer

I find it uncomfortable to have a page that won't validate when I can make it valid. I think it's worth the time it takes to write the JavaScript expression in the `<head>` tag.

To write the JavaScript and place it in the correct position for validation, follow these steps:

1. In the page's code, either before or after the `<style>` content, write:

```
<script type="text/
javascript" lan-
guage="javascript">
```

2. Write the opening tags for both hiding the script in non-compliant browsers and opening the character data identification, which forces the browser to read the text as characters, rather than code. The tags are written as:

```
<!--

<![Cdata[
```

3. Write or paste your JavaScript expression to follow the character data identification code.

4. To finish the script, close the character data tag, comment tag, and script tag by writing:

```
]]>

//-->

</script>
```

When defining the expression for the width, you can use the less-than sign, or ‹, rather than the characters `&lt` shown in the script in the previous steps.

When you validate the page's code, you may receive this warning:

character "‹" is the first character of a delimiter but occurred as data.

To specify the page width, follow these steps:

1. Insert a `<div>` tag within the `<body>` tag because the `<body>` tag can't have a minimum width assignment. Write the code as:

```
<body>
    <div class="container">
```

2. Write the style for the `<div>` tag to specify the minimum width for the page. I decided my example page must be at minimum 720px wide; the style is written as:

```
#container {
min-width:720px;
}
```

3. Internet Explorer doesn't understand the `min-width` property. Instead, you can specify the width in a JavaScript command either within the style or within the `<head>` tag. In the example

page, to maintain the minimum page width, the expression is included in the `#container` style, and written as:

```
width:expression(document.body.
    clientWidth &lt720? "720px":"auto");
```

SPECIFYING THE MAXIMUM PAGE WIDTH

You can specify the maximum width for a page along with its minimum. For the maximum value, use `&gt` in the expression instead of `>` to prevent errors or warnings when validating the page.

The code for writing the JavaScript for Internet Explorer is valid if included within the `<head>` tags and written as:

```
<script type="text/javascript"
 language="javascript">
<!--
<![Cdata[
```

```
width:expression(document.body
  .clientWidth &lt720? "720px":
  document.body.clientWidth &gt950?
  "950px":"auto");
]]>
//-->
</script>
```

The style that can be read and processed by other browsers is written as:

```
#container {min-width: 720px;max-
  width: 950px;}
```

PRINTING YOUR WEB PAGES

You can print any Web page, right? So why do you need styles?

You should include print styles when there is a potential for your users to print your page, such as with pages containing instructions or technical support documentation.

Defining styles for printing takes care of problems such as navigation menus showing on each printed page, or pages that are too wide.

ADJUSTING A PAGE FOR PRINTING

Here are some general tips to keep in mind when writing print style sheets:

> **Hide the navigation links.** Your viewers don't have any use for a visible menu on a printed page, like the one shown in figure 12-7.

12-7

> **Remove the underlines from in-text hyperlinks — or not.** Some like to remove the underlines because the links aren't active; others like to keep the underlines to indicate to the reader where there is linked content online. You say potato. . . .

> **Remove background colors or graphics from the page.** Image-intensive pages make the print job more complex and lengthy, and don't contribute much to the value of the content.

> **Change text to dark colors.** For most browsers, designating print as the desired media output strips a colored background, like the one shown in figure 12-8. In the print version, however, the text is still very light, making it difficult to read when printed.

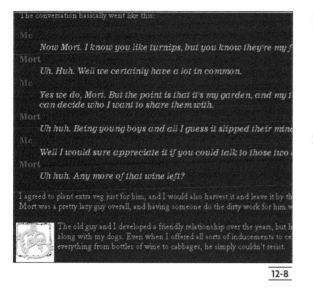

12-8

> **Decide what content is irrelevant in print.** You don't need navigation links. Do you need advertising? Or the privacy and terms-of-use disclaimers? Not likely. Any element not required for the print version should have a `display:none` ruleset applied.

> **Separate text from graphics.** Instead of using an image of a graphic with overlying text, separate the elements. Your print results are better using separate content streams. For example, the print preview of the banner shown in figure 12-10 doesn't display very clear text. Removing the text from the graphic and adding a heading, as in the title below the graphic, produces smoother text.

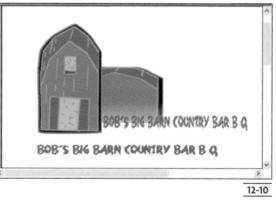

12-10

> **Modify the font size if necessary.** Points are the correct unit of measurement for print media styles, such as:

```
font-size: 12pt;
```

NOTE

Refer to Chapter 2 for much more on font and letter styling.

> **Evaluate your images.** Some images aren't suitable for both online and print. GIF images sometimes lose their meaning when printed, as you can see in the upper examples in figure 12-9. Transparent color assignments shown in the online version of the GIF images are replaced by white, effectively losing the curve of the first pie shape.

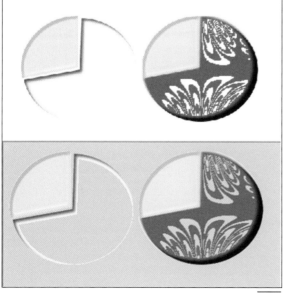

12-9

APPLYING OTHER PRINT STYLES

Once the page's display and content has been decided upon and the print media styles written, you can turn to additional properties that apply only to print media styles.

The print media properties and their descriptions and values are listed in Table 12-2.

Table 12-2: Print Media Properties

Property	Description
orphans	Specifies the minimum number of lines for a paragraph that must be left at the bottom of a page.
marks	Specifies if any marks should be rendered outside the page box. Your choices are none, crop, or cross marks.
page	Sets a page type to use when displaying an element.
page-break-after	Specifies how a page breaks following an element, such as a heading. Choose auto, always, avoid, left, or right.
page-break-before	Defines behavior for a page break before an element. The choices are the same as those listed for the page-break-after property.
page-break-inside	Defines how page breaks occur inside an element. Choose from auto or avoid values.
size	Specifies the orientation and size of a page as one of auto, portrait, or landscape.
widows	Specifies the minimum number of lines for a paragraph that must be left at the top of a page.

WRITING STYLES FOR HANDHELD DEVICES

The screen on your desktop computer is a far cry from the little screen on your PDA. Viewing regular Web pages on a handheld device can be disorienting and involve a lot of scrolling.

The browsers on PDAs and telephones are not standardized. As a result, the design you specify in your style sheet should be as uncomplicated as possible. That doesn't imply you should strip everything from the handheld version of your site — merely that you should use the styles judiciously.

PRO TIP

CSS commands in the handheld CSS file override any equivalent commands in the main CSS document.

The simplest way to make sure your pages look good across a suite of different devices is to use a consistent method for applying styles to keep track of what you are specifying. For example, I usually start with headings, styles for other tags, links, and then specific styles.

REDESIGNING THE LAYOUT

How your Web site appears to handheld users is different from how it appears in a traditional Web browser; consequently the viewer's expectations are different.

For example, you may have your site's pages laid out with an elastic column design, like the form shown in figure 12-11.

On a handheld device, your carefully crafted layout is wasted because there is room only for a small part of the form, as you see in figure 12-12.

Follow these steps to create a style sheet for handheld use and adjust the layout for the page:

1. Make a copy of your page's default style sheet to use for the mobile style sheet.

2. Specify the style by using a `link` element. Include a tag to link a handheld style sheet, such as:

```
<link type="text/css" rel=
"stylesheet"
href="MMMedia_handheld.css" media=
"handheld" />
```

12-11

12-12

12-13

> **NOTE**
>
> Some handhelds don't recognize `@import` or `@media` at-rules. Others apply screen styles as well as handheld styles, and still others ignore both. To be safe, use a `<link>` element instead.

3. Remove `width` rulesets and let the content wrap. The goal is to let your users view content on a PDA to see the width of the page without scrolling.

> **NOTE**
>
> The width of a handheld screen varies from 150px to more than double that width, making it impractical to specify a precise width. In my example using a form, I did specify a `max-width:220px` ruleset to configure the form's contents.

4. Remove margins and padding because there isn't enough extra space on a handheld screen to warrant using precious pixels for spacing; and, with such a small screen, there isn't the need to separate content as you would on a larger screen.

5. Test the page; my results are shown in figure 12-13. Because the page I am using contains a form, I maintained the right margin for the label style, which is applied to the labels for the check boxes.

> **NOTE**
>
> If your page contains columns, remove them from the layout. You may have to adjust or delete a fair number of styles including widths, floats, clear properties, alignments, positions, and so on.

MODIFYING TEXT AND IMAGES

Text and images seen on a small handheld screen should be simplified and modified as compared to their full-size Web browser counterparts.

Follow these steps to evaluate and adjust text and images:

1. Simplify the text styles if necessary. It's difficult to determine some slight differences in font styles, face, or color. Reducing the number and complexity of styles makes it simpler for the PDA to display the page.

2. Combine all the header information on your Web site into a single graphic to use as an interesting entry to your site without a lot of file download time. Either use an image for the page or specify a background image for the page's style sheet to place the header element, like the example shown in figure 12-14.

12-14

PRO TIP

My preference is to use a background image, but placing an image works equally well. You might have to make a composite image to replace what you could construct on your Web page using a header image and headings.

3. Restyle or replace the images shown on the page because an image too wide for the handheld screen has to be scrolled to view properly. Hide or modify the images in your handheld style sheet by either using the `display:none` ruleset, or specifying a `max-width` ruleset for the image.

PRO TIP

It isn't necessary to strip images entirely from a handheld version of your Web page. In some cases, you want to have images displaying, such as with instructional material.

My general rule is that if it isn't advancing the content in some definable way, it likely isn't worth the download and display time required.

CHANGING NAVIGATION

You need to modify the navigation structure and type of links used in a handheld to make it simpler for your users to access your information and get around the page.

Follow these steps to adapt your navigation system:

1. Add navigation anchors to your page. Scrolling a PDA screen vertically takes time, and the small screen size makes it difficult for users to orient themselves to page location. Use both content links and back-to-top links, like those shown in figure 12-15.

Canary Grass Seed	95 - 105
Fababeans	105 - 115
Corn (Grain)	110 - 120
Potatoes	110 - 140
Sunflowers	120 - 130
Sugar Beets	120 - 140

back to top   index   tables   home

Table 2: Base Temperature for Selected Crops and Insects

12-15

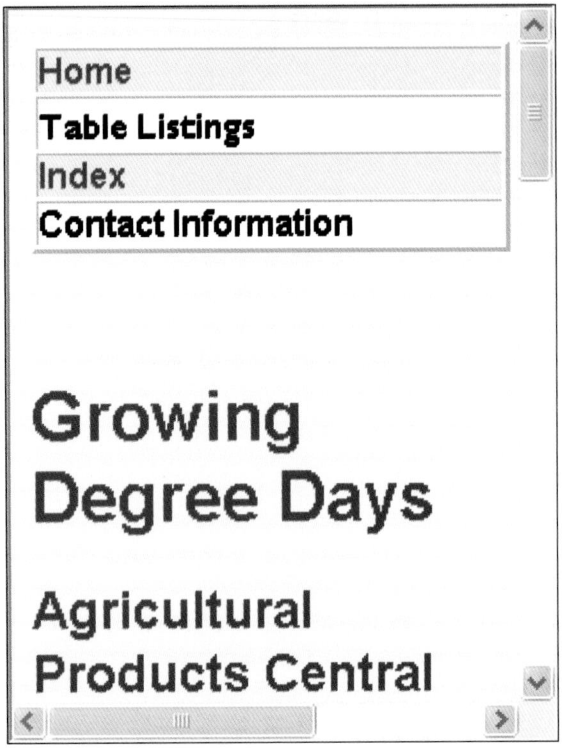

12-16

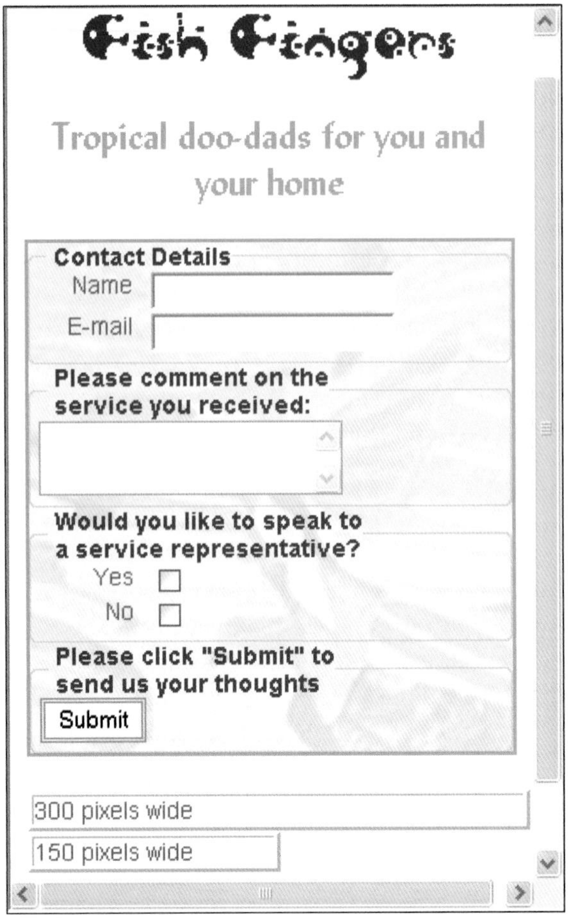

12-17

2. Revise the location and appearance of your menu. If you have the menu in a column, remove it from that location; if your menu is configured like the example in figure 12-16, consider making a horizontal list rather than a vertical list for the menu.

NOTE

Refer to Chapter 10 for information about constructing and using different types of menus.

3. Check out the site using a browser window sized at 150px to 300px wide to test how the user will see the pages on a handheld screen. The example shown in figure 12-17 is 300px wide. I have added a notation on the page showing the 150px width for reference.

NOTE

The W3C has integrated different mobile devices such as telephones and PDAs into a common category called mobile Web applications. Read about best practices for mobile Web applications at: www.w3.org/TR/mobile-bp.

BROWSING WEB PAGES ON TV

Some folks prefer to do their Web browsing and e-mail via television. Although a system such as Microsoft's WebTV interprets the styles in a regular Web page, the layout isn't necessarily what you want to portray.

The introduction of Internet terminals that use TV as a display medium has started to close the gap between Web design and broadcast design. You can build style sheets that let you define a predictable page appearance for this group of users.

NAVIGATING A WEB PAGE ON TELEVISION

Navigation is different because a set-top box doesn't use a mouse. Instead of a mouse, you navigate through pages using arrow buttons on the keyboard or a remote control on a TV browser display. The visible response on the Web page is a yellow selection box — regardless of your page's styles — like the one shown in figure 12-18.

A television browser can't scroll horizontally. To compensate, if the layout is defined solely by the TV browser the page is extensively reorganized, as in the page shown in figure 12-18: its actual layout is quite different, as you see in figure 12-19.

Adjusting the structure

If you want to control the appearance of your page, look into these structural items:

> Revise your page's layout to use a maximum width of 544px.

> Convert all the fixed-width lengths and values to relative values to compensate for the smaller size of the television display.

> Remove width and height properties from images to allow them to resize automatically.

> Don't assign heading styles and then resize the style; the TV browser reads the heading tag and applies the default rather than a custom size.

Figure 12-20 shows a page that retains the same appearance regardless of the medium on which it is displayed. There aren't any fixed style lengths, headings, or images that have to be reinterpreted differently for the narrower TV screen.

12-18

LAYING OUT THE WEB PAGE

Web pages on a television receiver are viewed at a nominal size of 544px x 372px.

New
Introductions

F.J.
Grootenhorst

Daffodil
Hill

Hardy
rugosa.
Long
history of
growing
without
winter
protection
in very cold
regions.

Back to: New Introductions   Roses   Perennials   Home

12-19

Petersen Electronics

custom vehicle monitoring and security controls

At Petersen Electronics we make it our business to offer a full range of custom and stock monitoring and security equipment for all makes of domestic and import vehicles.

How many categories do you or your business fit?

- customized vehicles, including boats and RVs
- sports cars
- vintage and antique vehicles of all types

Petersen Electronics Home

12-20

Checking out the color

Take a look at your color scheme as well. On TV, light and bright colors like pure white or yellow, or pure bright color like red or green, produce a vibrating effect.

Midrange colors, like a medium blue or gray, are the best options for backgrounds.

PRO TIP

In Photoshop CS and CS2, you can use a filter to convert your image's color. Choose Filter ⇨ Video ⇨ NTSC Color to apply a common TV-safe color palette.

Displaying text

A TV receiver doesn't display thin lines like those that make up text. To allow text to be readable on-screen, the default font size should be about 18pt Helvetica font.

The TV browser wraps text elements to fit in the window and the designated column. Using the smaller screen and larger text size results in very short lines of text in a columned Web page. Remove the column structure from the page to make the text easier to read.

The page shown in figure 12-21 is a good example of text that wraps independently of the screen size. The page has no columns, and the lines wrap comfortably.

PRO TIP

If you are concerned that your viewers won't be able to correctly navigate through a Web page, consider displaying status bar messages responding to mouseover actions. You need to use JavaScript `onmouseover` and `onmouseout` events to control the messages, which can be up to 35 characters.

If you like, go one step further and include an `onLoad` event in the `<body>` tag that displays an alert about the messages when your page is viewed on Web TV.

If you aren't the JavaScript type, changing your navigation from small images to large text, for example, will enhance the visibility and users' navigation experience.

years ago. Or at least I thought we had. We discussed the problem over some delicious chokecherry wine one night on the back porch.

The conversation basically went like this:

Me
> Now Mort. I know you like turnips, but you know they're my favorite veg.

Mort
> Uh. Huh. Well we certainly have a lot in common.

Me
> Yes we do, Mort. But the point is that it's my garden, and my turnips, and I can decide who I want to share them with.

Mort
> Uh huh. Being young boys and all I guess it slipped their minds.

Me
> Well I would sure appreciate it if you could talk to those

The Hare and the Porcupine Redux. ...

12-21

THE ORGANIC WEB

"Organic" isn't a term most of us immediately associate with the Internet and the Web. Yet there are significant parallels between the Web and any other organism, as you can read in this essay by Web designer, Faruk Ateş.

When the Internet bubble burst in 2000, many people left the Web behind, labeling it uninteresting, a failed medium, or not profitable. Yet there were those who felt the Web had become much more interesting than it was before. To them, the bubble was a first sign of the Web's organic existence. It wasn't just some computers connected to each other on a global scale — the Web was living, breathing; alive!

Back then, the people most fascinated by the Web started spreading Web standards, evangelizing semantic markup, and using CSS for presentation. This movement, embodied by the Web Standards Project (WaSP), was the first trigger in the Web's new evolutionary cycle.

THINKING OUTSIDE THE BOX

As Web standards became more widespread and the adoption rate for applying standards increased, people started thinking outside the box. With the restraints from the table-based layout approach cast off our shoulders, our creative juices started to flow once again. New CSS-powered layouts inspired others to come up with new concepts entirely, which in turn inspired brand-new applications and a simplicity that was never seen before.

The Web solidified its Darwinian existence when investors once again took notice of it. New startups and innovative sites created an online ecosystem, where community life and connectivity reigned supreme. These focused, organized groups of target audiences — so well-intertwined and exponentially growing — were ripe for harvest, and one after another were bought up by large corporations.

Communication between our friends as well as complete strangers (preferably those who share our interests) is becoming a more integral part of the Web than ever before. The explosion of blogging and content syndication paved the way for this development, and already we see companies capitalizing on the trend to enrich these technologies with new possibilities and implementations.

Application Program Interfaces, or APIs, are an interesting development on the Web today, and accurately represent its organic nature. Rather than expanding through completely new, isolated Web sites, the Web is currently growing by the merging of existing Web sites using their open APIs. People are combining the APIs of large sites to create entirely new platforms and solutions that make keen and clever use of the Web's new abilities. Syndication is again an integral part that allows this to happen.

PREDICTING THE FUTURE

So where is all this going? In five years, the Internet will become a more integrated part of our everyday lives. What Apple Computer currently offers with iChat AV — incredibly easy four-way video conferencing with our friends and family — will move into the living room, and we'll "call" others over the Web and see each other using tiny cameras built into our plasma TVs.

Surfing the Web won't be limited to desktop computer and handheld browsers, but various content — especially multimedia-rich content — will take place in the living room. Rather than only searching for Web sites with text content, we will browse Web sites for their streaming video, and enjoy content from the Web in a fashion similar to our current-day habits of zapping across TV channels.

Web sites will evolve and become a much more inter-active experience, where we no longer switch from one static page to another, only to be "enriched" in liveli-ness by flashy banner ads, but instead living pages that respond much more naturally to our actions.

The Web is alive, now more than ever, and its expan-sion has been one that can only be seen as organic growth. Where will it truly be in five years? Nobody knows for sure, but what is certain is that it's only going to get more interesting from here.

I am planning a style sheet for users viewing my site on a handheld device. How do I figure out what to leave and what to remove?

Many Web sites use a three-column layout, with the left column displaying navigation; the main, central column used for content; and the right sidebar used for ancillary information, advertising, and so on. There is far too much scrolling involved to use that sort of a page layout for a handheld screen.

Look at your Web page from a different perspective. One of the real advantages to online information is the virtually endless capability to hyperlink. While that advantage exists for handheld devices as well, it's not always the primary requirement for users. Instead, they more often want to find the key information and not be served a lot of pretty but extraneous information.

Viewing my Web site on a television is so frustrating. Why is the area of my page displayed so small compared to the large size of the TV screen?

A broadcast signal uses 525 horizontal lines to draw the image, rather than filling pixels with color as on a computer screen. The screen dimensions of 544px x 372px represent the *safe area,* or area that is dependably displayed on the monitor. Based on Microsoft Developers Network data, the dimensions are calculated as:

1. 525-42=483 lines, which has an equivalent screen resolution of 640px x 480px. The Vertical Blanking Interval (VBI) is a part of the signal equal to 42 lines, reserved for synchronizing the screen redraw and other purposes such as closed captioning text.

2. 640px x 480px - 80px x 60px = 560px x 420px. Broadcast signals aren't very efficient and may *overscan,* or lose up to 20 percent of their signal.

3. 560px x 420px - 16px x 48px = 544px x 372px. Some of the screen area is reserved for the Web page interface, including the border and status bar.

ABOUT THE CONTRIBUTORS

I was extremely fortunate to have several contributors give their time and expertise to bring you different perspectives on Web design and using CSS.

Read bios about the contributors and learn about their own Web sites in this appendix. I asked them two questions, and their responses are included as well. The questions are:

> What is your philosophy on Web design and the use of CSS in particular?

> What constitutes "good" CSS in a site?

DENYER

Denyer is a Web designer, programmer, and photographer living in the United Kingdom whose original university training was in electronic engineering. Not quite content with designing circuits that no one would ever see, he decided to pursue a more creative, yet still technical field of work. Having come "late" to the game by picking up Web development just a few years ago, he started learning about standards compliancy and technologies like CSS without being burdened with a history of working with older methods like table layouts.

A lot of his work comes through referrals from other Web design companies that don't have the necessary skills in-house to produce clean, standardized CSS layouts, or simply need a good job done fast. It is in part due to the subcontracting nature of this work and the accompanying non-disclosure agreements that he thinks his company Sozu isn't perhaps as well known as it should be.

Although keen on both designing and programming, Denyer likes nothing more than the challenge of taking someone else's Photoshop file and making it work on someone else's code — all the while appearing to enjoy it. The most appealing thing about Web site development for him personally is the fact that it seems to strike a nice balance between creativity and technicality, like the interface for the Sozu site shown in figure A-1, though that's not to say he wouldn't drop it all for the opportunity to be a professional photographer or a drummer in a rock band.

NOTE

The image shown in figure A-1 is located at www.sozu.co.uk/index.php?id=15&pic=3.

Q What is your philosophy on Web design and the use of CSS in particular? What constitutes "good" CSS in a site?

My philosophy is there are two sides to Web design: information and appearance. CSS lets one (the appearance) live in hopefully blissful abstraction from the other (the information). There is a certain purity in knowing that the data a search engine or newsreader will see and the visual presentation are two totally separate entities, both remaining flexible because of this. In Web design there's nothing better than totally overhauling a site by simply replacing the CSS and the graphics folder!

For me, good CSS is either code that makes terrible markup work, or something that works with good markup to make it whatever the designer can dream of!

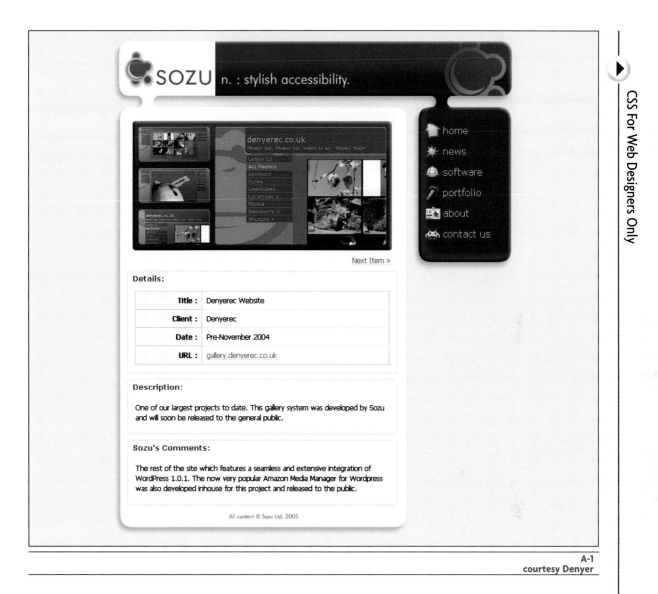

A-1
courtesy Denyer

FARUK ATEŞ

Faruk Ateş is a Web Kaizen Specialist, focusing on the continuous improvement and innovation of Web sites and applications. As an all-aspects-of-the-Web consultant, Faruk aims to improve the overall quality of Web sites by introducing better principles and techniques to not only developers, designers, and content producers, but also to educators and project managers.

Besides his blog, shown in figure A-2, Faruk writes for books and online magazines on topics ranging from XHTML and CSS to JavaScript, Accessibility, SQL, and design. When not writing on these subjects, Faruk can be found doing workshops and speaking about them at conferences. His personal ideas and projects, made to help shape the Internet, include technologies such as FACE, an innovative approach to giving life to static Web sites.

Q What is your philosophy on Web design and the use of CSS in particular? What constitutes "good" CSS in a site?

When you say "Web design" many people think of the visual styling of a site, nothing more than the way it looks, but they couldn't be more off-target. Web design is not just about crafting a visual presentation for a Web site; it is about creating interaction, creating a complete user experience. Visitors don't just look at Web sites — they interact with them. They rescale text, scroll through pages, click on links, drag objects around, and fill in forms. Web design is about placing yourself in the user's perspective and figuring out how to make optimal use of white space, content, interactivity, and so much more.

In the old days of the Internet, the Web designer was limited in his tools of trade. Nested tables, font tags, and spacer GIFs left no room for true Web design. The design goals and focus in the past were a misguided attempt to reduce Web design to what it is still often seen as today: print design in a digital world. The coming of CSS changed this for good, calling in a new era: the era of true Web design.

Today, Web designers have the freedom to express themselves in truly beautiful Web sites where CSS performs a key role in separating structure from presentation. CSS allows us to create meaningful pages with clean markup, and present them any way we'd like to the visitor. When used optimally, CSS allows us to restyle and even redesign entire Web sites quickly and painlessly, providing complete freedom in design and interaction, and utilizing clean code that others can learn from.

MARGARET WERDERMANN

Margaret Werdermann is an instructional designer based in Winnipeg, Canada. She has ten years of experience in various forms of adult education. Her work focuses mainly on creating Web-based learning solutions, but she is also a talented classroom facilitator and writer.

She has enjoyed varied careers from teaching and curriculum design to database development and administration. These experiences have led to a unique skill set that combines technical know-how with educational expertise.

Margaret has a degree in Education from the University of Winnipeg and is currently in the final year of a Masters degree in Distance Education through Athabasca University.

Q What is your philosophy on Web design and the use of CSS in particular? What constitutes "good" CSS in a site?

My philosophy regarding Web design is that "it's all about accessibility." There's no point whatsoever in designing a site that can't be used by a significant portion of my intended audience. Using CSS enables me to create accessible Web sites that still look attractive.

To me, good CSS works "with" the site, not "against" it. What do I mean by that? I mean that a site must still be able to function without the CSS — this harkens back to accessibility issues — but that it is made more attractive, more streamlined, and far easier to manage with the CSS in place. A combination of templates and good CSS should make any formatting or layout updates to a large site inconsequential.

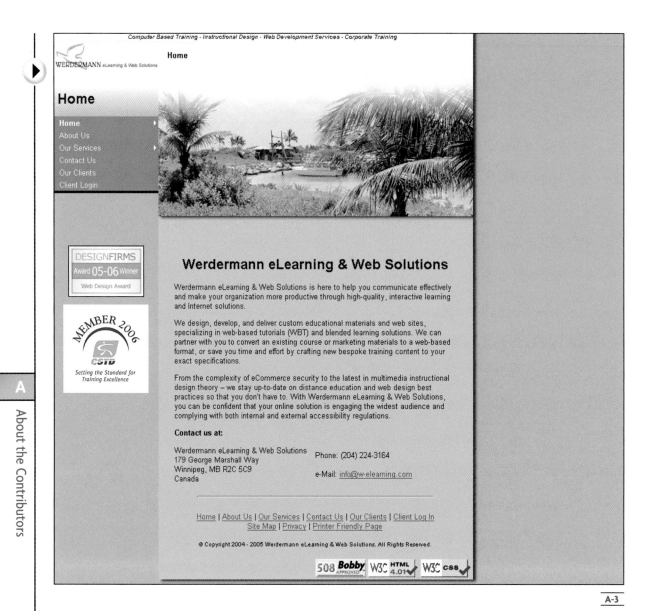

CHRISTOPHER WARE

Christopher Ware is a graphic/Web designer based in Birmingham, Alabama. He has many years of professional experience, and is proficient in Web site interface layout, XHTML, CSS, typography, and traditional print design.

NOTE

Chris was in the midst of a complete site redesign at the time of writing. The page shown in figure A-4 is the home page active in April, 2006, located at www.exploding-boy.com.

FAMILIAR TO DOZENS
EXPLODING BOY

HOME | ABOUT | CONTACT | ARCHIVES

Realization   4 comments
Published April 9th, 2006 in Design.

I noticed something a while back, but was recently reminded after visiting some of the CSS gallery sites today. The most harsh, attacking comments about webdesign always seem to come from people with either no site of their own, or people with some super-basic, horrid design they try to pass off as minimalism.

Is Boot Camp Good or Bad?   5 comments
Published April 6th, 2006 in Apple.

By now most everyone has read the news about Apple releasing an application called Boot Camp, which will be included in OS X 10.5, Leopard. For those who haven't yet read about Boot Camp. The application lets you create a boot disc with all the proper Windows drivers so you can safely install Windows XP on your Intel Mac. This in essence can be a huge move for Apple's hardware sales, but I have my concerns.
Continue reading 'Is Boot Camp Good or Bad?'

RECENT POSTS   RSS

» The Douche Card
» CSS Tabs Showcase
» Who Do You Blog For?
» Realization
» Is Boot Camp Good or Bad?
» Boot Camp
» Suckerfish HoverLightbox
» Pimp Rims Go High-tech
» Watching a Ripper

RECENT COMMENTS   RSS

» Christopher on Centered Sliding Doors Menus: Rocket: The...
» Rocket on Centered Sliding Doors Menus: well...it doesnt...
» Josh on Live Thumbnails: That script is pretty cool. I...
» Ollie on Easy Top Corner Banners with CSS: Hey, I have...
» Ian on Centered Sliding Doors Menus: Thanks Chris :-)
» Edwin Durning on Realization: it's pretty similar to spec...
» Christopher on Centered Sliding Doors Menus: Ian: I...
» Ian on Centered Sliding Doors Menus: This is excellent :)...
» Tim on Add a Newsvine.com Link to your Blog: I like your...

ELSEWHERE   RSS

» Tired of arguing with complete morons? Tired of getting into bar room brawls? Try The Douche Card. (0)
» CSS Tabs Showcase — A lot of good references to css navigation techniques and huge showcase of css menus. (0)
» Who Do You Blog For? — When a blogger develops an audience demands begin to be made on that blogger by the audience. (0)
» Apple will include technology in the next release of OS X that lets you install and run the Windows XP on your Mac. (0)

FLICKR   RSS

XHTML | CSS | WORDPRESS | DREAMHOST

A-4

My primary goal with design is to make it as simple as possible for users to achieve their goals throughout the site. I strive to make all information on a Web site easy to read and understand, and even easier to find. What good is a beautiful Web site if no one can accomplish anything on the site?

Using good CSS helps separate the style and layout of your HTML from its content. In this way, you can control the position, spacing, fonts, colors, and other aspects of a Web document's elements without compromising its structure. It helps speed up site maintenance, reduce load time, and create search engine friendly pages.

CSS PROPERTIES AND VALUES

Throughout the book you have seen multiple references to properties and their values. In this appendix, style categories are set into tables listing properties and their values. In addition, I have included the browser version numbers to indicate which browsers recognize and process a particular property.

The tables' properties are listed alphabetically or in logical groupings, such as width, min-width, and max-width. A shorthand property is listed as the first item in the table where it exists.

Table B-1: Units of Measure and Color Values

Unit	Description
in	Inch
cm	Centimeter
mm	Millimeter
em	The current font size of the current element has a value of one em; used as a constant for sizing other elements
ex	The x-height of a font; that is, the height of a lowercase "x" is its x-height, used as a constant for sizing other elements
pt	Point; 1pt is equivalent to 1/72in
pc	Pica; 1pc is equivalent to 12pt
px	Pixels; a color dot on a computer screen
%	Percentage

Color Unit	Description
color_name	A color name, for example aqua
#RRGGBB	A hexidecimal number, such as #FF00CC, which is bright pink
RGB(R,G,B)	An RGB value, such as RGB(255,255,0), which is yellow
RGB(R%, G%, B%)	An RGB percentage value, such as RGB(100%,100%,0%), which is yellow

Table B-2: Background Properties and Values

Property	Values	IE	F	N
background	background-color background-image background-repeat background-attachment background-position	4	1	6
background-attachment	fixed scroll	4	1	6
background-color	color-hex color-name color-rgb transparent	4	1	4
background-image	none url	4	1	4
background-position	top left top center top right center left center center center right bottom left bottom center bottom right x-pos y-pos x-% y-%	4	1	6
background-repeat	no-repeat repeat repeat-x repeat-y	4	1	4

Table B-3: Font and Text Properties

Font Property	Values	IE	F	N
font	font-style font-variant font-weight font-size/line-height font-family caption icon menu message-box small-caption status-bar	4	1	4
font-family	family-name generic-family	3	1	4
font-size	small medium large x-small xx-small x-large xx-large smaller larger length %	3	1	4
font-size-adjust	none number	-	-	-

Font Property	Values	IE	F	N
font-stretch	normal wider narrower condensed semi-condensed extra-condensed ultra-condensed expanded semi-expanded extra-expanded ultra-expanded	-	-	-
font-style	normal italic oblique	4	1	4
font-variant	normal small-caps	4	1	6
font-weight	normal bold bolder lighter 100 200 300 400 500 600 700 800 900	4	1	4

Continued

Text Property	Values	IE	F	N
color	color-hex color-name color-rgb transparent	3	1	4
direction	ltr rtl	6	1	6
text-align	left right center justify	4	1	4
text-decoration	none underline overline line-through blink	4	1	4
text-indent	length %	4	1	4
text-shadow	color length none	-	-	-
text-transform	none capitalize uppercase lowercase	4	1	4
white-space	normal pre nowrap	5	1	4
letter-spacing	normal length	4	1	6
word-spacing	normal length	6	1	6

Table B-4: Dimension Properties

Property	Values	IE	F	N
height	auto length %	4	1	6
line-height	normal number length %	4	1	4
max-height	none length %	-	1	6
min-height	length %	-	1	6
width	auto length %	4	1	4
max-width	none length %	-	1	6
min-width	length %	-	1	6

Table B-5: Border and Outline Properties and Values

Border Property	Values	IE	F	N
border	border-color border-style border-width	4	1	4
border-bottom	border-bottom-width border-color border-style	4	1	6
border-bottom-color	color-hex color-name color-rgb transparent	4	1	6
border-bottom-style	border-style	4	1	6
border-bottom-width	thin medium thick length	4	1	4
border-color	color-hex color-name color-rgb transparent	4	1	6
border-left	border-left-width border-style border-color	4	1	6
border-left-color	color-hex color-name color-rgb transparent	4	1	6
border-left-style	border-style	4	1	6
border-left-width	thin medium thick length	4	1	4
border-right	border-right-width border-style border-color	4	1	6

CSS Properties and Values

Border Property	Values	IE	F	N
border-right-color	color-hex color-name color-rgb transparent	4	1	6
border-right-style	border-style	4	1	6
border-right-width	thin medium thick length	4	1	4
border-style	none dashed dotted double groove hidden inset outset ridge solid	4	1	6
border-top	border-top-width border-style border-color	4	1	6
border-top-color	color-hex color-name color-rgb transparent	4	1	6
border-top-style	border-style	4	1	6
border-top-width	thin medium thick length	4	1	4
border-width	thin medium thick length	4	1	4

Continued

Outline Property	Property Values	IE	F	N
outline	outline-color outline-style outline-width	-	1.5	-
outline-color	color-hex color-name color-rgb transparent invert	-	1.5	-
outline-style	none dashed dotted double groove inset outset ridge solid	-	1.5	-
outline-width	thin medium thick length	-	1.5	-

Positioning Property	Values	IE	F	N
right	auto length %	5	1	6
left	auto length %	4	1	4
top	auto length %	4	1	4
bottom	auto length %	5	1	6
position	absolute relative fixed static	4	1	4
vertical-align	bottom middle top baseline sub super text-top text-bottom length %	4	1	4
clip	shape auto	4	1	6
overflow	visible hidden scroll auto	4	1	6
z-index	number auto	4	1	6

Continued

Classification Property	Values	IE	F	N
display	none	4	1	4
	inline			
	block			
	list-item			
	run-in			
	compact			
	marker			
	table			
	inline-table			
	table-row-group			
	table-header-group			
	table-footer-group			
	table-row			
	table-column-group			
	table-column			
	table-cell			
	table-caption			
clear	both	4	1	4
	left			
	right			
	none			
float	left	4	1	4
	right			
	none			
position	absolute	4	1	4
	fixed			
	relative			
	static			
visibility	visible	4	1	6
	hidden			
	collapse			

Classification Property	Values	IE	F	N
cursor	default	4	1	6
	crosshair			
	pointer			
	move			
	text			
	wait			
	help			
	url			
	auto			
	e-resize			
	ne-resize			
	nw-resize			
	n-resize			
	se-resize			
	sw-resize			
	s-resize			
	w-resize			

Table B-7: Margin and Padding Properties and Values

Margin Property	Values	IE	F	N
margin	margin-left margin-right margin-top margin-bottom	4	1	4
margin-bottom	length % Auto	4	1	4
margin-left	length % Auto	3	1	4
margin-right	length % Auto	3	1	4
margin-top	length % Auto	3	1	4

Padding Property	Values	IE	F	N
padding	padding-left padding-right padding-top padding-bottom	4	1	4
padding-left	length %	4	1	4
padding-right	length %	4	1	4
padding-top	length %	4	1	4
padding-bottom	length %	4	1	4

Table B-8: List and Marker Properties and Values

Property	Values	IE	F	N
list-style	list-style-type list-style-position list-style-image	4	1	6
list-style-image	none url	4	1	6
list-style-position	inside outside	4	1	6
list-style-type	none circle square disc decimal decimal- leading-zero lower-alpha upper-alpha lower-roman upper-roman lower-greek lower-latin upper-latin hebrew armenian georgian cjk-ideographic hiragana hiragana-iroha katakana katakana-iroha	4	1	4
marker-offset	Auto length	-	1	7

Table B-9: Table Properties and Values

Table Property	Values	IE	F	N
border-collapse	collapse separate	5	1	7
border-spacing	length	-	1	6
caption-side	top bottom left right	-	1	6
empty-cells	show hide	-	1	6
table-layout	auto fixed	5	1	6

Table B-10: Pseudo-Class and Pseudo-Element Properties and Applications

Pseudo-class	Purpose	IE	F	N
:active	Assigns a unique style to an active element	4	1	8
:focus	Assigns a unique style to an element when the element has focus	-	-	-
:hover	Assigns a unique style to an element in response to a mouseover event	4	1	7
:link	Assigns a unique style to an unvisited link	3	1	4
:visited	Assigns a unique style to a visited link	3	1	4
:first-child	Assigns a unique style to an element that is the first dependent of another element	-	1	7
:lang	Specifies the language to use for a particular element	-	1	8

Pseudo-element	Purpose	IE	F	N
:first-letter	Adds a unique style to the first letter of a text string	5	1	8
:first-line	Adds a unique style to the first line of a text string	5	1	8
:before	Inserts content before a specified element	-	1.5	8
:after	Inserts content after a specified element	-	1.5	8

Table B-11: Properties and Values for Print Styles

Print Property	Description	Values
size	Specifies the orientation and size of a page	portrait landscape auto
page	Specifies a page type used to display an element	identifier auto
marks	Specifies whether printer marks are shown outside the page box or not	crop cross none
page-break-before	Specifies how a page breaks before an element	always avoid left right auto
page-break-after	Specifies how a page breaks after an element	always avoid left right auto
page-break-inside	Specifies how a page breaks within an element	avoid auto
widow	Specifies the minimum lines of a paragraph that must be left at the top of a page	number
orphan	Specifies the minimum lines of a paragraph that must be left at the bottom of a page	number

PRO GLOSSARY

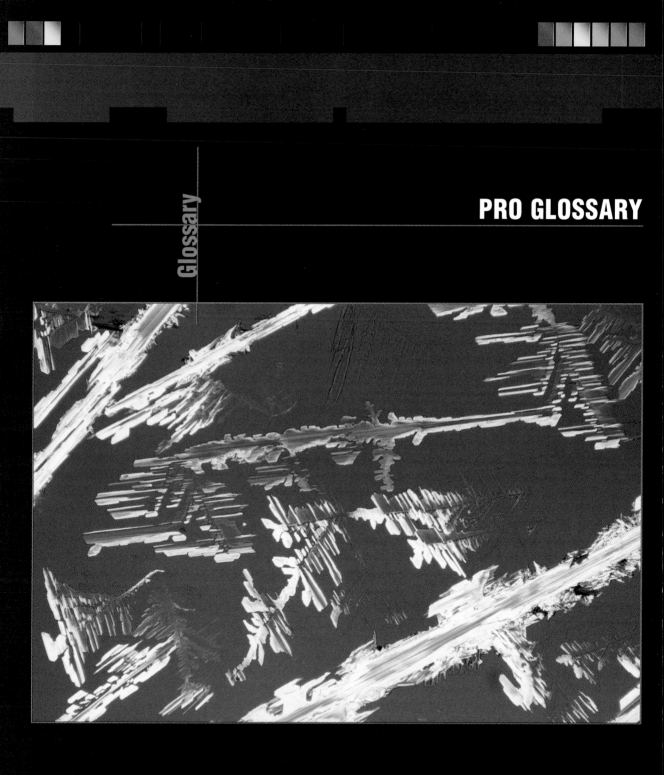

! important: Declaring a style as important overrides all other styles regardless of their origin, or whether the element is specified. The `!important` keyword is a declaration, not an attribute, but it can be attached to any attribute. In the following example, using the declaration means that regardless of styles applied via other means, the paragraph's text is bold: `p {font-weight: bold !important;}`.

absolute length: A unit of measure used to define a length for a property's value expressed in a defined unit, such as `mm`, `cm`, `in`, or `pt`. Values are expressed as the number followed by a two-letter abbreviation without a separating space.

actual value: The property appears using local settings such as monitor settings. Actual and used values are usually the same.

anchor pseudo-class: A browser that supports CSS can show several link states that can be styled using pseudo-classes. A link that is active, visited, unvisited, or in contact with your mouse can have separate styles. The order is important, and must follow this sequence: `a:link` (the unvisited link); `a:visited` (the visited link); `a:hover` (the link during the mouseover state); and `a:active` (the selected link).

aspect ratio: The proportional ratio of width to height is the object's or screen's aspect ratio. Fonts use an aspect ratio to define their proportions, as do monitor, screen, and other user agent displays.

background properties: Use one or more of the five available properties to define a background on a page or for an element. Specify a value for the `background-color` to display a color other than the default white, or include a background color if you use an image smaller than the full-page size. Use an image defined by the `background-image` value. If you want an image to remain stationary while the page scrolls, define the `background-attachment` as `fixed`. Both `background-position` and `background-repeat` properties can use several values — see separate entries for each property.

background: Use the shortcut attribute to set up to five separate background attributes for a background's style in one statement. The values can be in any order and are delimited by a space. You can include `background-attachment`, `background-color`, `background-image`, `background-position`, and `background-repeat`.

background-position: Specify the location where the background color or image starts on the page. A color fills from the specified location; an image is placed at the specified location. Define the value on x-axis and y-axis coordinates, or use keywords including `top`, `center`, `bottom`, `right`, or `left`. For example, a style written as `body { background-position: 0px center;}` places the image or starts the background color at the left margin and at the center of the page.

background-repeat: There are several ways to specify how an image defined by the `background-image` property is shown on the page. `No-repeat` shows the image once, by default at the upper left corner of the page. The default display tiles the image both horizontally and vertically. Use either `background-repeat:repeat-x` or `background-repeat: repeat-y` to restrict the image repeat to one axis or the other.

border properties: Specify a width for a single border using a specific property, such as `img {border-right-width: 12px;}` using any value except a negative value. The border inherits the element's background; specify a foreground using a `border-style` value. Border styles can be applied to the entire border, or specified for each side as one of several configurations, from dashed to groove to solid lines.

border: The shorthand attribute, such as `h3 { border: 4px groove #663333;}` is used to set width, style, and color of the four borders of an element in one statement. If you don't specify an attribute its default value is used. Instead of using the border shorthand, you can use individual styles for each border property. Different browsers view borders differently, so specify the width and style properties at a minimum. Additional border shortcut styles are either appearance- or side-specific. For example, specify the border color for all or specific sides of an element in one statement, such as `h1 {border-color: silver red;}` which colors the top and bottom borders silver and the left and right borders red. Use a style such as `p {border-top: 5px dashed #999900;}` to specify the appearance for the top edge of an element's border.

cascading order: The fundamental principle of style sheets is the cascading order. Defined property values are applied from the most specific (the style closest to the element) to the most general (the default styles used by the browser displaying your Web page). The order from highest to lowest is: an inline style, written as a property within a tag, such as `<p style="font-size:1.6em"> </p>`; a `<style>` tag included in the `<head>` of the page's code, such as `<style> .group1 { font-size:1.6em;} </style>`; and an external style sheet, such as `<link rel="stylesheet" type="text/css" href="biz.css">`.

class: A class selector is a text string preceded by a period that is used to define a tag attribute, such as: `.special { font-family: "Gill Sans", Arial, sans; background-color:#330000; color:#FFFFFF; }`. In the code, the class is written as: `<p class="special">Be sure to ask about the daily specials!</p>`.

clear: When using CSS for positioning content on a page, use the `clear` property to define how an element appears in relation to other elements. Specify whether the element can have floating elements around it. Choose `both`, `left`, `right`, or `none`. The element is positioned below any floating element on the specified side. For example, a property written as

column3 `{clear:left;}` forces the column below any element floating to its left. Using a style such as `footer {clear:both;}` places the footer element below other page content that is listed in the page's code before the footer, regardless of that content's `float` property values.

clipping: Use a clip property to specify a visible area, thereby making the rest of the element's area transparent. Clipping applies only to an absolutely positioned rectangular element. Values are specified as `top`, `right`, `bottom`, and `left`, such as `{clip: rect (5px 30px auto auto);}`.

color unit: Color values are assigned to numerous properties using one of three different methods. A hexadecimal value is written as `{color:#FFCC66;}` and assigns color based on red/green/blue, preceded in the style by a hash mark or number sign (#). A percentage color value is based again on red/green/blue values, and is expressed as `{color:rgb (255%204%102%);}`, where each percentage represents each color value in sequence. Colors can also be written as names, such as `{color:navy;}`, which is interpreted by a browser as dark navy blue.

comments: Comments are strings of text — labels, information about styles or groups of styles, other information to store for future reference — that are stored within the style sheet. A comment string is hidden from the rest of the page's script and code. Anything within the opening /* and closing */ is hidden, even over multiple lines.

computed value: A value determined by inheritance, such as computing `ex` lengths to pixel or absolute lengths.

confetti menu: Create a special look for a Web page using a confetti menu. The menu itself becomes part of the page's design: each link uses a markedly different font, color, and layout on the page.

contextual selectors: One or more selectors delimited by spaces used to specify the circumstances under which the style is applied; only the last element in the pattern is modified. The following rule indicates the blockquote's text color will be olive green only if the `<blockquote>` is also within a `<div>` element: `div blockquote {color: #666600;}`. In the XHTML: `<div><blockquote> This one uses olive green text </blockquote> </div> <blockquote> This one doesn't display olive green text.</blockquote>`.

cursor: Rather than using a default cursor appearance on your page, you can specify one of numerous options for custom cursor appearances, such as `crosshairs`, `help`, `wait`, and `resize` of the active element in different directions. The appearance depends on the browser and your system settings. Specify a custom appearance by writing the ruleset such as `{ cursor: help }`.

definition list: Definition lists display a term and definition pair, like what you may see in a glossary, or a character's name and line of script like in a screenplay. A definition list is written like this: `<dl> <dt> list item term </dt> <dd> definition </dd></dl>`.

device-dependent length: A unit of measure used to define a length for a property's value based on the dimensions of the device displaying the page, expressed in pixels as `px`.

display: The `display` property overrides the default formatting applied to XHTML elements and tells the browser how to display the page based on the invisible boxes that make up the text and other elements on the page. The default value is `display:block`. Other common options include `inline`, which displays the content as an inline box; `list-item`, which displays the content as a list box in either an ordered or unordered list; or `none`. If you use the `display: none` value, the element is hidden and no space is reserved on the page.

div: Use a `<div>` element to hold other page content to which attributes can be applied as a single unit. A style such as `.top2 {border: 2px ridge #FF0033; margin: 8px;}` applies the properties and values defined in the `<div>` element's style to all tags within the `<div>` like this: `<div class= "top2"> <p> </p> <img /> <p> </p> </div>`.

elastic layout: A way to develop a Web page using only relative values expressed as percentages and em values. An elastic layout maintains the relative proportions of the Web page and its contents, regardless of the size of the browser window and how the user modifies the size of the display font.

element: An element is an object within a Web page, such as `<body>`, `<table>`, `<p>`, or `<div>`.

external style sheet: One or more external style sheets can be attached to a Web page, either for print, handheld, or screen reader versions in addition to a style sheet for regular browser viewing. Use a `<link>` tag to attach the style sheet to your site's pages, written as: `<link rel="stylesheet" type="text/css" href="biz_pda.css">`. An external style sheet lets you make changes within the sheet that are applied to all pages to which the sheet is linked.

fieldset: In a complex form `<fieldset>` tags are used to break the form into groupings of like fields or types of information.

first-letter pseudo-element: Apply a different style to the first letter in a block element to produce appearances such as drop caps. For example, if you write the style `p:first-letter {color: #336699; font-size: 1.8em;}` the paragraph to which it is applied displays the first letter in a dusty dark blue color at nearly twice the size of the regular paragraph text.

first-line pseudo-element: Apply a different style to the first line in a block element to produce a unique appearance from the rest of the text. To show the first line in bold, bright red text using all caps, write the style as `p:first-line {color: #990033; font-weight: bold; font-variant:small-caps;}`.

float: Use the `float` properties to define where an element is oriented on a page. Use a `float` property and one of the `left`, `right`, or `none` values. Float images to the specified side, such as `img {float: left;}` to let text or other elements wrap around it. The `float` property applies only to non-positioned block elements.

font family: A font family is a set of fonts you specify for a style defined by name. The property is written as: `(font-family: "font choice a", "font choice b", generic font-family;}`.

font properties: Specify the appearance of text on a Web page using font properties, including `font-style` (`italic`, `oblique`, `normal`), `font-variant` (`small-caps`, `normal`), `font-weight` (keywords such as `bold` and `lighter`, and numeric values `100` to `900`). Other font properties described separately are `font-size` and `font-family`.

font: Write one shorthand attribute to set multiple font attributes in a single statement. You don't have to include all the properties, but you do need to include `font-size` and `font-family`.

font-family: Declare a sequence of specific fonts to be applied to the target element in order of preference. The values are comma-separated, and multi-word font names are enclosed with quotes, such as `{font-family: "Dom Casual BT", Comic Sans, Arial, sans-serif;}`. The generic families that browsers display by default if none of the named fonts exists on a system include `serif`, `sans-serif`, `monospace`, `cursive`, and `fantasy`.

font-size: The size of a font displayed on a device can be defined using absolute, relative, or percentage values or keywords. Set the absolute size (`mm`, `cm`, `px`, `pt`, `in`), relative size (`em`, `ex`), or a percentage of the default size for the element. Use one of various keywords ranging from `xx-large` to `xx-small`.

grouping: Multiple selectors included in the same style separated by commas is a grouping; use groupings to assign styles to multiple elements simultaneously. The three heading tags based on this example are dark blue: `h1, h2, h3 {color: #333366;}`.

height: Specify the height of an element using the `height` property, such as `{height: 185px;}`.You can use the attribute for any block-level element, but can't use a negative value.

ID: An ID selector is used as an attribute for a tag. The ID is written as a string following a hash mark (#) that is assigned only once in a document. For example, an ID selector written as `#row5 { background-color:coral; }` is applied to the page's code like this: `<tr ID="row5"> Resource List </tr>`.

image gallery: An image gallery is a method of displaying images on a Web site. Thumbnail views of a larger image are shown on a page as a set of visual links; clicking a thumbnail loads the full-size image.

inheritance: All elements inherit formatting properties from the element in which they are contained, known as a parent element. All properties display a value, which is the browser's default value unless you write a custom value.

keyword: Values for some properties are expressed as keywords, such as `bolder`, `lighter`, `larger`, `smaller`, `xx-large`, `xx-small`, and so on.

length: Units of measure used in styles are called lengths. You must include a unit of measure for any length indication in your styles, except for a 0 length, which is 0 no matter what length you apply! The length is expressed as a two-letter abbreviation following the value without a space between the value and the unit. Lengths are in one of three categories, including absolute, expressed as a concrete value such as mm or pt; relative, expressed as an em or ex unit; or device-dependent, expressed in px (pixels).

letter-spacing: Space around any displayed character in a character string using a custom value for an interesting effect, such as h3 {letter-spacing: 5px;}.

linearize: A table-rendering process where the contents of the cells become a series of paragraphs (for example, down the page) one after another. The paragraphs occur in the same order as the cells are defined in the document source, and should make sense when read in order.

line-height: You can change the vertical distance between baseline values in an element by specifying the line-height, as long as you don't use a negative value. For example, increase the height of the space between rows of text in a paragraph by writing p {line-height: 1.2em;}.

liquid layout: Defining columns on a Web page using percentages. A page designed using a liquid layout changes the size of the components as the browser window's size changes, either larger or smaller.

list: A list is a common way to present information in either numerical sequence, as an ordered list, or in point form as an unordered list. Style all aspects of the list's appearance including the type of bullet or numbering used, whether an image is used in the list, and the position of the bullet or number inside or outside the margin in relation to the list's contents. Write the shorthand property as: ul {list-style: disc url(bullet06.gif) inside;}.

margin: A margin is blank space beyond the borders of an element between nested or adjacent elements. The shortcut attribute can set the margin width for one to four edges using space-delimited values. One value,

such as {margin:10px;}, sets the margin on all four sides of the element to 10px. Two values, such as {margin: 5px 10px;}, sets the top and bottom margin to the same value (5px in the example), and the left and right margin to the same value (10px in the example). Three values for the shortcut attribute, such as {margin:.8em 12px 5px;}, sets the top margin to the first value, or .8em in the example, the right and left margins to the second value, or 12px, and the bottom margin to the third value, or 5px. Using four values, such as {margin:10px 5px 20px 50px;}, assigns one value to the top, right, bottom, and left margins respectively.

marker: The character or image used in a list is called its marker; commonly called a bullet.

media: In CSS terms, media refers to the different user agents that can display a Web page, ranging from a computer screen to a television to a Braille printout.

overflow: When you specify absolute sizes for elements be sure to also specify the overflow, or how the browser handles the content when there is too much for the element's box to display. Specify visible, which displays all the content; hidden, which hides overflow content; scroll, which adds scrollbars if necessary; or auto, which lets the browser decide what to show.

padding properties: Specify the amount of padding for each side of an element by specifying its side, such as padding-right or padding-bottom, and a positive value. For example, ul {padding-left: .5in;} applies a half-inch padding to the left of the list element on the page.

padding: Use the padding shortcut property to specify the value for the overall padding for an element on all four sides, such as blockquote {padding: 2em;}. Negative values are not allowed. The element's background is inherited by the padding.

page-break: The two page-break properties, `page-break-before` and `page-break-after`, are used for defining how a printed page behaves. Page breaks don't work within a table. For example, if you have a `<blockquote>` on your page, your choices can include `auto`, to apply a page break only if there isn't any space on the page before/after the `<blockquote>`; and `always`, to break the page before/after the `<blockquote>`. Write a style for a `page-break` such as `<style> .blockquote {page-break-after: always} </style>`.

panorama: A panoramic image is an image that is too large or time consuming to download as a single file. Break the image into several segments and have it reassembled on the Web site as a single panoramic image using CSS.

percentage unit: Various properties use percentage values to define sizes in relative terms. A percentage is calculated against the element's default size. For example, a ruleset such as `{line-height: 150%;}` sets the spacing between the lines in an element to which the property is applied, such as a paragraph, to 150% of its default height.

position: Establish whether an element can be given a location on the page using a position property. Written as `#egform {position: relative;}`, you can use a value of `static`, which has no position defined; `relative`, which defines the position in relation to where it would be normally; or `absolute`, which defines where an element is in relation to the top left corner of the parent element.

pseudo-class: A pseudo-class is a separate style used to add special effects to selectors, such as anchors.

pseudo-element: A pseudo-element is a style used to add special effects to the first letter or first line of a piece of text. The style can include numerous properties, ranging from font and color to line height and spacing.

quirks mode: Using an incomplete or outdated DOCTYPE in a Web page, or no DOCTYPE at all, triggers the quirks mode, where the browser tries to parse the page in a backward-compatible way, reverting to previous versions, such as IE4. Quirks mode can be used for testing your Web pages against older browser versions.

relative length: A unit of measure used to define a length for a property's value expressed in a unit that is relative to other units in the page, good for creating scalable pages. Relative units include `em` and `ex` lengths.

shorthand syntax: Many properties can be defined in one statement in a style sheet using shorthand syntax. Values listed for a property are applied from the top clockwise. For example, writing `margin { .4em 0 .4em 1em }` is the same as writing `.announcements { margin-right:.4em; margin-left: .4em;margin-top:1em; }`.

span: A `<span>` tag is used for differentiating inline content, such as some of the text in a paragraph, to which separate styles can be applied. A style is written for a `<span>` like any other element, such as `.emph {font-weight: bolder; color: red; }`. Applying the style in an example like this one results in red bold text for the text within the `<span>` tag: `<p>You might be a <span class ="emph"> big winner! </span> in this year's contest.`

specified value: A value defined by the CSS specification, defined in this order: a value is used when the cascade produces a value; the computed value of the property's parent value is used when the property is inherited; and if neither case is true, the property's initial value is used.

stacking order: The position in which objects are layered on a page is its stacking order. Rearrange the order of element visibility by specifying a `z-index` value. The higher the value, the closer the element is to the top of the stack, and the more visible it is than elements with lower integer values.

style sheet: A style sheet is a file containing alphanumeric code that specifies the appearance of an element. A style sheet can define styles for existing tags, such as a color for the page background, or be assigned to a unique style, such as a paragraph used as a note on a page.

style: A specification of how a particular element should look; a style defines an element's attributes, such as font color, font size, and background color for a paragraph.

system fonts: Each type of font can be represented by a default font that is available on virtually every computer, including a default serif, sans-serif, and monospace font.

text-align: Set the horizontal alignment of text in a block-level element using the `text-align` property. Align the text in the usual way: left, right, center, or justify.

text-decoration: There are several types of text-decoration that can be used for your Web page, and the values can be combined. Choose from `none`, `underline`, `overline`, `line-through`, and `blink`. To remove the default appearance of links, use `{text-decoration: none;}`.

text-indent: You can indent the first line in a block-level element like an indented paragraph, written as `p {text-indent:1.5em;}`, or use a negative value for a hanging indent, written as `li {text-indent: -15px;}`.

text-transform: Changes the case of the letters in the element, regardless of the original text. Values are `capitalize` (capitalizes first letter of each word), `uppercase`, and `lowercase`. The style is written as `h1 {text-transform: uppercase;}`.

URL: A Universal Resource Locator, also called a Universal Resource Indicator, is a value defined for a property, such as an image, that specifies a location of a file. CSS lets you use a partial URL, which is written relative to the style sheet, not to the HTML document, such as `background-image: url(../images/lily_bkgd.jpg);`.

used value: The value results from converting a value to an absolute value based on display conditions. A style using a percentage value for a box parameter such as width, uses a value based on the width of the browser window that varies with the display size. Regardless of size, the value remains proportional.

user agent: A device used to interpret a Web page and display its content, such as a Web browser, hand-held device, or a television.

vertical-align: Use the `vertical-align` property to set the alignment of text within a line or the cell of a table using a keyword. For example, `.info {vertical-align: bottom;}` places the text at the bottom of its container, either a line or a cell table. Other keyword values include `baseline`, `middle`, `sub`, `super`, `top`, `text-top`, `bottom`, `text-bottom`.

visibility: You can define whether an element is hidden or visible by setting a visibility property, such as `#egform { visibility: hidden; }`. Using either value still preserves the space required for the element on the page. If you want to close up the space, use a display attribute instead. Visibility can be inherited — if a parent element is hidden, so are its child elements.

white-space: The `white-space` property specifies how the browser displays character spaces and line breaks used in the source code. XHTML usually ignores extra spaces, allowing you to break lines and add spaces as needed for good readability. If you want to have the spaces recognized, type `{white-space:pre;}` to convert your carriage returns and character spaces to line breaks and spaces. If you want to make sure the browser doesn't interpret your source code layout as content spacing on the page, use `{white-space:nowrap;}` to ensure the extra space is ignored.

width: Specify the width of an element using the `width` property. You can use the attribute for any block-level element, such as `table {width:60%}`, but you can't use a negative value.

word-spacing: Define the amount of white space between strings of characters by specifying a `word-spacing` value, such as `p { word-spacing: 0.3em;}`.

z-index: Set the `z-index` value to define whether an element is displayed above or below overlapping elements. Values may be written as `{z-index: auto}`, which means the elements are in the order they are read in the page's code, or as an integer. Elements with higher integer values are on top of those with lower integer values. For example, an element using `{z-index: 5;}` is above one using `{z-index: 2;}`.

index

continued

continued

271

continued